Vision, Rhetoric, and Social Action in the Composition Classroom

VISION, RHETORIC, AND SOCIAL ACTION IN THE COMPOSITION CLASSROOM

Kristie S. Fleckenstein

Southern Illinois University Press / Carbondale

13 12 11 10   4 3 2 1

The production of this book was partially funded by a
grant from the Humanities Area Council of the College
of Arts and Sciences, Florida State University.

Library of Congress Cataloging-in-Publication Data
Fleckenstein, Kristie S.
Vision, rhetoric, and social action in the composition
classroom / Kristie S. Fleckenstein.
      p. cm.
Includes bibliographical references and index.
ISBN-13: 978-0-8093-2955-7 (pbk. : alk. paper)
ISBN-10: 0-8093-2955-7 (pbk. : alk. paper)
1. English language—Rhetoric—Study and teaching.
2. English language—Social aspects. 3. Communication
in social action. I. Title.
PE1404.F585 2009
808'.0420711—dc22   2009011820

Printed on recycled paper. ♻
The paper used in this publication meets the minimum requirements of American National Standard
for Information Sciences—Permanence of Paper for
Printed Library Materials, ANSI Z39.48-1992.♾

To my father, John Lawrence Sealy
1921–2007

Contents

Acknowledgments

Blessed by a wide range of support throughout this project, I have many people to thank:

Steadfast friends and writing-group cohorts Nancy A. Myers and Sue Hum, who plowed through numerous ungainly drafts, pointing out faulty logic, taming recalcitrant prose, and pushing me to reach beyond my grasp. The virtues of this project are theirs; the shortcomings, unfortunately, remain mine.

Linda T. Calendrillo, longtime collaborator, who provided pragmatic feedback designed to keep me tethered to the here and now.

Carmen Siering, friend and former graduate student, who taught me by example the necessity of integrating activism and intellectual life.

James Weatherly, Lauren Brownell, and Christopher Cartright, extraordinary undergraduate research assistants, who tracked down resources and typos with equal passion.

Liane Robertson, generous and gifted graduate student, who proofread drafts and created the index.

My students and my daughters who allowed me to share their work and their lives.

Florida State University, for providing a summer research grant and funds necessary to complete this book.

The wonderful people at Southern Illinois University Press, beginning with Karl Kageff, who remained serene in the face of my frequent anxiety, and including Barb Martin, Editing, Design, and Production Manager, who made sure the trains ran on time; Wayne Larsen, Project Editor, who kept track of all the details; and Mary Lou Kowaleski, who meticulously and compassionately copyedited the manuscript. The pride they take in their work makes it a joy to publish with SIU Press.

Finally, my mother and sisters, who provided the fellowship and emotional support necessary to survive grief. I revised this project in the months following the unexpected loss of my father in December 2007. He was a man who, with little formal schooling, fiercely believed in the value of education for his daughters. Through that education, he hoped they would change their worlds. I dedicate this book to him.

Vision, Rhetoric, and Social Action in the Composition Classroom

INTRODUCTION
Vision and Rhetoric in Social Action

It was an old theme even for me:
Language cannot do everything—
—Adrienne Rich, "Cartographies of Silence"

A woman in her late thirties, a Buddhist by faith and a peace activist by conviction, dresses in black and joins a group of silent women on a street corner in Boulder, Colorado, protesting world violence with her quiet presence. A middle schooler, ostracized and ridiculed by her classmates, creates *The Mutt's Dark Side*, a cartoon saga of a puppy with power, that remediates in small ways the painful intolerance of her adolescent culture. A woman in her mid-thirties sits anxiously in her college composition class, reluctant to participate, reluctant to write. Seeking to change the course of her life and the quality of her children's lives by reskilling after a painful divorce, she brings herself to the threshold of academic life convinced that she has neither expertise nor anything to say.

These situations, explored in more detail throughout the ensuing chapters, highlight the complex category of experiences that I call *social action*: behavior designed to increase individual and collective human dignity, value, and quality of life. The first two individuals reveal different ways of proactively seeking change on a macro to micro level. From a woman serving as a voiceless testament to peace to an adolescent challenging social identities through a privately circulated cartoon, both activist and tweenager choose widely divergent methods to modify attitudes, beliefs, and realities that contribute to what they see as inhumane in the world. The third woman, the single mother returning to school only to sit anxiously in the classroom, manifests a one-step-forward, two-steps-back process of social action. A belief in the possibility of change returns her to college, but that belief is not strong enough to power forward her participation in the classroom or in the wider public sphere. Agency takes her only so far, then ebbs, leaving her marooned in silence.

These different individual experiences disclose important insights into the makeup of change. Whether proactive, reactive, or inactive, these three women draw from a knot of rhetorical *and* visual habits that influence their efforts to alter their worlds. Because, as Adrienne Rich warns, language cannot do everything, we cannot rely on rhetoric alone to enact social change. Our realities are a complex amalgam of vision and language; therefore, acting on and in those realities require a similarly complex amalgam of vision and language. Linda Martín Alcoff makes this very point in "Toward a Phenomenology of Racial Embodiment." She argues that a combination of perception and language creates social categories; therefore, disrupting those categories requires a similar combination of perception and language. Alcoff illustrates the role of the visual in category creation by turning to the emergence in the eighteenth century of racialized designations based on physical markers. As she points out, a visible reality and the racial categories that resulted when visible reality was parsed evolved from the development of a "special form of perceptual practice," a visual habit that cultural members learned (268–69). Seeing race as physiological required learning this perceptual practice. Thus, she contends, changing the biologically "self-evident" view of race requires changing that visual habit (269).[1] Because modes of perceptions and images contribute to the joint creation of reality, action designed to transform those realities must always be bolstered by the twin dynamic of rhetoric and vision.

Vision, Rhetoric, and Social Action in the Composition Classroom contends that any approach to social action, individual and collective, micro and macro, depends on rich repertoires of ways of speaking and ways of seeing, both of which coalesce to open up (or, conversely, curtail) options for protest and intervention. An individual's ability to improve the material conditions of her or his life depends on the ability to read and write in a range of symbol systems. Scholars concerned with both social action and education concur. For instance, Gunther Kress underscores the need to attend to the visual elements comprising activity in the public sphere: "If English is to remain relevant as the subject which provides access to participation in public forms of communication, as well as remaining capable of providing understandings of and the abilities to produce culturally valued texts, then an emphasis on language alone will simply no longer do. English will need to change" ("'English' at the Crossroads" 67). This urgency to integrate the visual and the rhetorical is even more pressing when we move from English writ large to composition studies where literacy—the practices by which people make meaning of and participate in the world—is intricately interwoven with concerns for justice, equity, and peace. The composition classroom serves as one gateway to the larger public sphere, and getting through that gate is a visual as well as a discursive process. As Robert Bernasconi points out, the political realm, the site of deliberative rhetoric, is also "the realm of appearance," which means that people manipulate reality by manipulating appearances (286). Disempowering a segment of the population requires rendering those individuals imperceptible, a strategy that serves to sustain both racism and sexism (287). To illustrate, he points to the systematic way in which African Americans, "who are most visible phenomenally for the dominant group," have been "invisible" in the public sphere, deliberately not seen by the dominant group (286). Without visibility in the realm of appearances, individuals have little hope of engaging in the dialogue of the political sphere, he emphasizes. Invisibility and silence go hand in hand (287). Neither racism nor sexism can be eradicated by "the policing of ordinary language" (287) because both are sustained by more than ordinary language. Addressing racism and sexism requires attending to the transaction between visual and rhetorical habits; therefore, that transaction is important to composition's agenda of social equality. To tackle the challenges posed by social action, we require visuality and rhetoric.

Acting for change in the world presents an array of problems, particularly in a postmodern world. If, as members of a culture, people are already entrenched in its taken-for-granted realities, how do they perceive the need for change? Martin Luther King Jr. believed that "the hope of a secure and livable world lies with the disciplined nonconformists who are dedicated to justice, peace, and brotherhood" (*Strength* 12). I concur; but such a belief begs the question: where do we find or how do we develop into King's disciplined nonconformists? In addition, once people perceive the need for change, is agency possible for everyone or only for certain segments of the population? Finally, if the need for change can be perceived and if agency can be enacted, what options might community members have for bringing about a new reality that does not repeat the problems of the old? *Vision, Rhetoric, and Social Action in the Composition Classroom* offers robust responses to these questions. By considering social action an outgrowth of the transaction of visual and rhetorical habits organized in response to the constraints presented by particular locations, this book addresses the possibility of perceiving the need for change, the possibility of enacting agency, and the possibility of a pedagogy that increases a student's repertoire (and desire) for creating a new vision of social reality.

Social Action: A Definition

My use of the term *social action* draws on and refines work in composition and communication studies. From the classical concern with rhetoric as the means for maintaining the well-being of the polis and its individual citizens to nineteenth-century preparation of male students to participate in the discourse of their world, teacher-scholars have focused on various incarnations of social action and cultural formation. The deployment of the term *social action* in various contexts and configurations on the edge of the twenty-first century reveals the continuing commitment to it. One trend in composition and rhetoric uses *social action* to highlight the communal and dynamic nature of language with little attention to the goal of eliminating social inequities and oppressions. For example, Marilyn Cooper and Michael Holzman argue that all language, especially writing, constitutes social action; that is, language constitutes a kind of social behavior, a contrast to an individualistic, isolated cognitive approach to language. In this context, *social* aligns with communal and *action* with any language act. Focused on the level of meaning, this view emphasizes the social nature of language but does not directly tackle the political ramifications of language. Absent from this use of *social action* is any emphasis on language specifically designed to alter circumstances in the world.

Complementing the first trend, a second use of the term *social action* highlights language as action. Carolyn Miller lays the groundwork for this perspective in her 1985 landmark study of genre, calling discourse structure a social action to highlight the ways in which genres afford certain kinds of actions while constraining others. She argues that a "rhetorically sound definition of genre must be centered not on the substance or the form of discourse but on the action it is used to accomplish" (151). Anis Bawarshi in *Genre and the Invention of the Writer* extends Miller's work to maintain that a genre constitutes a social literate practice by which individuals participate in the world, specifically emphasizing the connection between language and social agency. He defines genres as "sites of action," socioliterate practices that enable (and constrain) options for engagement (6). Although both Miller and Bawarshi highlight the dynamic and agentive nature of discourse, particularly genres, neither explicitly spins out the implications of this textual dynamism for direct action designed to change some aspect of an oppressive reality.

A third trend pushes the connection between discourse and social action toward active intervention in the world. For example, feminist scholars advocate a deliberate social-action agenda in and for their research, defining *social action* as collaboration between researcher and research participants during and after the project to improve life situations (Kirsch). This activist orientation is reinforced by efforts to expand the venue (and subjects) of academic discourse so that compositionists write to and in the larger public sphere. Ellen Cushman urges scholars to engage in, rather than merely study the mechanisms of, social action. She calls on compositionists to bridge the gap between university and community by grappling with issues that threaten the quality of life for so many people. Cushman's appeals are rendered even more urgent by the growing fear that the scope for social action—the public sphere within which an agenda for change is presented, debated, and deployed—is shrinking, thus limiting opportunities for and sites of social action (Welch, *Living Room*). By choosing not to engage in social action, activists lose the places within which they can protest; as venues for protest shrink, opportunities to alter unjust conditions in the world similarly shrink. Finally, another aspect of this third trend toward social action in composition studies concerns the growing pedagogy of social action, characterized by the desire to develop language-arts curricula that intertwine social change and students' experiences with literacy (DeStigter, *Reflections*).

Building on this rich array of definitions, I use *social action* to refer to a category of individual and communal symbolic acts motivated by the desire to improve aspects of reality that harm individuals and communities. Any symbolic act aimed at redressing inequities constitutes social action. Such acts are integral to our humanity. Without social action—which includes the recognition of oppression, deprivation, cruelty, and violence *as well as* the desire to change those ills—the web within which humans are interwoven disintegrates. Thus, the perception of and the desire for change are primary to any social action. Once individuals perceive the need for social transformation, they can act on various levels. Borrowing from Johan Galtung, a scholar in peace studies, who has developed a taxonomy for violence and, conversely, peace, I see social action functioning on three intersecting planes: direct, in which individuals seek to change conditions of their personal lives; structural, in which individuals, alone or in conjunction with others, seek to change institutions that support, explicitly or implicitly, unjust social conditions; and cultural, in which individuals, again alone or in conjunction with others, seek to alter the systemic threads by which a culture organizes itself, such as its rhetorical and visual habits. Each level is reciprocally linked to the others.

I also limit my use of social action to symbolic acts designed to bring about compassionate living, where the boundaries of the self are pushed outward through a painful awareness of another's undeserved misfortune and a desire to remedy that inequity (Nussbaum 300). Compassionate living consists of a vision of community in which people see each other as valuable and important; the suffering of another is not separate from self but intimately intertwined with one's own well-being. Arguing that compassion is the heart of social justice, Martha C. Nussbaum calls this responsiveness the *eudaimonistic* character of compassion: a person takes another "person's ills as affecting her own flourishing. In effect, she must make herself vulnerable in the person of another" (319). Motivated by compassion, people engage in social action by using semiotic systems to delineate a caring vision of reality, orient themselves and others to that vision, and work individually and jointly to enact that vision.

Vital to the aim of compassionate living is the necessary reciprocity between means and ends. Simply put, the how affects the what. The tools that activists use to change the world need to fit with—to resonate with—the vision of the world they are working toward. Ann E. Berthoff argues that composition pedagogy, to be successful, must possess "elements of what we want to end with ... in some form from the first or we will never get to them" (215). Richard Fulkerson echoes Berthoff, criticizing educators for a "consistent mindlessness," in which they fail to perceive the tensile relationship between means and desired ends (343). Both Berthoff and Fulkerson focus on the importance of creating a composition pedagogy that possesses the end within the means. That same reciprocity between means and ends is crucial to social action as I define it. If the goal of social action is compassionate living, then the symbolic acts designed to effect that change must possess elements that align with compassionate living.

Ends and means exist in a feedback loop, the one affecting the other. Visual systems that consistently situate certain members of the human community as objects of the gaze, as rightly appropriated by hegemony, do not support social action; rather they reproduce cultural violence. Rhetorical habits that function similarly replicate an inhumane status quo rather than work for compassionate living. Social change does not occur in a neat linear progression that moves logically from desire to language to beneficially changed reality, where each move is separate and distinct from the other. Nor does social action proceed in a similar linear progression from individual to group to seismic social change. Rather, social action results from a circular causality in which the means implicates the end. Therefore, to reach a desired social goal, that goal must be present in some nascent form in the means. To illustrate, certain actions, from the Weathermen-initiated riots of the 1960s to the Oklahoma City bombing in 1995, do not constitute social action according to my definition for two reasons: the ends are not compassionate, and the means to achieve those ends are not compassionate. Similarly, the violent choices of ecoterrorists also fall outside my definition of social action regardless of their ends.

The requirement that the how and the what relate does not mean that everyone is tied to the same vision of a compassionate reality. It means that everyone is tied to compassion, to making oneself vulnerable to other persons. For instance, from various perspectives, *Roe v. Wade* constitutes a compassionate and just reality in which women have control of their bodies and their reproductive systems. But the pro-life supporters protesting at family-planning clinics also have a compassionate vision of reality, one that considers the cost of control—the cessation of a viable pregnancy—as too high. Adherents of both visions seek to enact what they see as a social good, a compassionate good. What falls outside the category of social action—what betrays the goal of a compassionate reality—are symbolic actions that advocate, strategize, and justify bombing clinics, harassing women, or assassinating medical personnel as a means to bring about a desired end. Such acts do not foster the creation and maintenance of any kind of compassionate living. Such acts destroy it.

The reciprocity of means and ends in social action also requires that people take both a short and a long view of social change. To demonstrate, the desire to ensure that all children receive adequate education and that institutions are held accountable for such an education constitutes a laudable goal. However, the means to obtain that end—for example, the No Child Left Behind Act (NCLB)—may not be congruent with that goal if those means fail to articulate a caring vision or realize an agenda through compassionate actions. The systematization—or what Kenneth Burke would call the bureaucratization—of the desire to educate all children creates massive inequities, as well as serious educational dilemmas such as high-stakes testing and sapped revenues, all of which distort, in turn, the initiating desire of adequate education for children. The goal of compassionate living remains out of reach, subverted rather than supported by NCLB. Symbolic acts that are motivated by the desire for social action but fail to resonate with compassion culminate in institutional edicts that replicate the very inequities they are designed to ameliorate. While other symbolic acts can in turn be deployed to resist and redress the social ills resulting from any institutional edict, those symbolic acts also have the potential to reify rather than alter those ills unless their means manifest the end they wish to achieve.

In short, within this book, the term *social action* refers to symbolic acts motivated by the goal of compassionate living where means and ends function reciprocally. It is this form of social action that I believe is crucial to human life, both individually and socially. This form of social action helps people maintain the health of their communities, their individual spirits, and their cultures. Unchecked instances of political abuse, children who fall through the institutional cracks, people who are bereft of hope, and unassuaged acts of local or global violence each unravels the web of relationships that hold people together. Social action based on the reciprocity between compassionate ends and means reweaves and protects that fragile web.

The Necessary Integration of Vision and Rhetoric

Without a doubt, language is crucial to this definition of social action. Rhetoric is inextricable from social action. It is the vehicle by which communal and individual health—the well-being of the polis inextricable from the soul of the politicos—is defined and the method by which that health is achieved. As Gerard A. Hauser points out, "Rhetoric is communication that attempts to coordinate social action" (2); thus, rhetoric consists of language used to bring about collaborative change in the world. In the West, rhetoric was born with social action more than twenty-five hundred years ago in classical Greece. It evolved in response to and as a palliative for social disruptions in the communal weave. Initially a legal remedy for property disputes, then a means by which citizens mutually determined the course and quality of their communal life, rhetoric "is a mode of altering reality, not by the direct application of energy to objects, but by the creation of discourse which changes reality through the mediation of thought and action" (Bitzer 4). Via its power, community members decide who should and should not make decisions, what decisions serve the common good, and, perhaps most important, what constitutes the common good. As Greek citizens used rhetoric to define their world, they were simultaneously defined by that rhetoric.

Rhetorical habits are also crucial to social action because they serve as the vehicle of change. Rhetoric provides the *why* for language use, the predisposition to act through language for change. Rhetorical habits are the *how* of such change, the means by which people respond to, perhaps even shape, the why. Embedded within rhetoric are ingrained language patterns and conventions—systemic rhetorical habits—that dispose community members to use language in particular ways. Every culture develops a unique array of rhetorical habits that provide protocols for engagement with and performance of certain social actions. Such habits converge in and evolve out of what John Poulakos calls formal situations, a loose set of speaking circumstances that stipulate roles, dictate what is appropriate, and define what is exigent. Guidelines evolve as formal situations become codified, and those guidelines become habituated, directing who can speak, where language can be spoken, and how that language must be shaped to be worthy of attention. The possibility of agency and social action are entangled in rhetorical habits, for these habits authorize some speakers to raise certain topics while invalidating other speakers and their topics.

It is relatively self-evident, then, that any effort to address social change must include language use and rhetorical habits. Equally important, but certainly less evident, is the crucial role that images and visual habits play in social action historically. As art historian Barbara Maria Stafford points out, the fundamental visuality of past oral cultures has been insufficiently emphasized to date (*Good Looking* 46).[2] Redressing that emphasis would reveal the power of the individual image (or array of images) and visual habits to shape and transform realities. Such an agenda is even more urgent now, Stafford contends. In the twenty-first century, when images saturate Western culture to an unprecedented degree, we are returning to or, perhaps more accurately, creating a new oral-visual culture (*Artful Science* xxiii). Fellow art historian E. H. Gombrich reinforces Stafford's assessment of Western culture: "Never has there been an age like ours," he wrote in 1956, "when the visual image is so cheap in every sense of the word" (8). Over fifty years later, in the wake of the digitization of Western culture, that "cheap image" is even more widely distributed, evoking what Diana George calls an "aggressively visual" culture that instills particular modes of seeing impinging on social action ("From Analysis to Design" 15). Kress agrees. The landscape of public communication is "an irrefutably multisemiotic one; and the visual mode in particular has taken a central position in many regions of this landscape," he argues ("'English' at the Crossroads" 69). Cultural critic Nicholas Mirzoeff goes even further: "We are all engaged in the business of looking," a process that shifts across the borders constituting private and public actions (33). Given the emergence of a twenty-first-century oral-visual culture, it is absolutely essential to understand more fully the ways in which visuality impinges on social action, from the constitution of the public sphere to the images by which a community validates itself.

Mirzoeff's "looking" and Kress's "visual mode" are important to social action in two ways: through the construction and privileging of specific images and through the organizing power of visual habits that evolve, in part, from the proliferation of those visual images. When Kress speaks of the changing landscape of public communication, he refers to the increasing presence of graphic imagery and its impact on action, from the image of Rosa Parks on a Montgomery, Alabama, city bus to Bill Clinton playing saxophone on the Arsenio Hall Show. Grappling with the intricacies of social action, therefore, requires grappling with the dynamic by which a social cache of images unites people into a community, provides concrete goals to realize, and offers models for agency. That process begins with meaning because images, Stafford says, "help us organize and make sense of the floating world"; they are our first means of making sense of the world (*Good Looking* 39). In addition, images are our first means of coalescing as a community. Specific visual images—functioning like totems or other identity/reality markers—serve as the means by which communities define themselves, articulate a common vision, and determine strategies for achieving that vision. What constitutes "goodness" for a community—the goal of social action—is derived in part from that community's images of goodness. Burke refers to *god terms*: words of power that draw members into a cohesive group and serve as the shared ground by which strangers identify with (separate from) one another and organize their realities (*Grammar of Motives* 74). Certain visual images function as *god images*, weaving together diverse people into a cohort with a shared vision of an ethical life. For instance, the AIDS quilt has become a god image, integrating people into a cohesive group through their shared grief for lost loved ones and their desire to change AIDS intervention and society's attitudes. Joe Rosenthal's picture of the flag raising on Iwo Jima has become a god image, one that rallies and validates nation-building (Hariman and Lucaites, "Performing").[3] The activists involved in CODEPINK, a peace movement begun in 2002, are gradually turning a color into a god image, tying it to an affirmation of nonviolence. Finally, images are necessary to transform our realities. Gloria Anzaldúa emphasizes that "nothing happens in the 'real' world unless it first happens in the images in our head," a process that is both mental and material (*Borderlands/La Frontera* 87). Changing the world requires changing the images we hold of the world and of goodness in that world.

But visual images, as a tool for shaping meaning, communal cohesion, and social transformation, do not function alone, and here is the central argument of *Vision, Rhetoric, and Social Action in the Composition Classroom*. *What* we see is inextricable from *how* we see. The second way that vision affects social action is through visual habits: systems of perception that, through an array of habituated conventions, organize reality in particular ways leading us to discern some images and not others, to relate those images in characteristic ways to each other and ourselves, and to link those images to language in a uniform dynamic. Just as rhetorical habits are implicit within rhetoric, so are visual habits implicit within images, and those visual habits are integral to social action. To return to and slightly redirect Anzaldúa, we cannot change the world until we change *how* we see the world, until we change our visual habits, beginning with the recognition that we do in fact construct our identities and our worlds by means of those visual habits. A visual habit constitutes what Burke calls a terministic screen: a means of seeing some parts of reality by not seeing others (*Permanence and Change* 48–49). Thus, a visual habit works as a reality sieve or a set of blinders, directing our attention to some facets of reality while rendering others invisible. For example, Bronislaw Malinowski in his study of the Trobriand Islanders of New Guinea discovered that the islanders developed a kinship system in which matrilineal resemblances were neither recognized nor acknowledged. Children looked like their fathers, not their mothers. Furthermore, islanders did not see resemblances between siblings, either brothers, sisters, or brothers and sisters. Siblings could look like their father but not each other. If a visitor pointed out similarities between a child and mother, the community members pointed out, instead, the child's differences from the mother. Thus, a visual habit sifted out—prevented the perception of—an aspect of reality that would have been evident to someone with a different set of visual habits (Malinowski qtd. in Bolles 106–7).

According to historian Martin Jay, ways of seeing are not just reality sieves for individuals and communities; they are reality sieves for entire cultures. He equates visual habits with scopic regimes, a term he borrows from French film critic Christian Metz. A scopic regime constitutes a dominant way of seeing that shapes one's sense of reality *and* defines a culturally appropriate relationship to that reality. A scopic regime not only reflects by selecting, organizing, and deflecting but also structures and replicates power within a culture. Membership in a culture is predicated on one's ability to see and speak in the privileged mode. To be a member of a particular culture demands that one develop and deploy that culture's dominant way of seeing and speaking. Acquired through participation in cultural activities with cultural artifacts, ways of seeing feed back into what images can be perceived (e.g., family resemblances) and, thus, what god images can develop.

Just as images implicate social action, so, too, do ways of seeing privilege (or curtail) strategies for social action, such as stipulating who can speak on the basis of one's access to the political, social, or academic "high ground," the position with, ostensibly, the clearest "sight lines." Visual habits also dictate where one must speak (or can speak), serving to demarcate the permeable line between public and private. To be heeded, one must speak from the "public" venue providing the best possibility of being seen by either the most people or the most "right" people who then judge the rhetor's appeal on the basis of how the rhetor looks as much as on the basis of what that rhetor says. As Bernasconi highlights, the public sphere is the realm of appearances, so denying people power simply requires the deliberate refusal of the established order to see them (287). Finally, visual habits subtly organize how one should use language so that one's rhetorical choices reveal a culturally valid subject-object relationship and a shared perspective.[4]

Although more teacher-scholars are attending to the impact of proliferating graphic images on literacy and public communication, few recognize the impact of visual habits. Additionally, imagists, a term Stafford coined to describe people working at the interdisciplinary boundaries of visual studies, have not made explicit connections between visual habits and social action, a gap addressed in *Vision, Rhetoric, and Social Action in the Composition Classroom*. Because acting in ways that rectify what is inhumane in the world involves ways of speaking *and* ways of seeing, it is necessary to enlarge our disciplinary scope to include not just images but visual habits. Ways of seeing dispose people to perceive the world and relate to that world in one way and not another. It then organizes human beings into communities based on those shared visual vocabularies, protocols, and procedures. Similarly, ways of speaking organize the same people into language communities sharing common vocabularies, hierarchical relationships, and language patterns. Both rhetorical and visual habits are intrinsic to social change and to each other. Ways of speaking and ways of seeing combine to reinforce particular goals for social action and particular tactics for achieving those goals. Thus, without attention to both ways of seeing and ways of speaking, we cannot fully understand social agency, effectively teach writing as social action, or resourcefully engage in social action. Mapping more precisely the interconnections between speaking and seeing, between word and image provides insight into the dynamic of people acting, or failing to act, in the world.

The Possibilities for a Pedagogy of Hope

Without a doubt, I am drawn to this project because of my desire to map the fascinating intersections between vision and rhetoric in social action. But my engagement with this subject stems as well from my responsibilities as a teacher and a parent. I have regularly taught introductory composition classes in post-secondary institutions for more than twenty years, but I have never incorporated an explicit element of social action. I talk of exigency, of the impact of language on the writer, and of the influence of language and image on an audience, but my attention to rhetoric only indirectly engages issues of social action. I am increasingly troubled by my choices, for I fear that the absence of direct attention to social action might mean that I am teaching a weak or impoverished version of rhetoric, one that serves neither my students nor my community. If social action and agency erode, does not rhetoric likewise erode? If the two are reciprocal, might they not if split from one another undermine the power of the other?

Issues of rhetoric, vision, and social action continue to materialize as I grapple with the "so what" question in my teaching. If the means and ends are reciprocally linked, how do I make my daily engagement with teaching writing meaningful? Without directly focusing my composition classroom on the nexus point of rhetoric, vision, and social action, am I simply providing knowledge workers for the corporations and obedient members of the dominant social order? Am I advocating writing for its use value and exchange value but not for its action value?

Nor is my concern limited to teaching alone. It seeps into my home, into my parenting. Recently, my younger daughter, Lindsey, burst into the house after school in her typical manner, shedding coat, backpack, lunch box, and flute like a snake shedding skin.

"Mom, I need cans."

"Cans of what?" I asked.

"Food for the food drive. If I bring in ten cans, Mrs. DeNeal will give me ten extra credit points."

Food for points? For my daughter, civic action has been reduced or converted to notches on an academic yardstick. If she brings in cans of tuna fish or packages of Ramen noodles, she will grease her way to an A in social studies. Extrinsic rather than intrinsic reward motivates this social generosity. While I do not wish to discount the value of extrinsic reward, what concerns me in this instance is the invisibility, the absence, of an internal impetus for social action: the recognition of inequity *and* of one's ability to remediate that inequity through some sort of action. Instead, I fear that this scenario transforms social action into school action: the acquisition of academic capital in a social-studies class.

In addition, and perhaps even more troubling, this experience erodes the need for *rhetorical* agency by construing it so narrowly that it becomes negligible. The language that matters in this scenario is that of the teacher; it does not extend beyond the classroom, beyond the teacher-student dyad. The effect of the cans of food, the change brought about in a small portion of the world by the distribution of the food, remains hidden. The only opportunity that Lindsey has to use language that matters is in the parent-child dyad ("Mom, I need cans."), one in which she is already proficient. Thus, her rhetorical agency is restricted to the home, and social agency is converted to academic advancement. The opportunity to link social agency to an internal impetus, to a vision of compassionate living in which one is vulnerable and responsive to the undeserved pain of another, is lost.

My choices for the classroom and my hopes for my daughters are tightly knotted to the identity and teaching of rhetoric itself. The writing classroom is especially important for the fusion of visual and rhetorical habits because the classroom serves as a site of cultural production, reproduction, and resistance by inculcating the rules of a dominant culture's literacy practices. What we teach our students about writing and reading implicates how they construct their realities and their roles in those realities (Berlin). As Louise Rosenblatt points out, the kind of literacy pedagogy teachers practice directly affects the kind of citizenship that their students practice. Whether we acknowledge it or not, the classroom, as a place where visual habits and rhetorical habits are tightly knotted, instills privileged image-word relationships that configure (and limit) social agency in certain ways. Thus, if I am concerned, as I am, about my younger daughter's construction of social action as the price of classroom success, if I am concerned, as I am, about my students' reluctance to commit themselves except in superficial ways to a class writing assignment, then, might not one reason for the troubling separation between writing and action be found in the gradual erosion of social action, an erosion to which I might unwittingly contribute? How might I teach composition so that teacher and students jointly engage in the messy, occasionally contentious process of reality-building and possible reality-transforming? This book is impelled as much by a desire to understand how I might more effectively teach my students and enact that teaching in my own life as it is by the desire to map the beguiling intersections among vision and rhetoric in social action. *Vision, Rhetoric, and Social Action in the Composition Classroom* constitutes simultaneously a theoretical and pragmatic exploration of these concerns. It addresses our lives as scholars, parents, teachers, and citizens living with (and in) the possibilities of hope.

The Design of *Vision, Rhetoric, and Social Action in the Composition Classroom*

My goal, then, is two-fold: to explore the intertwined relationships between visuality and rhetoric, following up the implications of those relationships for one's ability to effect change in the world, and to develop strategies for teaching those intertwined relationships within the composition classroom. I explore social action in writing classrooms from the perspective of three visual habits: spectacle, which fosters disengagement; animation, which fuses body with meaning; and antinomy, which invites the invention of new realities. These habits evolve out of community members' interaction with different imagistic artifacts that circulate in Western culture.

Chapter 1 provides the theoretical frame for my analysis of the fusion of vision, rhetoric, and composition classroom in social action. I contend that particular protocols for (and goals of) social action emerge from the knotting of visual habits, rhetorical habits, and places, all of which are enacted and negotiated by people in their everyday lives. I use the metaphor *symbiotic knot* to highlight this transaction. The symbiotic knot provides a powerful explanatory construct in that it accounts for the existence and the attrition of social agency and provides a framework for exploring how social change can be envisioned, performed, dismissed, and resisted. Different tools for social action evolve out of different symbiotic knots, ranging from empathic social action in which bodies are the vehicle of the message to subversive social action in which contradiction disrupts status-quo versions of reality.

Chapters 2, 3, and 4 explore three different symbiotic knots, disentangling the rhetorical threads interwoven with specific visual habits and following those threads into the composition classroom. Each chapter is organized according to that analysis, presenting, first, a particular visual habit that is reciprocally linked to both imagistic artifacts and new modes of literacy; and, second, examining the interface between visual and rhetorical habits to trace the ways in which they combine to invite a particular mode of social action. Each chapter concludes with a description of the composition praxis reinforcing a symbiotic knot. In addition, each chapter addresses a question key to social action:

- What forces undercut an individual's belief in his or her ability to act? (chapter 2)
- When individuals seek to exercise agency, how might they evolve compassionate means of social action? (chapter 3)
- How might individuals evolve new visions of the world and new protocols to make those visions real? (chapter 4)

The conclusion describes a visually rich composition class based on a symbiotic knot of contradictions and suggests new directions for research that might lead to equally rich options for social action.

Walter Benjamin warns, "Whoever does not pay his dues to the picture treasury of the masses is bound to fail" (qtd. in Seyhan 229). I would add that rhetorical scholarship and teaching that do not pay dues to the visual habits of the masses radically reduce the possibilities for and effectiveness of acting in the world. I maintain that rhetoric should not be conceived solely or even predominantly in terms of language, which is the traditional venue of rhetorical studies. Nor do I believe that visuality should be conceived solely or even predominantly in terms of image, which is the focus of the current turn in visual rhetoric. Rather, I contend that images and language converge in diverse ways that affect the range of actions and identities available for social agency. *Vision, Rhetoric, and Social Action in the Composition Classroom* details in concrete ways that convergence in the classroom and in the world.

1. STRONGER HOPES
Symbiotic Knots and Social Action

> I once had stronger hopes than helping my students write
> good complaints if they were beaten up by the cops.
>> —Susan Wells, "Rogue Cops and Health Care"

In *The Incredible Disappearing Woman*, performance artist and social activist Coco Fusco creates a searing one-act play in which three characters on a single set bring dramatic attention to a cluster of social ills confronting Latina women in their home countries and in the United States: sexual exploitation, economic victimization, and domestic abuse. Throughout a complex narrative line focused on the Internet sex trade where unseen "clients" dictate the characters' actions, Fusco highlights the array of interlocking forces that conspire to destroy the lives of women in Mexico and South America, from the low-wage assembly-line factories in post-NAFTA northern Mexico to the secret police in Chile to religious precepts that sanction male dominance. *The Incredible Disappearing Woman* serves as both an indictment of those conditions and a strategy to change them through an art project that catapults Fusco's audience into the characters' brutal lives. This one-act play performed at various international venues constitutes social action. By soliciting outrage at the causes of her characters' pain, Fusco devises a compassionate means to bring about a compassionate end: the elimination of economic, social, and cultural constraints that render women of color silent, invisible, and damaged. Acting in the play and performing as an activist through the medium of the play, Fusco points to the possibilities of social action.

However, even as *The Incredible Disappearing Woman* enacts social action, it also points to the difficulty of social action, for while Fusco the author works to change the world, Fusco the character in the play cannot; she, along with her fellow sex workers, is powerless. The three women in the play manifest the absence of agency through the myriad ways they have been silenced and erased from the public's field of vision. First, the characters are invisible as human beings; rather, the clients—the "jo-blos" who have logged in to and paid for a live online sex show performed according to their specifications—control the women's actions. Representatives of the dominant culture's patriarchal eye, these clients dismiss the workers' humanity to focus on their utility as visual objects. Second, throughout the play, the characters reveal glimpses of lives in which options for action have been steadily eroded: Dolores, a victim of spousal abuse, follows the advice of her parish priest to transfigure violence into passionate prayer. Magaly, a former teacher in Chile, is mistakenly arrested by the secret police, tortured, and reported as dead. Her survival rests on accepting in silence that official death and in living invisible to the government eye. Finally, Chela, a worker in a post-NAFTA border factory, loses her job and is blacklisted because of a bungled sexual encounter with her boss; accused of being a union organizer, she is bereft of any official means to protest. In each case, the characters were barred from language, removed from the field of vision, and stripped of agency. Thus, while the play itself constitutes one mode of social action, the characters within it are blocked from changing the circumstances of their lives by economic, cultural, and political controls.

I open with Fusco's drama because it encapsulates the hope and the despair posed by individual and collective protest, a conundrum explored in this chapter. Three central challenges confound social action. First, how does an individual (or a group) perceive the need for change, especially if, as a member of a culture, he or she is already entrenched in what Roland Barthes calls the mythologies of that culture, its taken-for-granted realities? For example, Dolores, a devout Catholic, perceives no need for change, accepting the authority of her priest, who instructs her to transform domestic abuse into an invitation for fervent prayer. Second, even if the need for change can be perceived, do outlets or means for enacting agency exist? Here, Chela has no tool to counter through corporate channels her status on the blacklist. Lacking any vehicle for agency, she loses job, home, child, and life. Third, even if agency is possible, are venues available within which to alter rather than reinforce the unjust situation? Magaly has no safe forum from which to protest her mistreatment and to counter the story of her death disseminated through government-supported newspapers. She has no place from which she can speak, only places where she must be silent.

I tackle these three questions throughout *Vision, Rhetoric, and Social Action in the Composition Classroom*, addressing less dramatically but no less ardently than Fusco the possibilities and the impossibilities of social action. My overarching argument throughout this book is that social action—and the forces conspiring against it—emerge from the interplay of visual and rhetorical habits transacting in specific places. This chapter focuses on that interplay, arguing that vision, rhetoric, and place coalesce in a *symbiotic knot* from which social action may evolve. I map the intricacies of a symbiotic knot in four steps, beginning with visual habits, phenomena that, unlike rhetorical habits and place, leave few lingering traces of their presence and existence. I then integrate visual with rhetorical habits, moving to contextualize both with place. I conclude by considering a symbiotic knot as a totality, as more than the sum of its parts, arguing that such a perspective provides new insights into agency, the element most vital to social change.

This work lays the foundation for the ensuing chapters in which I examine more closely the configuration of different symbiotic knots and their connections to the classroom, a place important to the health of social action as Susan Wells points out. In a landmark essay on writing and social action, Wells poignantly articulates her desire to see writing do something more than defend her students against the barbarities of the world; she wants to see writing change the world so that her students are not subjected to those barbarities in the first place. Consciously untangling the intricacies of a culture's symbiotic knots supplies a first step in evolving a writing praxis that responds to Wells's fierce desire for a world in which her students are not beaten. Consciously reentangling these symbiotic knots offers hope that the women inspiring Fusco will no longer be invisible, silent, or injured.

A Symbiotic Knot: Organic, Artistic, and Accidental

Marked organically, culturally, and idiosyncratically, symbiotic knots provide matrices out of which different modes of social action emerge (see fig. 1.1). This metaphor provides a means to keep the threads distinct without eliding the complexities of the interaction. Possessing more explanatory and analytical power than a one-dimensional focus on vision or rhetoric or place (or individual agent), a symbiotic knot helps us puzzle out why social action is simultaneously possible and impossible, present and absent, successful and futile. And, in this puzzlement, we can harness the potential for compassionate living through compassionate means.

The term *symbiotic knot* highlights the organic, artistic, and accidental nature of a web of visual habits, rhetorical habits, and places. In one sense, a symbiotic knot resembles the odd biological creature *Mixotricha paradoxa*, a single-celled entity that lives in "obligatory symbiosis" with other organisms in the gut of a termite where it helps transform cellulose into carbohydrates (Haraway, *How Like a Leaf* 83). Donna J. Haraway refers to *Mixotricha paradoxa*, or mixed thread, as "an entity that interrogates individuality and collectivity at the same time" (83). Tightly intertwined, one organism cannot be excised from the collective without doing irreparable damage to the symbiosis. Although these organisms can be individually named, they can only live in a mutual relationship, in a symbiotic knot. In another sense, though, the term *symbiotic knot* links to artistry, to the craft of knotting. If *symbiotic* connotes an organic

Figure 1.1

Social Action

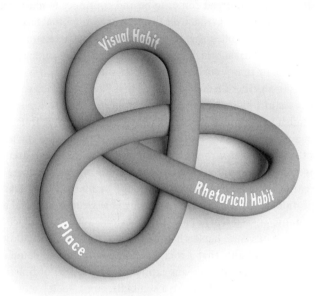

A Symbiotic Knot

mutualism, then *knot* connotes a deliberate, even artful, interweaving of threads into a locking pattern. *Knot* evokes a love knot, an infinity knot, a Gordian knot, a bullion knot, all complex, intertwining loops designed so that the viewer is unable to determine where one thread begins and another ends. In addition, *knot* conjures up sailors' knots, climbers' knots, Girl Scout knots, all of which are crafted to hold tight in all conditions or to hold tight until a skillful tug releases that binding. Knot as art and craft possesses an element of deliberate design or control. Paradoxically, both artistic and practical knots, perhaps, too, organic knots, call forth connections to disruption, the last connotation I want to integrate. While knots are artful and consciously crafted, they are also accidental, occurring outside the design of nature or culture. Thus, hair, yarn, embroidery floss, shoelaces, fishing line, and dog leashes mysteriously snarl while traffic lines, ticket lines, and bathroom lines inexplicably congest. Knots evolve into their own complex systems that defy, for good or ill, efforts to disentangle them, to tame them. In the process, these baffling knots undermine cultural control or relocate control to different sites.

The organic, artistic, and accidental natures of symbiotic knots emphasize the same qualities in the intertwining of visual habits, rhetorical habits, and place. First, each thread of the knot is organic, in that habits and place are anchored to the natural world of bodies, soil, air, and water. Also, like the *Mixotricha paradoxa*, each thread comes to be and continues to exist in a tangle with the others, an organism that lives through its own mutual feedback loops. Snipping out a visual habit, a rhetorical habit, or a place irreparably damages the symbiosis of the whole, which means that it irreparably damages the social action dependent on that symbiosis. In addition, the threads of a symbiotic knot come into being together through a process that Paul R. Ehrlich calls coevolution. In coevolution, biological phenomena influence the development of each other through a fine-grained process of change and response. Thus, a human, situated in a particular place, time, and culture, does not first form a visual habit that then calls forth a rhetorical habit. Rather, the threads are mutually constitutive; changes in one elicit changes from the others.

The organic and codependent qualities of a symbiotic knot have important implications for social action, suggesting that we look at social action as likewise organic and codependent. Social action cannot take place without the intertwining of visual habit, rhetorical habit, and place. In addition, the symbiotic knot highlights that a social action committed to compassionate living through compassionate means cannot define itself according to a single cause, a single injustice. Rather, like a symbiotic knot, social action involves a commitment to the well-being of all people. Similar to the butterfly effect in complex-systems theory, where butterfly wings flapping in Asia contribute to a hurricane in Florida, small local injustices proliferate exponentially with transnational effects.

Second, the symbiotic knot leads us to see social action as artistic. Even as visual habits, rhetorical habits, and place are tied to the materiality of the organic world, they are simultaneously tied to the materiality of the human-made world through sign systems, technologies, laws, architecture, city planning, green space, community involvement, and so forth. A symbiotic knot is produced, stabilized, and deployed through cultural exchanges, including the production, dissemination, and consumption of products. As a design constructed by a particular culture at a particular historical juncture, a symbiotic knot reproduces the ideologies and values circulating throughout various communities. No symbiotic knot is politically or economically neutral, a point important for social action. The effectiveness of one mode of social protest will evolve out of and depend in part on the web of ideologies and values within which it is immersed. Like a symbiotic knot, strategies for social change are shaped by people using the tools provided by their cultures in ways congruent with ambient visual habits, rhetorical habits, and places.

Finally, a symbiotic knot comes into existence accidentally, through neither the design of nature nor the design of culture, suggesting a similar dynamic for social action. Visual habits, rhetorical habits, and place can coalesce through chance or luck, and one component of that accidental organization is the individual community member. People *enact* visual habits and rhetorical habits, and in the process they decide how to combine various threads, a dynamic that sometimes creates new symbiotic knots or disrupts an established knot. As Michel de Certeau points out, people are low-level mischief-makers. They are notorious for using cultural artifacts and protocols in ways that serve their personal goals and momentary whims. Thus, a fork, contrary to its design, becomes a paperweight, a computer a footstool, a car a home. Although a fork, computer, and car have been constructed for specific tasks and purposes, people employ those artifacts in ways not initially envisioned by their designers. Visual-rhetorical habits and places likewise snarl in unexpected ways because of the idiosyncratic enactments of living, breathing people. In addition, although cultures and communities tend to be organized according to the intricate pathways of a single symbiotic knot, competing knots evolve and are enacted, ensuring that no single symbiotic knot has supremacy everywhere.

The accidental symbiotic knots and the disruption of long-standing symbiotic knots implicate social action on a variety of levels. Regardless of an individual's immersion within a culturally privileged way of seeing and speaking, opportunities always exist to resist that training. People ensure through their low-level machinations that no single symbiotic knot dominates and that no single habit controls a populace. Community members stumble upon and enact new modes of social action, from the Clothesline Project to virtual sit-ins, challenging entrenched ways of thinking and being in the world.

Organic, cultural, and accidental, symbiotic knots enlarge our understanding of social action, inviting us first to explore the individual threads and second to explore the gestalt formed by the interaction of those threads. My investigation of the makeup of a symbiotic knot begins in the next section with visual habits. Rooted in a dominant culture, individuals may have difficulty perceiving the need for change. Therefore, a key question posed by social action concerns how community members identify injustice, acknowledge the need to alter a situation, and devise compassionate strategies to accomplish their objectives. Visual habits provide insight into this dynamic. I begin with a description of visual habits as an amalgamation of bodies and cultures; a visual habit becomes an ingrained response to stimuli as a result of an individual's repeated interaction with a culture's imagistic artifacts. I then point out two ways in which visual habits are also transformative, ways in which a visual habit ensures that the need for social action can be perceived.

Thread 1: Visual Habits and the Im/Possibility of Change

Sighted people rarely think of vision in terms of habits. Vision is one of those seemingly transparent, natural senses that the sighted take for granted. If each member of a community possesses unimpaired vision, then the collective presumably sees the same thing in the same way. Thus, what I see when I look outside my kitchen window as I wash dinner dishes—the concrete birdbath that needs a good scrubbing, the graceful river birch shading the west family-room window, and the pet beagle Molly, nose to the ground, sniffing out rabbits—is exactly what I expect my daughters to see as they dry dinner dishes. The common misconception is that vision is not a habit we acquire through repetition or practice. Instead, it is commonly taken to be integral to our shared physiology: a simple decoding/recording of visual stimuli. But perception is far trickier than that. If Anna, Lindsey, and I *see* the same scene, it is in part the result of possessing similar visual habits as well as possessing similar visual organs.

I define a visual habit as a system of perception that, through an array of habituated conventions, organizes reality into particular patterns, leading us to discern some images and not others, to relate those images in characteristic ways to each other and ourselves, and to link those images to language in a uniform dynamic. Key to my definition is the transaction between bodies and cultures. On the one hand, visual habits encompass the bodies we are born with, the very real physiological processes necessary for seeing: cones, rods, optical cells, and neurological wet matter. For example, in "What the Frog's Eye Tells the Frog's Brain," physiological Jerome Y. Lettvin, Humberto R. Maturana, Warren S. McCulloch, and Walter H. Pitts explore the "synthetic a priori," the constraints exercised by a body on vision (153). In their examination of a frog's visual apparatus, they contend that a frog was able to see only objects in motion in its field of vision. Until an object moved, it remained invisible to the frog. As the authors point out, this kind of vision made the frog an excellent bug-catching machine. The human body similarly constrains human vision. Without technological extensions, human perception is limited to only a certain visual spectra, certain distances, and certain motions. Our physiological design restricts what we can and cannot see, functioning as our first reality sieve. Anthropologist Gregory Bateson notes that "the rules of the universe that we think we know are deeply buried in our processes of perception" (*Mind and Nature* 36).

On the other hand, the human body—the physiological processes of perception—is itself shaped by cultural conventions that are necessary to interpret or organize physiological processes. E. H. Gombrich notes in *Art and Illusion* that "the starting point of a visual record is not knowledge but a guess conditioned by habits and tradition" (89). While the majority of people are born with the physical mechanisms of sight, they are not born "seeing": rather, they are born impelled to learn how to see and equipped with the bodily mechanisms necessary to that learning. Neurologist Oliver Sacks's case study of Virgil illustrates the necessary reciprocity of vision and culture in "To See and Not See."

Sacks recounts the story of Virgil, a man who had had partial sight restored surgically after almost an entire life spent blind. When the bandages were removed from Virgil's eyes, however, there was no magical "ah-ha" moment. Instead, Virgil reported later that "he had no idea what he was seeing. There was light, there was movement, there was color, all mixed up, all meaningless, a blur" (114). He could not make sense of this chaos of light and shadow until the attending surgeon, who was standing before him, spoke. Throughout the next two years, before illness again eroded his surgically restored sight, Virgil struggled to make a place for himself in a sighted world. As Sacks observes, "his sight might be largely restored, but using his eyes, looking, it was clear, was far from natural to him; he still had many of the habits, the behaviors, of a blind man" (117). Virgil's sightedness lacked the crucial element of cultural ways of seeing. "One does not see, or sense, or perceive, in isolation," Sacks explains. "Perception is always linked to behavior and movement, to reaching out and exploring the world. It is insufficient to see; one must look as well . . . [W]ith Virgil . . . there was . . . a lack of capacity or impulse to look, to act seeing—a lack of visual behavior" (118). The confusion that Virgil continued to experience with a visual world, its collision with the world he had created tactilely and audibly, emphasizes the "learned" quality of vision. Sacks concludes, "When we open our eyes each morning, it is upon a world we have spent a lifetime learning to see. We are not given the world; we make our world through incessant experience, categorization, memory, reconnection" (115). Thus, Virgil could and could not see.

Kenneth Burke refers to this interplay between biology and culture in bodies as *second naturing*. Humans do not live in nature, he says; they live in a culture they create, and culture turns around to reshape the creator. As Burke explains, people are separated from their natural condition by instruments of their own making, instruments that craft for them a different "natural" condition (*Language as Symbolic Action* 13). Using the tools they construct, humans "make a set of habits that become a kind of 'second nature,'" become "a special set of expectations, shaped by custom, [that] . . . seem 'natural'" (13). Thus, nature is always "second natured." What is "given" in a body, endowed with a physiological heritage, results from people acting in the world through the tools they create and developing habits that sink below the level of conscious awareness. The organizational power of a culture and the tools constructed by a culture's members to address the problems posed by an environment impinge on biological bodies. Sociologist John O'Neill concurs: "Our bodies are the permeable ground of all social behavior; our bodies are the very flesh of society. . . . *Here is the incarnate bond between self and society*" (qtd. in Berman 56; emphasis in original). Fusing culture and bodies, second naturing underscores that humans are made as well as born.[1] This biological-cultural fusion means that vision is also made, which Marshall McLuhan emphasizes: "Every culture and every age has its favorite model of perception and knowledge that it is inclined to prescribe for everyone and everything" (5).

Nowhere is the second naturing of visual habits more vividly illustrated than in what my daughters see and I do not. Products of a different generation and citizens of a highly digital culture, my daughters (and my students) have developed ways of seeing foreign to me. For instance, Anna, my older daughter, organizes much of her realities according to a visual habit that resonates to Jeff Rice's rhetoric of cool. In the wake of the digital revolution, Rice argues, a new mode of meaning making—a rhetoric of cool—circulates through and shapes twenty-first-century culture. Marked by such qualities as appropriation, juxtaposition, commutation, nonlinearity, and reliance on imagery, a rhetoric of cool aligns with the way of seeing Anna deploys so easily. She is the family resident techie, proficient with PhotoShop, digital cameras, MovieMaker, and other software/hardware combos. Active in Internet communities, Anna began designing Web sites for her own pleasure before I did more than navigate them. Whereas I perceive images as relatively stable phenomena that invite opportunities for identification, interpretation, and/or critique, my older daughter perceives images as unstable phenomena that invite opportunities for invention. Like many of the students who enter my classroom, Anna considers images fertile occasions for improvisation. She dismantles, mismatches, and recontextualizes images, enacting a kind of visual remixing in her online and off-line activities.

Lindsey, too, has developed a visual habit I do not share, one intimately connected to the gaming culture she inhabits. My younger daughter, a video-game junkie, enjoys an array of role-playing games, particularly the fantasy-oriented *The Legend of Zelda* (and more recently *World of War Craft*). While I share with Lindsey a love of science fiction/fantasy, a taste for sugar cookies, and a delight in goofy socks, I cannot share *Zelda* or any video game with her because I have not developed the visual habit—a kind of digital integration—necessary for gaming success. I perceive jerky, disconnected, and incomprehensible images on-screen whose quick movement makes me slightly nauseated (and thoroughly impatient). I read only a bewildering array of individual images on the page of the official game guide. I cannot work out the connections among the individual images, the descriptive/instructive text, or the purpose of the game. But Lindsey looks at the on-screen moving graphics and constructs an interactive world with a coherent narrative, a hero, and a moral imperative: rescue the princess, save the world, and beat Ganondorf. She smoothly navigates a maze of images and words on the screen, through the cheat sheet, and from her own body. As she links to the game through the controller, the separation between her body and the graphic image and the various texts dissolves; in some mysterious fashion, she becomes a part of the game while I remain a fairly unremorseful exile of both game and cheat sheet. I am, as my daughter teases, a gaming illiterate. I am blind to *Zelda*.

Vision requires habits cultivated in bodies through time and across time, and those habits depend on the imagistic artifacts an individual experiences. The phenomenon of shared vision in one context (watching Molly sniff out rabbits) and disjunction in another (digital cool and digital gaming) underscores the connections among visual habits, a culture's imagistic artifacts, and the mediating role of humans. People acquire their individual and collective visual habits not only through the gifts of birth but also through interaction with cultural artifacts, especially imagistic artifacts, that permeate their culture. However, and this is a crucial point, artifacts do not, cannot, imprint a visual habit; the individual user negotiates among artifacts, physiological predisposition, and cultural positioning to develop (or not) a visual habit based on this complex array of factors. Thus, despite being immersed in a similar visual culture and in the same array of imagistic artifacts in our home environment, Anna is more comfortable with cool than gaming, Lindsey more comfortable with gaming than cool, and I, tightly bound to print books, am comfortable with neither. Artifacts invite the coevolution of a visual habit by lending themselves to one predominant use over another, a use reinforced by the ambient community.[2]

Both examples emphasize the culture-body interface of vision, countering the Western predisposition to conceive of vision as solely a physiological act, one separate from our cultural sphere. Seeing requires more than physiology; it requires visual habits, the tacit cultural rules that transform stimuli into the experience of sight. Historian Martin Jay describes the dynamic between body and culture in terms of *vision* and *visuality*, arguing for a permeable boundary between physiological vision and cultural visuality (*Downcast Eyes* 9). According to Jay, visuality involves the acquisition of a culturally dominant way of seeing, a scopic regime. A scopic regime consists of the prevailing, culturally sanctioned conventions fusing how we see with what we see. It directs our attention so that our perception and interpretation of stimuli create particular content out of that raw material. Thus, Virgil, blind since birth, had vision after his operation but lacked the requisite visuality to see.

The idea of a scopic regime is absolutely essential for understanding how social action is construed, misconstrued, or nonconstrued. A culture's imagistic artifacts help second-nature visual habits that then serve to mold an individual's and community's perceptions of the world and actions in the world. Barry S. Brummett points out that "we are socialized by our cultures to see the world and to make the world in certain ways" (xiv). The second naturing of any visual habit creates a fine-grained reality sieve: it renders invisible some aspects while rendering visible other aspects of reality. Specific images and networks of reinforcing images across a variety of media, then, can be tools for controlling communal and individual identities, raising "questions concerning who has agency—and therefore responsibility—for these repeatedly circulating cultural products" (Geisler 11). Visual habits can work to prevent people from seeing the need for change.

Such cultural blindness to the need for change motivates and circulates through Fusco's *The Incredible Disappearing Woman*. Invisibility, core to the play and to Fusco's efforts to alter what and how her audience sees, operates on three levels in the play. First, the focal point of the play is the body of a deceased woman who is never present, only alluded to. As Fusco explains, the play's narrative was inspired by and built around a late 1970s transgressive performance-art project in which a male artist, as a prelude to a vasectomy, audiotapes his last "live" ejaculation in the body of a corpse that he had traveled to northern Mexico to "rent" ("In Conversation" 8). Initially, the project languished without a showing because of outrage in the art community, but it was resurrected and received a museum opening in the 1990s. In the controversy swirling around that art project, both originally and two decades later, the deceased woman was invisible; she was simply not perceived as important or germane to the discussion ("In Conversation" 9). Throughout the play, the action circles the examination table with sheeted mannequin, but the violated woman from the 1970s transgressive-art project remains visually elusive.

Second, the characters in the play are in essential ways also invisible. The play opens with the characters donning costumes for the evening's work. Thus, the identities they have assumed to enact the sexual fantasies of their clients are seen, but they themselves are unseen, disregarded as unimportant. Third, two other groups of invisible women, both of whom inspired Fusco, ghost through the play. The first group consists of the more than 220 women, most of them young workers at low-wage factories (*maquiladoras*) in Juarez, Mexico, who literally disappeared, believed murdered, between 1993 and 1999, disappearances that received little local, national, or international attention (Fusco, *Bodies* 202). The second group, connected to the first, includes the cadre of women, again in low-wage factories, who put together the computers Fusco's fictional clients use to access the sex club and communicate their orders (*Bodies* 194–200). The computers are built on the women's bodies even as those bodies remain invisible to the users. The incredible disappearing woman, then, is not just one woman but all women whose presence and plight are unseen by the dominant political, cultural, and economic eye. As Fusco explains, "Through their stories of being silenced, 'disappeared' and effaced from their homelands, I hope to show how the political agency of Latin women is repressed by the family, the Church, the state and neoliberal economic forces" ("Incredible Disappearing Woman").

If the formative power of a scopic regime—its normative influence—were the entire story, then Fusco's play would not be possible, nor would there be a need for this book. People would all be trapped in the reigning visual habit of a culture, constructing out of the flux of reality one flat, narrow view. However, change exists, and social action occurs, both testifying to the possibility that visual habits, while definitely normative, can also be transformative. Fusco's *Incredible Disappearing Woman* challenges a patriarchal-imperialist scopic regime and spotlights that which is invisible. Echoing Fusco's agenda, Brummett maintains, "If we could see how we are influenced to do so [to see and make the world in certain ways], if our repertoires for making reality were broadened, we might make the world into something different" (xv). The paradoxical nature of a visual habit is, not unexpectedly, the key to such critical reflection, the first step to transformation.

First, just as multiple visual artifacts exist within a culture, so do multiple visual habits. A culture is marked by more than one way of seeing, and these multiple habits compete, providing diverse ways to perceive reality. Any one historical period habituates multiple visual habits because any one culture possesses more than one kind of imagistic artifact. A culture is never organized by means of a single, totalizing scopic regime. Instead, competing ways of seeing clash and contend for organizational power within a culture (Jay, "Scopic Regimes of Modernity"). For instance, in the early part of the twenty-first century, the highly participatory way of seeing that Ernest G. Schachtel calls *allocentric perception* contests the entrenched detachment of rational Cartesian perspectivalism. Allocentric perception is characterized by a "profound interest in the object, and complete openness and receptivity toward it, a full turning toward the object which makes possible a direct encounter with it" (220). Such perception yields insights impossible through Cartesian perspectivalism as Barbara McClintock, a Nobel laureate in plant cytology, illustrates. McClintock describes her research approach as acquiring a "feeling for the organism," in which she opens herself up to what the "material has to say" (qtd. in Keller, *Feeling for the Organism* 198). McClintock describes studying corn plants in the field and through her microscope so intently that she achieved an unexpected intimacy, which was a necessary prelude to her insights concerning the transposition of genes (198). Thus, Evelyn Fox Keller, McClintock's intellectual biographer, can conclude that the long delay in scientific recognition of McClintock's remarkable discoveries resulted, in significant part, from a way of seeing that differed radically from the more conventional Cartesian perspectivalism that dominated science.

Just as multiple visual habits coexist within any one culture, multiple versions of reality avail themselves for world building. We stitch together these bits and pieces of divergent realities, finding gaps impossible to suture. Such spaces among multiple ways of seeing hold the hope of revealing different aspects of material realities. Even as we are immersed in our cultural mythologies, even as we attempt to sew together a seamless visual reality from the threads of different visual habits, we prick our fingers, finding in the dilemma of oppositions the need for a different pattern. To illustrate, Fusco attempts a little metaphorical finger pricking by juxtaposing a disembodied, detached way of seeing with a participatory, engaged vision fostered by performative art.

Fusco fears that digital technologies pose a potential problem for social change. Despite a performative element intrinsic to virtual realities, digital media, through ease of manipulation, replication, and distribution, also tend to disengage bodies from minds, expelling bodies from the virtual-visual imaginary (*Bodies* 188). The enfleshed body is not on-screen; an imaginary construct with no anchor or referent in the material world and therefore no stake in that world is on-screen. Thus, Fusco worries that digital technologies, particularly the Internet, constitute a potential threat to social action. These media, she argues, promote a disembodied way of seeing that objectifies life and positions the user as a detached spectator. Digital technologies disconnect the viewer from the viewed, habituating a disengagement that creeps into real life.

Concerned with this disembodied visual habit, a habit that she believes reinforces the patriarchal-imperialist gaze, Fusco revised her published 2001 version of the play in a deliberate effort to evoke and simultaneously disrupt that way of seeing. In her original text, the action occurs in a diorama of the museum where the characters work as custodians preparing for the opening of a show. However, in the 2003 performed version, Fusco sets her one-act drama in a live Internet sex club where clients, through digital (audio and typed) commands, direct the actions of the characters. The original stage set—a recreation of the transgressive-art project—becomes a set within a set for a play within a play. The mock Web cams and computer technology invite the clients' disembodied vision; however, that vision is disrupted by the characters who cross the fourth wall separating viewer from viewed. Confronted with sex workers who respond to commands in unexpected ways, the clients lose control of their detached way of seeing.

A second source of transformation resides in the circular relationship between image and habit that constitutes the dynamic of second naturing. Visual habits exist through the reciprocal movement, the creative tension, between image artifact and habit, which resist as well as complement one another. Potentially new and compassionate perceptions lie in those differences. This circularity of and the intrinsic differences between image and visual habit are at the heart of Fusco's feminist agenda, for she employs a subversive array of visual, graphic images to disrupt the patriarchal-imperialist gaze so closely intertwined with digital disembodiment as a means to alter women's realities. For instance, exposed to an array of specific, networked images that present certain representations of women, women raised in the West are taught to align themselves to the patriarchal gaze in submissive ways. Laura Mulvey calls this "to be looked-at-ness" (11) while John Berger calls it the habit of "watch[ing] themselves being looked at" (47). However, because there is no isomorphic match between image and experience or image and visual habit, the stitches suturing image to reality, image to visual habit unravel, opening up gaps where the possibility of new images and new ways of seeing can flourish. Feminist artists capitalize on these differences to create feminist insurgency tactics that challenge the patriarchal gaze (Meyers, *Being Yourself*). Fusco's insurgency tactics stem from her selection of images from the most tenacious of patriarchal paradigms: the objectification of women within pornography and the perception of women as simply a collection of body parts. Then, she systematically twists the images to skew that objectification and perception. The characters talk back to the clients and each other; the characters subtly accommodate and resist the clients' orders through a variety of strategies: outright opposition, irony, and parody. The images become subversive, ripping apart the ostensible seamlessness of a patriarchal-imperialist way of seeing.

To summarize, then, a visual habit is an amalgamation of a culture-body interface. Image artifacts within a community rebound on that community to (re)shape particular ways of seeing that initiate members into a cohesive cohort. As such, a visual habit is formative. However, it can also be transformative: it can reveal new (alternative) images that, in turn, can nurture new ways of seeing. Integral to the possibility of social action, a visual habit provides a means to recognize the need for social action. The fabric of this possibility is woven from the threads of visual habits, discussed above, and of rhetorical habits, discussed below. The prevailing means of verbal persuasion within a period or a single situation cannot be separated from the prevailing visual habit of that period or in that situation. We might snip one from the other for various purposes, but this is an artificial separation at best. The next section explores how visual habits work with *and* against rhetorical habits, and contends that options for change lurk within the interface between the visual and the rhetorical.

Thread 2: Rhetorical Habits and Options for Change

The previous section asks, "Is it possible to perceive the need for change?" Regardless of the formative power of a visual habit, the conflict within and among visual habits as well as the mediation of individuals ensures that injurious material and social conditions can be perceived, identified, and acknowledged. The affirmative answer, then, leads to another question: how do we act on that new perception? Social action poses a methodological problem. What symbolic options for change can community members exercise that will not reinforce a harmful status quo? Or, to reprise the terms of my introduction, what compassionate means for action might community members deploy that will bring about the goal of compassionate living? One answer lies in the interweaving of visual and rhetorical habits, the second loop in a symbiotic knot. A culture's and an individual's options for social action lie within the visual-rhetorical connection, a connection formed by the various ways in which images *and* words relate. Community members evolve rhetorical habits—persuasive strategies calling forth a particular social action—in conjunction with (or in resistance to) a set of normative, historically situated visual habits. Social action emerges from the interweaving of the two. Therefore, understanding means-end reciprocity requires understanding the looping of visual habit with rhetorical habit. This section explores that looping in two steps: first, highlighting the intersection of visual with rhetorical habits historically and second, looking into the contributions of that intersection to new options for social action.

Vision and language are not independent systems either physiologically or culturally; they are interdependent, developing contiguously yet asymmetrically. Because our visual activities are linked to our linguistic activities, we perceive and enact social action within this nexus. To understand the reciprocity and coevolution of visual and rhetorical habits, we can begin by teasing out the visual habits already operating in conjunction with the rhetorical habits inherited from classical oratory.

Rhetoric grows out of an individual's experiences in the world, John Poulakos argues, and those experiences foster rhetorical habits that, in turn, become habituated responses to particular repeating situations. Through complex feedback and feed-forward loops, habituated rhetorical responses—rhetorical habits—not only evolve out of repeating situations but also serve to ensure particular situations continue to repeat. Rhetorical habits are both the product of situational repetition and the producer of that repetition. Intertwined in these rhetorical habits, even before the contemporary image-saturated age, is the visual element. The nature of the visual-rhetorical interface has changed historically, but the reliance of one on the other has remained a constant. For instance, Gombrich points out that Quintilian correlated alterations in rhetorical style with alterations in art. During the Second Sophistic, Quintilian associated the rise of Roman oratory particularly and its shifts from "rough vigor to smooth polish" with parallel shifts in art from the "hard" manner of archaic sculpture to the "soft" and "sweet" style of fourth-century sculpture (10). In addition, Gombrich claims that Roman scholars tied moral decay in oratory, identified by subtle shifts in style, to a similar decay in art. Other scholars defended contemporary styles of oratory and art, such as Tacitus who claimed, "Times have changed and so have our ears. We demand a different style of oratory" (qtd. in Gombrich 11). Not only have our ears changed with the times but so, too, have our eyes. We demand—and develop—different rhetorical habits in relationship to shifts in images and visual habits. To attend to these shifts is to attend to the possibilities for social action.

Two historical examples illustrate the existence of the interface of visual and rhetorical habits as well as the centrality of that interface for social action. The first example derives from classicist Simon Goldhill's argument that a regime of display—a way of seeing that relies for value and truth on the weight of the collective, not individual gaze—organized the rhetoric of fifth-century B.C.E. Athens. Integrating the visual and the rhetorical along with the visual and the spatial, Goldhill contends that judgment by the collective gaze of the polis played an integral role in social action during fifth- and fourth-century B.C.E. Greece. Citing three major public institutions that constituted a "supremely Greek" Athenian culture—the assembly, the law-court, and the theater—Goldhill claims that Greek society consisted of a performance culture: one's democratic citizenship intersected with one's participation as an audience member. The boundaries between spectator and performer were permeable, not only because spectator could so easily become performer but also because spectating itself constituted a performance, an enactment of one's democratic duty as a citizen. Spectating was the "doing" of citizenship and thus the "doing" of social action. Spectating was both an option for social action and the social action itself.

The participatory, collective character of classical Greek rhetoric, and thus of social action, in fifth-century B.C.E. Athens manifested itself in a variety of discrete visually oriented rhetorical habits. First, dropping one's cloak exemplifies the fusion of rhetorical and visual habits. Sociologist Richard Sennett in *Flesh and Stone* claims that the cityscape in fifth-century B.C.E. Athens was designed to promote "naked speaking," where rhetors figuratively and, occasionally, literally shed their clothes to engage in the ultimate act of display as an element of persuasive speaking. James N. Davidson in *Courtesans and Fishcakes* elliptically confirms such naked speaking, recounting a speech where the appearance of the accused's body in the Assembly served as evidence confirming the charges of conspiracy and immorality: "Only recently," Aeschines claims, "he [Timarchus] threw off his cloak in the People's Assembly and his body was in such an appalling and shameful condition thanks to his drunkenness and his vices that decent men had to look away" (qtd. in Davidson 219). Davidson also points to the role that the "cloaks" themselves might play in rhetoric, again citing Aeschines, who criticizes Demosthenes: "If someone were to unravel you from those lovely draperies of yours and the soft little chitons underneath . . . and let the jurors hold them in their hands, I think they would be unable to tell whether they had taken the clothing of a man or of a woman" (qtd. in Davidson 168). Dropping one's cloak or arraying oneself in a particular manner served as a rhetorical strategy, an option for social action, one that grew out of the visual-rhetorical culture.

The point I make here is not that fifth-century B.C.E. Athenian rhetors stripped to speak, literally or discursively. Rather, I underscore how rhetors twenty-five hundred years ago and throughout the centuries have evolved rhetorical habits—the means of bringing about a persuasive end—in conjunction with a set of visual habits widespread at the moment. Crucial to social action in fifth- and fourth-century B.C.E. Athens was its participatory, collective character, and that participatory, collective character was enacted through an array of rhetorical options that were visually inflected. The architecture of the buildings, the shape of the cityscape, and the elements of a speech did not evolve in a vacuum. These phenomena were fashioned in part to facilitate a particular way of speaking *and* a particular way of seeing to produce a particular way of acting. The physical and the social constitution of fifth-century B.C.E. Athens supported a participatory seeing where seeing easily morphed into speaking; that is, the see-er moved, from one moment to the next, from seeing to speaking. See-ers observed as speakers. Speakers shaped discourse as see-ers. Other eras supported other ways of seeing and ways of speaking, thus inviting other ways of acting, other options for social action.

Ekphrasis provides a second example of the fusion of visual and rhetorical habits in social action. A technique of verbal description, especially descriptions of art, dating from Homer's poetry, *ekphrasis* was an accepted rhetorical strategy in the fifth-century B.C.E. Through vivid verbal description, a rhetor brought before the listener's "mind's eye" a vision (and experience) of reality that validated his persuasive point and invited his listeners to participate in the lawfulness of that reality. Although generally associated with epideictic rhetoric, or speeches that honored specific occasions and reaffirmed the polis's cultural values, *ekphrasis* was potentially applicable in all rhetorical situations. In the fifth century B.C.E., governed by the scopic regime of display, *ekphrasis* served a mimetic function, a discursive way to drop one's cloak and reveal the validity of one's vision of reality.

Without a doubt, both the techniques of dropping one's cloak and *ekphrasis* exist today. Dropping one's cloak has its modern counterpart, for example, in taking off one's suit jacket during a political debate or in a business meeting. Like the ancient gesture, it remains today something that men can do but women cannot. Similarly, *ekphrasis* continues to be a powerful rhetorical option today as reflected in political speeches that rely on descriptive anecdotes and well-told stories. But the configuration of these rhetorical habits has changed in concert with changes in visual habits. How, when, and where a rhetor drops his cloak depends on a community's prevailing visual habit. So, too, with *ekphrasis*, where a culture's dominant visual habits affect the rules and canons of enactment.

Ruth Webb notes this fluidity in her exploration of the literary and rhetorical representations of sacred space during the Byzantium period. She reveals the way in which *ekphrasis*, the "textual aesthetics of description, the rhetorical strategies favored by authors in presenting their subject matter," assumed different forms in different times (62). Such differences highlight the extent to which rhetorical habit and visual habit coalesce within historical eras to shape options for social action.

Conceiving of visual habits and rhetorical habits as intertwined enables us to tackle tough questions concerning individual and/or societal change. If visual-rhetorical habits are formative—controlling who sees/speaks, what is seen/said, where it is seen/said, and how it is seen/said—what options might community members use to change reality without inadvertently reinforcing the very reality they seek to change? In addition, if the objective of social action is compassionate living, how do community members develop the means—the visual-rhetorical habits—that are themselves compassionate?

The first way in which we can create new options for and visions of compassionate living consists of knotting rhetorical and visual habits in startling combinations.[3] Nowhere is this better manifested than in metaphor, a powerful rhetorical strategy that links disparate images to concepts to create new or alternative meanings.[4] A metaphor teeters on the edge of a rhetorical habit and on the edge of a visual habit, deriving generative power from both. Drawing on the work of Donald Davidson, Richard Rorty claims that metaphors serve as the transition between one vocabulary, or language regime, and another; intellectual history is the history of metaphor (16). Thus, the epistemological shifts effected by such thinkers as Galileo, Hegel, and Yeats resulted from new vocabularies, "thereby equipping them with tools for doing things which could not even have been envisaged before these tools were available" (17).

Galileo's development of $v = gt$, the formula plotting the speed of a falling body as a function of time, provides an example of this (re)visionary visual-rhetoric fusion. Given the Greco-Christian tradition during Galileo's life that privileged space rather than time, the treatment of time as an element of an object's speed constituted a conceptually revolutionary step. Because of space's conceptual prominence, French philosopher Michèle Le Dœuff argues that it would have been "stunningly unnatural to relate acceleration to time alone. To make time a parameter of speed meant breaking with solidly rooted mental structures" (36). This break—what Rorty would call a shift into a new vocabulary—was effected through what Le Dœuff calls analogical or metaphorical thinking. Using key passages from Galileo describing the evolution of his theory, Le Dœuff argues that Galileo shifted from an Aristotelian vocabulary to a new vocabulary by means of metaphorical thinking: using the alchemical notion of affinity to wed time, rather than space, with movement. Metaphor stands at the crossroads of rhetorical and visual habits; as a result, it can serve as the vehicle of intellectual and social change.[5]

The second way that the tangling of visual and rhetorical habits serve social action concerns their differences. Visual habits and rhetorical habits might evolve in relation to one another, but they are not the same. There is no one-to-one correspondence between word and image, between a way of speaking and a way of seeing. As a result, gaps always exist as community members participate in their worlds by juggling modes of seeing and saying. In some cases, that juggling results in a misalignment where one subordinates the other. Thus, a critical awareness of such misalignment can lead to new, productive visual-rhetorical linkages that open up opportunities for change.[6] Todd DeStigter highlights this dynamic and its possibilities for either stifling or reconfiguring modes of action in his ethnography of Latina/o students at a rural Michigan high school. Specifically, he notes the failure of what he calls *cosmetic multiculturalism*: staged performances, such as Cinco de Mayo days, that are designed to emphasize the value of cultural diversity in the public school system and redress racial inequalities.

As a predominantly visual strategy, cosmetic multiculturalism fails to initiate the dialogue integral to change, DeStigter says. Instead, it placates, leaving unchallenged the pedagogies and/or districtwide procedures that deter democratic participation of students of color.[7] In addition, at the same time it discourages rhetorical engagement, cosmetic multiculturalism encourages a visual rebellion divorced from discursive rhetoric and thus equally futile at effecting substantive change in the status of marginalized students. Drawing on his research, DeStigter explains that many Latina/os in the school he studied responded to cosmetic multiculturalism by evolving their own transgressive visual performances. They sought to counter visual trivialization by dressing, looking, and acting on a daily basis in ways that disrupted the "good Mexican student" status quo and affirmed the bone-deep, versus cosmetic, nature of Latina/o identity. Such visual performances signaled the students' contempt for the school's superficial efforts to respond to their needs and signaled their awareness of the disjuncture between cosmetic multiculturalism and unaddressed institutional inequities. But, while such visual tactics successfully signaled defiance, they, like cosmetic multiculturalism, failed to alter the students' situation because they were not linked to rhetorical tactics. Visual resistance without discursive resistance reinforced rather than challenged the subordinate position of Latina/os within the school and the culture at large. Students skipped school and rejected academic culture in myriad ways, with the end result that they dropped out, took low-paying jobs, and continued to fill the low-income labor pool.

The misalignment between visual and rhetorical habits underscores two important points. First, the differences between a visual habit and a rhetorical habit can generate new perceptions of reality, new alternatives to injustice, and new modes of social action. Second, the differences between the two habits can erode the possibility of social action by privileging one habit over the other. When we engender social action through a solely visual or a solely rhetorical means, we limit both the scope and the effectiveness of that action. In certain cases, as with cosmetic multiculturalism and visual resistance, we may even undermine our efforts to change the status quo. Social action relies on the integration of the two. In addition, social action relies on the integration of the two *enacted in specific places*. Weaving throughout this discussion of visual and rhetorical habits is a third thread in a symbiotic knot: place. From sex workers in a chat room to Latina/o students in a southwestern Michigan high school to rhetors in fifth-century B.C.E. Athens, physical environment has been necessary for the existence of both vision and language. To account for social action, we need something more than the interweaving of visual habits and rhetorical habits because neither exist nor function in a vacuum. Rather, both are enacted contextually and interpreted locally. They are emplaced; they require bodies *as* places and bodies *in* places to exist.

Thread 3: A Place of and for Social Action

The paradoxical nature of visual habits ensures that community members, even while immersed in a culture's mythologies, can perceive the need for change. The interweaving of visual and rhetorical habits ensures that community members can develop options for change that do not replicate the status quo. The third thread in the symbiotic knot—place—provides venues for social action as well as venues within which visual and rhetorical habits are developed. This section integrates place with visual-rhetorical habits, delineating the implications such knotting poses for social action. I begin with the web of places that exist within any one location, including the writing classroom. Next, I detail the constraints and challenges that place poses for social action.

Place in and of itself is a tricky phenomenon because any single location consists of a web of interlocking places, both material and ideological. The first place that must exist for any hope of (or need for) social action is the body itself, which also comprises a set of interlocking places from cells to organs to organism. Without a body as a place, an individual cannot be in a place. While the body is certainly not a self-contained entity clearly circumscribed by the shell of the skin, it still exists as a site albeit a permeable one (Fleckenstein, "Writing Bodies").[8] Second, bodies as places are also in places themselves, from room to home to neighborhood, community, cityscape, and so forth. Bodies cannot exist without an environment that not only contains bodies but also affects the constitution of those bodies. Third, the constant interplay between physical places and bodies is subject to cyber-places (computers, networks, rooms, avatars) that fill the interstices between material locations and separate bodies, sometimes even supplanting both. Fourth, bodies, places, and cyberplaces link to and through the larger ambient visual culture, the wildly picture-oriented place of television, videophones, video games, videoconferencing, manga, anime, massively multiplayer online role-playing games (MMORPGs), magnetic resonance imagings (MRIs), Internet cafes, and Hubble telescopes. People within this highly visual culture live life on-screen, Nicholas Mirzoeff says, and that screen as the medium of expression constitutes a fifth place. Gombrich emphasizes the importance medium plays in both visual and verbal expression. An artist can only render what the medium allows: "[T]he artist's desire to create, to bring forth a second reality, finds its inexorable limits in the restrictions of his medium," Gombrich says (96). In addition, the medium creates a mental lens that predisposes the artist to see only those aspects of scene that can be expressed through a particular medium (86).

These five facets of place—body, natural or constructed environments, cyberspace, visual culture, and medium—hint at the complexity of place, a complexity that is integral to social action because place affects the rhetorical and visual strategies people deploy to bring about change. In addition, each facet of place is inextricably linked to (even in a sense produced by) the others, which means that change on one level is reinforced and/or contested on other levels. Compassionate social action does not limit itself to a single cause in a single place because place is never singular; place interconnects with an array of other places. Injustice in one locale bleeds into other locales. Therefore, by necessity, compassionate social action concerns itself with the well-being of all people in all places. *The Incredible Disappearing Woman* emphasizes the importance of interlaced places in compassionate social action by working to destabilize the audience's sense of a discrete place. Through deliberate spatial confusion, Fusco highlights the diffused nature of injustice and the importance of addressing injustice through a range of places because redressing a wrong in Havana depends on redressing a similar wrong in Juarez or San Salvador or rural Michigan.

Her provocative construction of a web of overlapping places begins with the characters' bodies, ensconced in multiple places simultaneously: the actual stage on which Fusco and her cohorts perform; the set on that stage, which consists of (a) Room #13 of the live, online sex club, which the Web cam transmits in real time and beams into the clients' "home" places, (b) a museum scene created for the clients with a penchant for necrophilia, (c) the transgressive-art project itself within that museum scene, and (d) a filmed version of the museum opening with docent, artist, and spectators interacting via a screen at the back of the stage. These levels constantly interact, confusing who the characters are and what they can be, say, and do. Dolores, the victim of spousal abuse who, counseled by her parish priest, takes sanctuary in prayer, offers a harrowing illustration of this confusion of places. When the sex workers Chela and Magaly clock in for work, they wheel Dolores out of a closet where, as half human and half robot, she is stored until the sex show begins. With a laptop built into her body, Dolores serves as the medium through which the clients communicate with the sex workers. She manifests in physical form the confusion of places and the dynamic by which insult in one place circulates throughout the entire complex web. Finally, the play itself constitutes a place as the medium through which Fusco shapes her social protest: as a one-act portable play performed four different times at four different venues. That medium constrains what Fusco can and cannot say, offering one kind of social action while closing off others.[9]

These individual layers of place and the reciprocity of those layers enable us to address the conditions necessary for social action. As *The Incredible Disappearing Woman* highlights, the first requirement for social action is a place *for* social action. Wells concurs, arguing that "if we want more for our students than the ability to defend themselves in bureaucratic settings, we are imagining them in a public role, imagining a public space they can enter" (326). If the first requirement for social action is to have a place for social action, the second requirement is to construct that place. As Wells contends, the public sphere is "always constructed" (326). Nancy Welch reinforces that argument. She notes in "Living Room" that "ordinary people *make* rhetorical space," which she defines as "public space with the potential to operate as a persuasive public sphere" (477; emphasis in original). They do so through a "concerted, often protracted struggle for visibility, voice, and impact against powerful interests that seek to deny visibility, voice, and impact. People *take* and *make* space in acts that are simultaneously verbal and physical" (477; emphasis in original). In addition, people take and make places in acts that are simultaneously verbal and visual, which brings us back to the important connections among place, visual habits, and rhetorical habits in a symbiotic knot.

Crucial to taking and making a public place for social action are the raw materials of construction. As part of a symbiotic knot, place coevolves with visual and rhetorical habits, and that conjunction both constrains and enables social action. The design of domestic spaces provides an illustration of the ways in which place, visual habits, and rhetorical habits conspire to limit options for social action by specifying *where* and *who* can speak or be seen. Greenpeace activism illustrates the power of place to configure *when* someone can or should speak. And the jeremiad provides an example of the way in which place influences *how* someone shapes an argument.

In her feminist critique of architecture, *Discrimination by Design*, Leslie Kanes Weisman reveals the interaction among place, image, and visual habit. She contends that human beings are shaped by their "built space," and a built space begins in the visual design. She explores in depth the design of homes as gendered places, particularly the evolving shapes of kitchens. For instance, Weisman argues that the 1930s open-kitchen arrangement directs who can see (mother), what can be (over)seen (the family), and where that seeing has primacy (the home). It also dictates who can be seen (the mother) and where that individual can be seen (the home). Introduced by Frank Lloyd Wright in the Malcolm Willey home in Minneapolis, this flowing design does not hide women in the kitchen "like servants"; rather, it positions women so that they can see/supervise the children and so that they can be seen but only in the home. The open concept was motivated by Wright's efforts to create "flowing interior spaces" that "brought family members physically together more often" (92). Place was thus created out of an image (architectural design) that then in turn created an image (family unity) and inculcated a visual habit, one based on surveillance and control by women and of women within the domestic sphere.[10]

In addition, language contributed to the design of Wright's kitchen area, with the design turning around to reshape the possibilities of rhetoric. Wells refers to local civic spaces—"the place where we decide to strike vote, hire a new minister, form a block watch"—as "scraps of discursive space" (326). The same argument can be applied to private places: they, too, are scraps of discursive space that intersect with civic spaces. The open design of kitchens in the 1930s positioned the mother visibly and firmly in the kitchen, in the home; the texts circulating publicly during this the same time reinforced the design. Weisman specifically points to the widely popular *The Personality of a House* by Emily Post, a work that was reprinted annually for almost a decade (93). A maven of social etiquette, Post set forth domestic behavior, advocating the design of rooms for women based on "how they [women] look" and the design of rooms for men based on "what they do" (95–96). Post's book, Weisman argues, "promotes home design that creates the illusion of security and family stability through traditional styles and symbols of a strong and active male presence and a dependent and passive female counterpart" (97). Once constructed out of words, place turns around to constrain speaking. Thus, the codification of the open-floor plan established the scene of women's power, a continuation of the nineteenth-century angel in the house, reducing women's rhetorical options by confining them to the domestic sphere. Reinforced imagistically and discursively, design excluded women from the public sphere and circumscribed their ability to enact social change. Circulating through this visual-discursive construction of domestic place, then, is a patriarchal ideology specifying who can see and speak and who is seen and spoken to, a realization vital to understanding the complexity of the public sphere.[11]

Contiguous to dictating where something can be said or seen and who can see or say it, place also constrains *when* something can (or should) be said.

Place is kairotic, Jerry Blitefield argues: "Place provides the pages upon which *kairoi* can get written and across which *kairoi* can endure" (73). Drawing on Aristotle's *Physics*, Blitefield points out that for a discourse to be kairotic, for it to be timely and opportune, it must occur somewhere, and that somewhere affects the timeliness—the appropriate moment—of the discourse. Greenpeace, for example, is a past master at acting on the *kairos* of a place, as Kevin Michael DeLuca demonstrates. DeLuca recounts a 1975 incident involving Greenpeace activists' attempt to disrupt Soviet whaling. Six Greenpeace protestors in three Zodiacs (small, rubber boats) interposed themselves between a Soviet whaler's 160-pound exploding-grenade harpoon and its sperm-whale target. The kairotic moment occurs between the loading of the whaling spear and the firing of the spear; the rhetorical forcefulness of the image event is tied to the timeliness of the action, which in turn cannot be extricated from the place of the action: on the sea in a bobbing inflatable dingy within the sights of a 90 mm cannon. Although DeLuca states that Greenpeace's efforts failed as direct action (that is, the whaler fired over the heads of the activists and killed the whale), the protestors did succeed in creating a persuasive communication; in the words of the then Greenpeace director, they transformed "the way people view their world" (qtd. in DeLuca 1). They did so by acting on the *kairos* of a place.

In addition to where, who, and when, place also impinges on *how* something can be said, for instance, how an argument is shaped and which proofs are used. Places where arguments occur implicate the structure that argument might take and the strategies used to make that argument persuasive. One example of the reciprocity between place and ways of speaking is the jeremiad employed by African American abolitionists in the nineteenth century. This rhetorical habit evolved in conjunction with the places where African Americans were speaking: in physical situations dominated by White audience members, which required African American speakers to tap into the White zeitgeist. According to Keith D. Miller, the jeremiad has been a dominant form of African American rhetoric for more than 150 years (200). From Jeremiah, the author of Lamentations in the Old Testament, a jeremiad consists of an essay or speech expressing grief over a current situation as a prelude to arguing for specific changes in that situation. Citing David Howard-Pitney, Miller explains that the African American jeremiad features three elements: past promise, current failure, and eventual fulfillment (201). Miller argues that this rhetorical form evolved in response to White epistemology and rhetoric. For example, orators from Frederick Douglass to Martin Luther King Jr. claimed the Declaration of Independence (all men are created equal) and the Bible (all men are brothers) to establish the promise of equality. They referred to the immediate situation to highlight the failure of that promise. Then, they followed with a specific course of action that would realize that promise. The claim to a past promise based on documents central to those White audience members was necessary to establish a point of adherence between speaker and listeners.

However, place also circulates through the logic of the jeremiad. To illustrate, King's "I Have a Dream," a jeremiad presented in Washington, D.C., on the steps of the Lincoln Memorial, evolves in conjunction with the Lincoln Memorial. Although King's ostensible audience consisted of the predominantly African American protestors gathered below and around him, his powerful secondary audience consisted of White voters watching through a different medium and from different places. The choice of the Lincoln Memorial constituted an appeal to that secondary audience because, first, the monument served as a concrete manifestation of past promise and, second, it evoked a current identity in which the White audience was invested. Without a doubt, that place and those rhetorical choices also invested King's primary audience in that White identity, which is Miller's point, but that double move does not undercut the power of place to influence rhetorical choices.[12]

Place—where one speaks—contributes to who can speak, when one should speak, and how one should speak. Where, who, when, and how emphasize the necessity of place to visual-rhetorical habits, simultaneously leading to the third implication posed by place for social action: its disappearance. If place is essential to visual-rhetorical habits, then the erosion of places to speak and to be seen speaking will likewise erode a community's occasions for speaking and repertoire of visual-rhetorical habits. Welch articulates this concern. Composition teachers dedicated to encouraging their students to engage in public writing that aims to challenge social inequities face "dramatically shrinking material and virtual spaces" for such endeavors ("Living Room" 474). She narrates an anecdote involving one of her students who was picked up by the police for posting a poem of protest in a "nondesignated area." Nondesignated areas where public writing and protest are restricted—where they cannot be seen—are increasing in this era of neoliberalism, Welch contends.[13] During a historical moment when we have "liberalized speech and assembly rights," neoliberalism, or the move to privatize public spaces, services, and resources, has "greatly reduced the locations in which we are able to exercise these rights" ("Living Room" 474, 475). An impoverishment of visual and rhetorical habits as well as an impoverishment of places for social action results from these "encroachments on voice, visibility, and movement" ("Living Room" 475).

DeStigter takes the impoverishment of place as a given in his analysis of Latina/o students. His goal is to alter the situation of Latina/os in school and in the culture at large by opening up new public venues for speaking, seeing, and acting. It is not enough to establish affective ties in the classroom and the community, he says, although such ties are essential for democratic action. Instead, those relationships must extend into the public sphere to change the conditions that limit Latina/os and other people of color. In "Public Displays of Affection," a title that captures his goal of extending communal ties of affection into public political action, DeStigter points to the work of Tammi, a counselor at the Chicago Latino Youth Alternative High School, who steadfastly labored to help her students enter public spheres for public speaking: Pedro, with Tammi's encouragement, attended a Chicago Public School Board meeting to protest funding cuts to alternative schools; dozens of Latino Youth students, with Tammi's help, organized a rally at Daley Plaza to protest police violence. According to DeStigter, Tammi acted on her belief that fostering community and nurturing literacy among marginalized young people were not enough. She had to help them create and participate in public places of protest. Any attention to social action requires a construction of places for speaking and acting. "All speakers and writers who aspire to intervene in society face the task of constructing a responsive public," Wells points out (328–29). Constructing that responsive public constitutes DeStigter's primary goal, which requires increasing civic engagement in a multitude of places so that a population's options for compassionate social action likewise increase.

DeStigter's work to expand civic engagement by expanding the places of engagement returns me to the starting point in this section: the interlocking quality of place. In short, compassionate social action cannot be effected on a single level of place nor can it be effected by focusing on a single thread in the symbiotic knot of vision-rhetoric-place. Marxist geographer David Harvey agrees, contending in *Spaces of Hope* that effective social action must be carried out on the micro and macro levels of place. Thus, the knotting of place with visual-rhetorical habits directs our attention to the necessity of *engaging* on multiple levels the places of public writing and speaking and *enlarging* the scope of those places. In addition, the knotting directs our attention to the ways in which visual and rhetorical habits, while growing out of places, also create places. Place impinges on the development of visual-rhetorical habits, which are second natured in response to the arrangements of artifacts in places (and perhaps places as artifacts). Even as visual-rhetorical habits are shaped and fashioned by an individual's immersion within multiple, intersecting places, those places are simultaneously constructed out of those visual-rhetorical habits. This Gordian knot means that engaging in and enlarging places for action require a consideration of the interplay of place, visual habits, and rhetorical habits.

A Symbiotic Knot of Agency

Despite my separate exploration of visual habits, rhetorical habits, and place in the above three threads, I maintain that all three exist interwoven with the others. The collectivity of the symbiotic knot itself presents the final value for understanding the possibilities and impossibilities of social action. A look at the totality of a symbiotic knot offers new insight into agency, crucial to social action because without both the belief in one's ability to act in the world *and* the ability to act, no social action is possible. Agency—who has it, who does not—is inextricably tangled up in symbiotic knots. As archeologist Andrew Gardner points out:

> The problem of agency is, in many respects, the problem of the human condition. It concerns the nature of individual freedom in the face of social constraints, the role of socialization in the forming of "persons," and the place of particular ways of doing things in the reproduction of cultures. In short, it is about the relationships between an individual human organism and everyone and everything else that surrounds it. (1)

A symbiotic knot provides a useful metaphor for examining relationships between an individual and "everyone and everything else that surrounds it." The power to see, speak, and act in the world and to influence how others see, speak, and act in the world is tangled in the loops of a symbiotic knot. Agency emerges from individuals negotiating the intertwined threads of visual habits, rhetorical habits, and places.

First, the concept of a symbiotic knot enables us to better understand how a segment of a population—such as the disappearing women in Fusco's performance art—can be denied agency. Symbiotic knots both confer and defer agency, different knots configuring different identities for agents and different modes of action for those agents. Any system of visual habits, rhetorical habits, and places serves to endow some segments of a community with agency in a particular arena (such as women in the kitchen) while withholding agency from others (such as women in the public sphere). A way of seeing intertwines with a way of speaking, and that pattern is replicated in subtle, sometimes brutal, ways in the construction of specific places to see and speak, thus hiding—rendering invisible—the reality that some people within a community are denied any right to see or to speak. That lack of agency becomes an ingrained aspect of a community's reality, difficult to perceive and difficult to change. In addition, the tighter the knots among those threads—the denser the connections—the greater and more deeply entrenched becomes one group's agency and another's lack of agency. The more that a visual habit, a rhetorical habit, and a place reinforce, the more rigid and codified becomes the assignment (or withholding) of agency. The denser the interconnections among classrooms, boardrooms, and backrooms, the more deeply seated is the power of a knot to configure reality and the individual's agency within that reality.

Second, even as a symbiotic knot confers and defers agency through a complex process of socialization that involves vision, language, and environment, it also keeps alive the hope of agency for those denied it. From the perspective of a symbiotic knot, agency is not the sole result of a discursive and a scopic regime replicating across different places. Instead, it is the result of the interplay of the three in one symbiotic knot that is part of a larger network of symbiotic knots within any one culture. This dynamic relationship highlights that there are multiple positions and multiple loops constituting reality for a community. Thus, an individual is not part of just one loop. Rather, each person is engaged in active and constant negotiation among places, words, and images no matter how tightly knotted those threads might be. Welch underscores how rhetorical space is not simply the product of "well-intentioned civic planning" (or imagery as design) or the exercise of a "few sound and reasonable rhetorical rules of conduct" ("Living Room" 477). Rather, it is the product of people making and remaking design and rules of conduct. From the perspective of a symbiotic knot, agency functions similarly: it erupts in unexpected places because people inhabit a network of symbiotic knots and constantly negotiate different visual-rhetorical habits. As a result, a group of people denied agency in seeing, or speaking, or being in one place can disrupt that status quo because they operate among and through different visual-rhetorical habits.

Third, a symbiotic knot stresses that the specific enactment of agency is always situational. An individual may have agency in one situation and not in another. Susan Zaeske says that agency is not "a thing possessed by an agent"; rather, "agency is more an energy that exists in a particular situation." Understanding rhetorical agency, then, requires looking "to the situation, the context in which that agency was exercised," she states. Conceiving of agency as part of a symbiotic knot emphasizes the importance not just of agency but also of *agencies* and of working to expand the situations within which one can perform as an agent.

Finally, a symbiotic knot highlights that agency relies on an act of the imagination, one in which the individual envisions himself or herself being heard *and* being seen. To return to Wells, "If we want more for our students than the ability to defend themselves in bureaucratic settings, we are *imagining* them in a public role, *imagining* a public space they can enter" (326; emphasis added). A symbiotic knot provides the raw materials for that imaginative act, resonating to Karlyn Kohrs Campbell's contention that agency emerges as an expression of artistry or craft: it is of the imagination and evolves as an act of the imagination. Agency flourishes within the gaps between image and visual habit, between visual habit and the word, between the rhetorical habit and place. In puzzling moments when we are pulled up short, startled into asking what a phenomenon might be and who am I to define it as such, imagination flowers, and the potential for agency exists. The failure of social action, then, is not always a failure of language or of vision or of place. Sometimes, it is the failure of imagination.

Immersion in a culture of images fosters visual habits that link image and word in different ways, feeding into visions of rhetorical agency linked to specific sites for action. The individual—free-floating, disembodied, Cartesian self—may be dead, but agency is not. The symbiotic knot enables us to consider agency as both a collective and an individual enactment. To understand the limits and the possibilities of social action, then, we cannot look merely at visual habits or environment or rhetorical habits. Rather, we must look at each and at the entire symbiotic knot. How visual-rhetorical habits coevolve in response to cultural images, how these habits converge to form a matrix for social action, and how that matrix affects agency in and out of the writing classroom are questions I explore in the next chapters.

2. A KNOT OF SILENCE
Spectacle, Rhetorical Compliance,
and the Struggle for Agency

> For one to whom the real world becomes real images, mere
> images are transformed into real beings—tangible figments
> which are the efficient motor of trancelike behavior.
> —Guy Debord, *Society of the Spectacle*

In his memoir *Dreams from My Father*, Barack Obama recounts a decisive moment in his work as a community organizer with low-income residents in Chicago's Roseland area and in the Altgeld Gardens public housing development on the city's South Side. Despite the fifty members of a core group of citizens who collaborated to improve their neighborhood in concrete ways, from community cleanups to lobbying for improved sanitation services, Obama fears that "*real* change" is just not attainable (229; emphasis in original). Because the constraints on change are too complex, too deeply ingrained, he dreads that he, like Chicago Mayor Harold Washington, might be "an inheritor of sad history, part of a closed system with few moving parts, a system that was losing heat every day, dropping into low-level stasis" (231). Rather than an agent of change, Obama dreads that he, along with Washington, has become a prisoner of fate, doomed to alleviate the symptoms but never the causes of social ills.

Obama's doubts come to flash point when, on the steps of a local elementary school, he and a fellow activist seek to enlist parents living in Altgeld Gardens to travel with them on a waiting school bus to the Chicago Housing Authority. The cohort plans to pressure the CHA for information concerning asbestos in the housing development. Buttonholing residents as they bring their children to school, Obama urges them to join the community action, only to be met with vague, murmured excuses about conflicting appointments, commitments, and engagements. As school begins and parents dissipate, only eight community members rattle over Chicago city streets to face the CHA goliath.

At this crisis in his life, Obama witnesses the debilitating erosion of agency as people excuse their lack of participation, their passivity, in the face of collective action. Obama perceives, and rightly fears, the entropy of agency: the unarticulated but deeply seated conviction within many people that agency is something others might enact but not them. Belief in one's agency constitutes a key element of social action. If people cannot imagine themselves as agents of change, if they cannot envision themselves acting, then they disengage. As argued at the end of my previous chapter, agency is as much about imagination as it is about action. To work toward a goal of compassionate living, individuals must believe, if only cautiously and locally, in their power to affect the world around them. Without that belief, they have no hope for their actions and thus no hope in the outcome of those actions. Understanding the complex factors contributing to or undermining an individual's belief in the capacity to act in and on the world becomes a first step in expanding the scope of agency and the scope of social action.

This chapter, then, is about agency: the belief in it, the constraints on it, and the struggle for it. It extends the discussion begun in chapter 1 where I detailed four ways that the metaphor of the symbiotic knot provides new insights into the complexities of agency. Here, chapter 2 examines the impact of a specific symbiotic knot—a knot of silence—on agency, asking how a particular complement of visual habit, rhetorical habit, and place can conspire, first, to strip people of their belief in their ability to act and, second, to offer them only a simulated agency that possesses little power for bringing about substantive change (see fig. 2.1).[1] Throughout *Vision, Rhetoric, and Social Action in the Composition Classroom*, I maintain that all social action, individual to collective, micro to macro, depends on a rich repertoire of visual and rhetorical habits that coalesce with places to shape unique modes of social action. But visual habits can also interweave with rhetorical habits and places to curtail social action, combining to limit belief in agency and encourage passivity in the face of injustice or suffering. A symbiotic knot of silence—comprising spectacle, rhetorical compliance, and monologic places—blocks nascent social action by eroding an individual's and a community's belief in personal and collective agency. It promotes disengagement by curbing visions of engagement.

My exploration of the symbiotic knot of silence begins with the visual thread of spectacle, arguing that this way of seeing is characterized by three processes—attending exclusively to the present, erasing expertise, and imparting a false sense of unity—each of which undercuts belief in agency and the possibility of social action. The rhetorical habit of compliance, the second thread, intertwines with spectacle to foster a simulated agency, one where the writer mimics the protocols for agency that have been dictated by dominant cultural forces. This mimicry provides the appearance of agency without the substance. The third

Figure 2.1

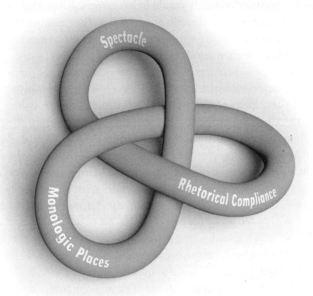

Disengagement

A Symbiotic Knot of Silence

thread of the symbiotic knot, the monologic classroom, reinforces passivity and simulated agency through the deployment of a remediated presentational pedagogy, pseudo-assignments, and rigid style requirements. Finally, I end with a consideration of the entire symbiotic knot of silence, suggesting ways to create what Charles R. Garoian calls a counterspectacle pedagogy: a way of teaching that aims to disrupt a knot of silence, confirming rather than undermining students' belief in their ability to act through compassionate means to redress local and global injustice.

Thread 1: Spectacle and the (Im)probability of Change

Agency is a complex phenomenon, Karlyn Kohrs Campbell explains, comprising a pool of factors, including material limitations, linguistic constraints, historical positioning, and cultural designations. Regardless of impediments, individuals negotiate among institutional powers, cultural-historical situations, and a repertoire of heuristic skills to invent agency. Because agency is crucial to social action, we need to understand the exact nature of the restrictions that undercut agency and the negotiations that surmount those restrictions. Why do some people become more effective inventors of agency than others?

Without a doubt, the obstacles to agency, especially for some segments of the population, are considerable. It should be no surprise, then, that the residents of Altgeld Gardens who declined to participate in the neighborhood-led civic action underscore anecdotally a growing trend of noninvolvement in the United States that cuts across gender, class, and racial boundaries.

The majority of Americans at the end of the twentieth century suffer from a crisis of agency, sociologist Robert D. Putnam claims. In *Bowling Alone*, he argues that participatory citizenship, which includes people voting as well as engaging in other civic activities, has steadily declined within the past three decades. "For the first two-thirds of the twentieth century," he says, "a powerful tide bore Americans into ever deeper engagement in the life of their communities, but a few decades ago—silently, without warning—that tide reversed" (27) Using the term *social capital*, a term reminiscent of civic virtue and one that refers to connections among individuals, Putnam contends that social networks have eroded and with them "the norms of reciprocity and trustworthiness" from which social action arises (19). Without the support of the ties of community, without access to social capital, people cease to believe in their ability to leverage change in the status quo. Along with the failure of imagination and belief, they develop an attitude of passivity, a habituated response of murmured excuses when faced with invitations to alleviate the ills afflicting their own community.

Nor is that malaise limited to the streets. It creeps into classrooms as well. Mike Rose chronicles the plight of at-risk students in a university setting who are unable to participate in the verbal give-and-take of the classroom. Myriad economic, social, and cultural factors contribute to the entropy of agency, and, as Rose points out, one important contribution is the different ways of using language that students bring with them to the classroom. However, another important contribution consists of the visual habits a student brings into the classroom. Visual habits, like other material constraints and cultural factors, influence an individual's belief in and imagination of agency. Thus, a student's reluctance to engage in classroom dialogue, to take up the tasks of the day proactively, stems as much from a particular way of seeing as from a particular way of using language. For instance, one visual habit that undercuts classroom participation and civic engagement by eroding belief in one's agency consists of spectacle. Associated with increased exposure to television and reinforced by family environment, economic status, and attitudes toward knowledge, spectacle reciprocally evolves with mass-mediated imagery to undermine agency's activism by encouraging passivity in and out of the classroom.

The goal in this section is to trace the various components of spectacle to better understand the challenges facing individual and collective social action in the beginnings of the twenty-first century. I open with a deliberately strong case for spectacle, highlighting the feedback and feed-forward loops between the ubiquity of television in the West and the ubiquity of spectacle, a concept I borrow from French Situationist Guy Debord. To highlight the omnipresent influence of television in the West, I emphasize the alarmist orientation that characterizes the discourse of much media criticism from the 1970s to the present moment, an orientation that Kevin Maness argues is currently unpopular (45). Teetering on the verge of technological determinism, an alarmist orientation relies on an imprinting narrative. For instance, cultural-media critics from Theodor W. Adorno to Neil Postman imply that a medium, sans active intervention, invariably affects, or imprints, all people in similar ways. To elaborate, in his controversial *Amusing Ourselves to Death*, Postman claims television fosters a way of seeing that undermines complex dialogue essential to politics and the classroom because the nature of the medium itself cannot sustain intellectual content. Consequently, community members shaped by sustained exposure to television cannot maintain the quality and quantity of conversation required for education and civic discourse. Television inevitably dumbs down viewers. In addition, skirting close to an alarmist orientation, Putnam suggests that television functions as a significant contributor to community disengagement. Repeated interaction with television's flickering images invites and reinforces passivity and isolation. Thus, the imprinting narrative circulating through an alarmist orientation posits that if we introduce television into a household, family members will magically become passive couch potatoes by automatically developing visual and verbal habits of disengagement.

Obviously absent from an alarmist orientation or alluded to only as a mitigating factor is the powerful role that individuals and contexts play in negotiating any medium, even television. No medium is deterministic, and exposure to television does not inevitably result in addiction. Clearly, individuals manage to resist television's addiction, because, although some kinds of civic participation and social action might be declining in the West as Putnam contends, neither civic participation nor social action has disappeared. The dynamic at work in habituation consists of both acquiescence *and* resistance. However, I initially take an alarmist orientation in order to grapple with the lure of acquiescence as a way to foster resistance. The goal for us as teachers consists of supporting resistance, but to do that we must understand the nature of a medium's attraction. As Postman argues, understanding the ways *and* the extent to which television shapes our lives is a necessary first step to understanding the ways and the extent to which we can shape it. So I delineate carefully the implications of a strong position as a prelude to developing a writing pedagogy that counters acquiescence and capitalizes on the resistance.

To that end, I begin with television and its interdependence with spectacle. I describe three key qualities of spectacle, each of which undercuts belief in agency. Spectacle focuses on the immediate moment, erases belief in expertise, and creates a false sense of unity. Connecting spectacle to language, I detail illegeracy, which Jeff Smith defines as a media-influenced literacy that skims the surface of meaning and avoids the responsibility of change. Finally, after exploring the challenges posed by spectacle for agency, I conclude with the importance of the individual and the hope of agency in the face of spectacle. Here I return to the eight parents from Altgeld Gardens who travel with Obama to confront the institutional power of the Chicago Housing Authority, providing an example of people resisting the acquiescence of spectacle for the activism of social change.

Spectacle evolves interdependently with mass-mediated images, particularly those disseminated through television. First introduced in the United States at the 1939 World's Fair, television is a crucial technology of Western popular culture. The way people know, behave, and interact has been radically reordered by television, a point Jerzy Kosinski makes in *Being There*. Kosinski calls the process by which television colonizes viewers' dreams, desires, and actions *vidiocy* and those susceptible to it *vidiots*. In Kosinksi's satiric novel, people under television's influence "just watch." A subject of critical review as well as satire for more than four decades, television has been parsed and analyzed, with scholars concluding that television constitutes a powerful tool for socialization. Everyone who consistently watches television for entertainment—and in the United States, 99 percent of all homes have at least one television and most homes have more televisions than bathrooms or family members—is vulnerable to television's co-optation and the lure of visual passivity: just watching (Rapping 21).

Beyond the content of its mass-mediated images, the medium itself—the flickering images—contributes to the habituation of passivity. For instance, a benchmark study of the effects of television on viewers conducted by Robert Kubey and Mihály Csikszentmihályi and published in 1990 confirms the connection between television and passivity. Based on Csikszentmihályi's Experience Sample Method in which subjects were given beepers and asked to report on what they were doing and feeling every time the beeper nudged them, the researchers concluded that television fosters feelings of compliance and lowered alertness. In other words, television predisposed viewers to sit and watch. In a 2002 *Scientific American* article, Kubey and Csikszentmihályi revisit their earlier work to argue that television watching can become a kind of addiction. Drawing on an array of studies, they argue that the formal features of television—the cuts, edits, zooms, pans, and sudden noises—attract and retain the viewer's attention without necessarily engaging any critical faculty. In addition, Kubey and Csikszentmihályi point out that viewers who spend hours a day watching television—and this involves most of the population in the United States, especially children who watch without parental intervention—erode their ability to apply sustained attention to a task. A rise in tension or general restlessness accompanies the decline in concentration. As the effects of television become ingrained and viewers return to television to feed those effects, they experience a decrease in mental acuity and physical activity. In other words, they become simultaneously more passive and more anxious.[2]

Roy F. Fox in *MediaSpeak*, an exploration of three "voices" in America—Doublespeak, Salespeak, and Sensationspeak—comes to similar conclusions: "Each communication vessel—TV, film, radio, computer—carries its own biases and strengths" (191). By accepting media passively, something that television invites, individuals are structured by those media (194). "It's not just a matter of the information that is conveyed through them, but also of the channel itself that can dispose us one way or the other" (191). Unless individuals view media actively—"discussing and exploring it with other people, and reflecting on how it connects to their own lives, families and communities"—they will not develop their own "internal symbol systems of imagery and language" (194). They drift into Kosinski's vidiocy. Without a doubt, the specific images deployed repeatedly by television and then repeated in consumer products shape viewers' beliefs, desires, and actions. But the medium itself encourages viewers to develop a passive way of seeing; viewers organize their realities and their identities in those realities according to that habit of passive perception. More specifically, television and complementary mass-mediated imagery work in tandem to foster the development of spectacle, a way of seeing that threatens social action in the West.

A concept first introduced by Debord in his 1967 classic *Society of the Spectacle*, spectacle results from a lifestyle inculcated by mass-mediated images, especially those disseminated through television. Spectacle fosters trancelike behavior; the prototypical image of this consists of the family on a sofa in a dark room held in silence and in thrall by the flickering lights flashing across the television screen. This trancelike behavior, Debord says, undermines one's ability to act, especially in ways that will beneficially change the world. In addition, though, and perhaps first in line, it undermines an individual's belief in the ability to act.[3] Although primarily concerned with social critique, Debord contributes to a critical understanding of the impact of spectacle on writing classrooms and the difficulty of acting for social change when influenced by spectacle.[4]

In his elliptical and nonlinear text, Debord explores the cultural implications of a society in which image silences word and crafts a passive populace who merely watch rather than participate in reality.[5] As a Situationist, Debord seeks to expose the forces that block individual and societal change. He declares in a position statement for the Situationist Internationale, "We think the world must be changed. We want the most liberating change of the society and life in which we find ourselves confined. We know that this change is possible through appropriate actions" ("Report" 17). But Debord claims that a major obstacle to change is *the* spectacle, becoming the first critic to place a definite article in front of spectacle (Jonathan Crary qtd. in Evans 19). To change the world, then, to make room for the possibility of agency, Debord believes that we must challenge spectacle and the passivity it fosters.

Echoing other media critics, Debord argues that the preponderance of imagery within the West has transformed *Homo sapiens* into *Homo spectator*. No part of Western society can escape the controlling influence of the spectacle. As Debord explains in the preface to the third French edition of *Society of the Spectacle*, his agenda involves, as a first step in fostering change, dismantling the specular society that has given birth to *Homo spectator* (2–3). Spectacle is not just a collection of images, although it embraces imagery; instead, "it is a social relationship between people that is mediated by images" (12), producing a reality of image-events inextricable from consumer culture. Life in societies organized by commodification "presents itself as an immense accumulation of *spectacles*. All that once was directly lived has become mere representation" (12; emphasis in original). The spectacle, at the "very heart of society's real unreality," epitomizes "the prevailing model of social life" (13), Debord argues. He commits himself to exposing spectacle because it negates life and belief in agency, belief in the possibilities of change. Through spectacle, negation "has invented a visual form for itself" (14).

A way of seeing that emphasizes the consumption of images for visual pleasure and a habit of passivity, spectacle undermines or discourages agency, rendering change improbable. Spectacle consists of a one-way process of communication marked by three qualities: the tyranny of the immediate, the erasure of expertise, and the promulgation of a false unity (*Society* 19). Each erodes in different ways an individual's belief in agency. First, spectacle attributes social significance only to the immediate, and through that immediacy, it outlaws history. As Debord describes, spectacle "always replac[es] another, identical immediacy" with that which has come before it, tying us to the eternal present (*Comments* 12, 15; however, in contrast, see *Society* 50). Focused only on the present, individuals experience a life flattened to immediate gratification. Nothing exists long term; therefore, community members lose the ability to recognize the need for change or imagine the possibility of change. As the memory of historical change fades, concrete examples of past enactments of social transformation also fade. With that loss, people cease to consider change a viable possibility. Debord notes, "The spectacle, being the reigning social organization of a paralyzed history, of a paralyzed memory, of an abandonment of any history founded in historical [versus spectacular] time, is in effect *a false consciousness of time*" (*Society* 114; emphasis in original). As spectacle buries history, it buries the probability of change (137).

Second, spectacle also renders change improbable because spectacle erases an individual's belief in his or her expertise, a belief necessary for individuals to envision themselves as agents and to act on that vision. Part of the process of silencing history involves "dispossessing producers": sharply curtailing the number of people in a community who have access to and proficiency with a culture's dominant symbol systems. The sheer volume of images and words produced always by others, never by oneself, inculcates the belief that community members possess no power, no control, no capacity to contribute to (or alter) the barrage of symbols flying at them. People come to believe that they can be recipients of someone else's words/images, but they cannot produce their own. Always a person separate from the immediate community, the expert "controls at will this simplified summary of the sensible world" (*Comments* 27). This expert "decides where the flow will lead as well as the rhythm of what should be shown, like some perpetual, arbitrary surprise, leaving no time for reflection, and entirely independent of what the spectator might understand or think of it" (28).

As a result of an expertise always possessed by someone else, the community member's belief in her or his personal ability to make and shape—the source of all creativity, invention, and change—evanesces. Only experts who now are experts only because they are credentialed by the state have ability: "all experts serve the state and the media and only in that way do they achieve their status. Every expert follows his master, for all former possibilities for independence have been gradually reduced to nil by present society's mode of organization" (*Comments* 17). Essentially, the visual habit of spectacle inculcates the belief that individual community members do not have the capacity or the training to act. In addition, it inculcates the belief that to acquire that capacity, the community members must replicate rather than improvise on the expertise of the state-trained "masters."[6]

Third, the tyranny of the immediate and the erasure of expertise combine to impart the illusion that reality is known, shared, and unified. Debord argues that spectacle promulgates a false sense of unification by eliding the gaps or differences that exist within an image-event; instead, spectacle presents an absolute, seamless reality. Part of the process relies on spectacle's power to "silence anything it finds inconvenient," which it does by isolating "all it shows from its context, its past, its intention and its consequences. It is thus completely illogical" (*Comments* 28). As a result, spectacular power, while fostering the illusion of unity, does, in fact, isolate. "Separation is the alpha and omega of the spectacle" (*Society* 20), for "specular discourse leaves no room for reply," no room for dialogue (*Comment* 29). What results is a one-way, a monologic, channel of messages, starting from the expert producers who send the image-event down the conduit for the consumption of the inexpert viewer who, without expertise or credentials, can never be the producer. Isolated from each other and persuaded that they share the same immediate and unproblematic reality with everyone else, community members remain silent in the face of that onslaught.

As described by Debord, then, spectacle contributes to the erosion of social action, of individual participation in collective protest. As a reality sieve, it limits one's perceptions of reality to those that others craft for the viewer's easy consumption. Specifically, spectacle eats away at agency, thereby preventing social action from taking place by preventing it from starting. It propagates a learned helplessness by inculcating the belief that one's role in society consists of passively consuming the image-events created by others. Even more alarming, the *degree* of passive consumption engendered by television correlates with an individual's cultural positioning. When reinforced by other dynamics within an individual's culture and place—or, to reprise my vocabulary from chapter 1, when densely intertwined in a symbiotic knot—the habit of spectacle becomes particularly pernicious, impoverishing a child's and an adult's belief in her or his ability to act.

Spectacle is at its most powerful when tightly knotted with cultural constructs such as class, gender, and race. For instance, as Loretta Alper and Pepi Leistyna's video *Class Dismissed* illustrates, the working poor are represented through television programming as buffoons or social misfits, a process that disenfranchises members of the working class and functions to silence those in the real world who watch the scripted antics. Winner of the Studs Terkel Award for Media and Journalism, the 2007 video dissects the way in which television has become "the babysitter and the role model" for many working-poor youth, a process that disempowers young people by persuading them they have nothing worthwhile to say to members of the larger social sphere. The effects of this misrepresentation are further exacerbated by gender and race categories.

Feminist critiques of the media, emerging during the 1970s, focused attention initially on the power of mass-mediated images to reflect and generate standards for gender roles separate from class. However, since the 1980s, feminist media scholars have begun exploring the intersection of gender and class in television, plotting the power of these mass-media images to persuade a generation of working-poor women to submit and subordinate themselves to television's "realism" just as they do to fathers and male employers (Press). Television habituates passive submission to a larger patriarchal and middle-class ideology. Adolescent girls in working-poor families, then, are encouraged by upbringing and socialization to configure themselves as responsive to someone else's agency, to subsume their needs to the needs of others. They are encouraged to take instruction obediently and avoid backtalk. They are encouraged to be passive. These cultural forces coalesce to predispose working-class women to organize their behavior in and out of the classroom according to spectacle's dictates.

The seduction of spectacle becomes even more acute when race is integrated into the gender-class equation. "Television and mass media," bell hooks argues in *Killing Rage*, constitute "great neo-colonial weapons" that diminish "the spirit of resistance" among African Americans by colonizing minds. The content of television counsels African Americans to remain quiescent, to do nothing about social ills because those ills are figments of their imaginations. Common representations of both black and white individuals on television, hooks contends, send the message "that the problem of racism lies with black people—that it exists in our minds and imaginations" (110). Ergo, because racism exists as a problem only in the imagination, no need exists for concerted action aimed at substantive systemic social change. Through this lie, television corrodes belief in agency and belief in the need of agency even in the face of everyday injustice. In addition, although television communicates messages of passivity to every viewer, regardless of race, Carolyn A. Stroman notes that television's neocolonial power may be greater among African American children because of two factors: time spent watching and a predisposition to use television as a source of guidance.

Stroman contends that many children from African American homes, especially among the working poor, watch more than eight hours of television per day, frequently spending more time watching television than their parents spend working a forty-hour workweek. Furthermore, many African American children in working-poor families watch television without any adult or community interaction. Bereft of opportunities for critical viewing, Stroman argues, many African American children consider programming content as a source of social guidance, providing role models for dating behavior, patterns of consumption, and career possibilities, a conclusion Carolyn M. Orange and Amiso M. George reinforce. Without mitigating interactions, too many African American children are drawn to "watch passively under the hypnotic influence of the remote control," they assert, resulting in a generation of viewers being "seduced and lured away into aggression, underachievement, and apathy" (294–95).

When cultural forces such as class, gender, and race reinforce spectacle, a child will be more inclined to grow up doubting her or his agency or believing in a narrowly circumscribed version of agency. Nor does the disempowerment stop with spectacle, for spectacle leaches into language, shaping language behaviors that undermine classroom and civic agency. Children carry with them into the classroom literacies honed by spectacle, deploying in school what Smith calls *illegeracy*: "a problem arising from a simultaneous and interlinked failure of the systems of mass media and education; low educational achievement combined with, and supporting, public passivity; esp. characteristic of American culture in the 1990s" (200).

Like Debord, Smith associates illegeracy with mass media, arguing that media encourages public disengagement; however, he is less concerned with tracking the complex causes of illegeracy than he is with defining it, illustrating its effects, and offering praxis to disrupt it. Illegeracy is marked by three traits, Smith says, and these three traits align with the three protocols of spectacle, highlighting the passive turn in students' knowledge making. The first involves an inability to make sense of one's cultural situation, which consists of an inability to read between the lines, to perceive "anyone *not readily visible in the transaction itself*" (202; emphasis in original). In Debord's terms, students are trapped in the immediate moment without the resources necessary to disentangle themselves from that moment and sift out the invisible forces at work. The visible constitutes the only thing with value because the memory of what is *not* present, the memory that would give weight and importance to what is absent, has disappeared.

The second trait involves a failure to see one's life as open to choice, which corresponds to Debord's conviction that spectacle in a one-way system of communication, monologic instead of dialogic, because it conveys the message that the same reality is shared by all; therefore, no one has anything to say that has not already been said. As Smith describes, an illegerate individual fails to see any "*point* in questioning the current set up" (204; emphasis in original) because "if things are just the way they are, what's the *point* of sitting down and arguing on paper for one view or against another? What good can it do? Who's gonna care? (205; emphasis in original). Finally, illegerates abdicate their political power, "in choosing the direction of society" because they do not think those choices are theirs to make (207), a direct link to Debord's belief that spectacle erases expertise and, in the process, erases the belief that one has the right to choose on the basis of expert knowledge.

Both Debord and Smith do important work, Debord in identifying the existence, scope, and implications of spectacle and Smith in returning spectacle to the classroom. Debord directs attention to the way in which spectacle organizes culture; Smith directs attention to the way spectacle organizes students' performances in our writing classrooms. Both emphasize a key component of spectacle, one that is responsible for its increasing dominance in the West: the linkage between this pernicious way of seeing and mass-mediated images, particularly those disseminated through television. Thus, both provide important insights into the nature of acquiescence to mass media. But what neither Debord nor Smith provides is insight into resistance. Acquiescence constitutes only half the dynamic. Crucial to spectacle is the role of the individual interpretant, who, as Fox points out, can and does become a canny, critical respondent to television imagery. As robust users of culture, humans actively negotiate the interface between medium and visual habit. Thus, even as television's flickering images invite viewers to consume quiescently—to just watch—an invitation that grows more insistent in direct ratio to the time spent watching (Shrum, Wyer, and O'Guinn) and to other reinforcing (or mitigating) cultural factors, these invitations are resisted. Campbell points out that, regardless of the constraints, the limitations, or the pressures of cultural positioning and historical circumstances, people continue to imagine and invent agency. Our role as teachers is to devise classroom approaches that emphasize the importance of negotiation between image and visual habit so that students can imagine agency, believe in their own agency, and envision concrete ways to enact that agency. The resolution of Obama's crisis of faith illustrates the victory of agency over spectacle and provides inspiration for a writing pedagogy that aims to counter disengagement.

Obama's dark moment of doubt does not end in despair on a bus with eight anxious novice protesters headed for the CHA. If it had, perhaps Obama, crushed by the sheer weight of his dream of real change, might never have chosen a course for his life that led to his election as the forty-fourth president of the United States. Instead, the fight these eight parents waged, led particularly by Sadie Evans—the small, shy wife of a minister in training—reconfirmed Obama's belief in the possibility of individual and collective social action. Confronted with an office manager's efforts to block the eight parents from access to the CHA director, Evans stepped forward to assert the right of the eight to keep their appointment. Her unexpected forcefulness, combined with supportive media coverage, enabled the group to push forward their agenda and within a few weeks garner more than 850 neighborhood supporters. Wavering on the edge of leaving community activism, Obama explains that the bus ride with the parents to and from the CHA changed him in a fundamental way. It hinted at "what was possible" and therefore spurred him on: "That bus ride kept me going, I think. Maybe it still does" (*Dreams from My Father* 242). Because the eight parents learned to believe in their own agency, they learned to invent agency and exercise that agency in the face of overwhelming obstacles to their collective action.[7]

By witnessing agency in action, Obama transforms a crisis of faith into an affirmation of faith. Doubts do not necessarily lead to passivity; spectacle does not necessarily lead to impoverished visions of the future. Agency does exist, and it exists, even for marginalized members of a community, because humans are always negotiating the complex linkages connecting ways of seeing with ways of saying. The payoff for such understanding is what Obama calls the audacity of hope: "hope in the face of difficulty. Hope in the face of uncertainty" ("Audacity of Hope").[8] As teachers, then, our goal is to foster both resistance and engagement in the midst of acquiescence, a tricky balancing act in the classroom. The next section focuses on a potential middle ground between passivity and social action, describing one student's efforts to come to voice in a writing classroom by initially configuring agency according to the parameters set by spectacle and its companion, rhetorical compliance.

Thread 2: Rhetorical Compliance and a Simulated Agency

To emphasize the importance of belief, I ended my last section with audacious hope and courage in the face of spectacle's constraints on agency. Within a culture infused with mass-mediated images, spectacle works to isolate and alienate. It functions to close off dialogue by trapping individuals in the immediacy of the current moment so that awareness of change and belief in one's own expertise disappear. Simply put, spectacle seduces people into passivity by undercutting their conviction in their own agency. Bound by passivity, tied to the failure of the moment, and bereft of places to speak, individuals grow to believe they have no agency because they have nothing relevant to say, no right to say it, and no ability to say it well. They lose their faith in their visions of the future and in their power to act on those visions. Against the backdrop of spectacle's pessimistic malaise, then, the triumph of the eight parents evokes respect and inspiration. This small cohort demonstrates that spectacle can be resisted. A group of eight can swell to a group of more than eight hundred; grassroots community action can tackle an institutional monolith like the CHA and elicit changes that improve in substantive ways a community's quality of life.

This section explores that resistance more minutely, asking how people who engage in individual or collective protest move between low-level stasis and dynamic activism. What is the nature of the middle space between passivity and activism? Obama's narrative highlights that people can believe in agency and act on that belief. Our students also confirm that spectacle is contingent rather than totalizing. For instance, Bronwyn T. Williams in *Tuned In*, a quasi-ethnographic study of fifteen first-year students at the University of New Hampshire, emphasizes the critically savvy processes that these students use to "read" television. They do not enter his classroom passive consumers of mass-mediated images. Instead, they are canny manipulators of television's flickering images; they sift, select, critique, and combine those images in sharp, highly literate ways. According to Williams, then, the goal of the composition classroom centers on tapping those critical abilities to hone a parallel critical literacy. Like Obama's experiences on Chicago's South Side, Williams's experiences in the classroom highlight that television might foster spectacle, but it cannot imprint spectacle.

While Obama and Williams give us hope, they do not give us direct insight into the nature of resistance and thus do not point to ways that we as teachers can encourage that resistance in our professional lives and in our classrooms. In fact, an implicit counterimprinting narrative characterizes Williams's study, a kind of reverse technological determinism. Rather than television automatically fostering passivity, an unspoken assumption in Williams's study is that television automatically fosters critical consumption.[9] The either-or formulation—either students passively consume television or students critically consume television—hides the complexity and challenges of resistance. The either-or thinking creates problems in Williams's classroom, for the smart, media-literate students struggle to transform their critical viewing skills into critical writing and reading skills. They have difficulty shifting their analytical acumen from one domain to another. Thus, an unaddressed question haunts both Obama's narrative and Williams's study: how did the eight parents come to engage proactively in community protest? How did Williams's students became sharp, hip consumers of television's imagery? One possible answer to these important questions lies with rhetorical compliance, which develops codependently with spectacle to offer a middle step between passivity and activism. Rhetorical compliance consists of an uncritical reliance on a formulaic agency that while lacking reflective critique or inventive imagination still enables the individual to act in sharply prescribed ways.

Spectacle does not function alone in the symbiotic knot of silence. It co-evolves with a way of speaking that reinforces—that confirms and replicates—spectacle's identity. All visual habits and rhetorical habits in any symbiotic knot mutually constitute the other, codeveloping the same set of markers. While the former deploys those processes throughout the visual system, the latter deploys those processes throughout linguistic symbol systems to invite the writer to rely on certain patterns or protocols for persuasion. Thus, the three core processes organizing spectacle—the tyranny of the immediate, the erasure of expertise, and the illusion of unity—similarly organize rhetorical compliance, spectacle's companion rhetorical habit.

In what follows, I explore the elements of immediacy, erased expertise, and false unity in rhetorical compliance, attending specifically to the implications of this habit for belief in and enactment of agency. I argue that rhetorical compliance interfaces with spectacle to tempt students to interpret agency as obedience to a set of arbitrary rules established by the dominant culture. Then, rhetorical compliance restricts that obedience to the immediate moment, with limited consideration of the future or the past. Finally, rhetorical compliance encourages students to believe that writing agency consists of a static construct restricted to monologic exercises where feedback flows through a top-down, teacher-to-student channel. Within the parameters of a knot of silence, agency may lack critical substance because it acquiesces to the rules and power structures of the dominant order, but it is a starting point for belief in the possibilities of action. Although rhetorical compliance leaves little room for imaginative agency, it still serves as an important placeholder, a middle step between passivity and activism. I illustrate the limits and possibilities of rhetorical compliance through the story of one student's struggle to come to voice in a writing classroom.

Gloria entered my spring-semester composition class late for both the class and the start of the semester. A short, stocky African American student in her late thirties, Gloria was a business major, pursuing an academic career in addition to a full-time job and the demands of single-parenting three boys. A child of working-poor parents, Gloria began her college writing career in a yearlong class designed for underprepared writers and came to my writing course convinced that she could not write. She announced this baldly during the first of our many meetings: "I'm just not a writer. I don't have anything to say to anybody." Yet she came to college, to class, and to my office despite that lack of faith in her writing because she was determined to carve out academic success.

The nature of the class also generated anxiety for Gloria as well as for many of her fellow students. A second of a two-semester first-year writing requirement, this class focused on critical writing in response to various texts, culminating at the end of the semester in a research paper. However, I drew the texts for the course from speculative fiction, ranging from award-winning science-fiction short stories, to a fantasy novel, and, finally, to the film *Blade Runner*. I designed the course, described more fully later in the chapter, with a mix of conventional and unconventional requirements to position students on the cusp between imagination and action, between the visual and the discursive. Students engaged in a variety of traditional writing tasks with a heavy emphasis on analysis and critique. But they also took on a range of atypical writing tasks, such as transforming a short story into a political speech, writing a motion for legislative action, and proposing a treatment for a documentary. In addition, they performed an array of visual tasks, from storyboarding short stories to designing cover art for their critical essays. I wanted to encourage them through this pedagogy to develop processes that served them well in traditional academic writing (a program requirement). At the same time, I wanted to encourage them to transform those processes into robust strategies for imagination.

For much of the semester, Gloria organized her writing identity guided by the three qualities of immediacy, erased expertise, and false unity. She defined and interpreted her writing agency based on the protocols provided by rhetorical compliance. Remarkable about Gloria's story, as well as the stories of myriad students caught within the spectacle-rhetorical compliance interface, were her steadfast efforts to claim agency for herself even within the restricted acquiescence of rhetorical compliance. Remarkable as well was her use of rhetorical compliance as a bridge to more active and critical enactments of agency. Despite her conviction that she was "not a writer," a conviction reinforced at various turns by rhetorical compliance, Gloria invented a writing agency for herself in which she was an active producer of meaning. Her story highlights the tenacity of hope and the possibility of agency in spite of a symbiotic knot of silence. It confirms that belief, like hope, should be, maybe even must be, audacious. And that story begins within the parameters of rhetorical compliance.

Like spectacle, the first limitation imposed by rhetorical compliance lies with the lure of immediacy. Intertwined with spectacle, rhetorical compliance erases history by imprisoning people in a series of present moments. Immediacy strips individuals of any time to reflect, of any ability to act or react. It confines people in "being" with no hope of "becoming." The tyranny of the immediate manifests itself rhetorically in the dismissal of memory. Dismissing memory constitutes a crucial element of rhetorical compliance, for without memory of a personal or cultural history with repeated illustrations of change, a writer cannot easily maintain a belief in agency or any hope of change through social action. Belief in agency is predicated on belief in one's ability to change self and world; that belief erodes if an individual possesses no evidence of change, no model, historical and otherwise, of change. Clearly, these models exist, but the lure of the immediate elides everything except the current moment. No past or future survives, merely the constancy of the now. Dismissing memory, then, traps the writer in the eternal present, persuading the writer that the immediate writing situation is the only writing situation.

As a result, immediacy creates a tenacious terministic screen that obliterates past successes and contributes to students' persistent passivity. In addition, immediacy traps writing students in an eternal present fraught with pain not pleasure, failure not accomplishment. Configurations of agency cannot transfer from past writing experiences because those past experiences do not coexist with the immediacy of the moment. Thus, many students struggle in every writing class and in every writing situation to shape agency anew. For instance, Gloria could not easily integrate into her current situation significant images of her past academic (and life) successes; she could not easily leaven her current struggles with the certainty of past victories in her prior yearlong composition sequence or with the certainty of successful writing outside of the academy. Instead, she was caught in a composition class bereft of her memories of and confidence in those victories. At the end of her first day in class, during our first postclass conference when I reviewed the syllabus and textbooks with her, Gloria announced with conviction: "I'm going to flunk this class. I'll try, but I won't pass." She noted in an early journal entry that her success in her past writing class was a fluke: "I can't figure out how I got a B last year because I just can't write." What confronts her and what she experiences as real, are only the knowledge of the present struggle and of her immersion in that struggle. Each day she entered my classroom, then, she engaged in a battle with her own fears of failure.

In addition to stripping students of memories of agency, immediacy also renders inventing agency difficult. For Gloria, "I can't write" was a way of protesting that she did not know how to write, a belief totally at odds with her prior academic and personal history. By erasing memory, immediacy erases a tool by which one constructs agency. Memories of past victories provide the foundation for imagining future victories, and writers need that foundation to invent agency. As one of the five rhetorical canons, memory, the ancients said, connected intimately with creativity. A rhetor developed the arts of memory not as a means to memorize a set speech for delivery. Rather, memory served as a means to organize and locate available arguments that a rhetor would then tap into as needed (Yates). Thus, imagination and memory have traditionally intertwined. Built out of past experiences, past study, and a canny understanding of *kairos*, memory for the ancients constituted a strategy by which the writer took the material from the past to fashion arguments in the present to serve a vision of the future. Thus, the assault on and the insult to memory implicit within the immediacy of spectacle strips writers of the possibilities of rhetoric by stripping them of their belief in a past and their ability to imagine a future.

Like spectacle, rhetorical compliance encourages subordination to the immediacy of the moment by erasing expertise. It inculcates the belief that one lacks the proficiency to affect the world. Instead, proficiency lies in the hands of the experts, producers designated as masters by the state. Expertise is transferred through imitation of those experts; novices become proficient through mimicry. Within rhetorical compliance, then, writers come to voice not through invention but through duplication: they replicate the protocols of the experts, the masters, as a means to acquire the status of producer. Rhetorically, then, erasure of expertise means that writers abjure agency as anything other than a reproduction of the rhetorical roles surrounding them. The degree of agency they acquire depends on the degree of replication they achieve.

Such erasure of expertise manifests itself in the classroom as a search for formulas, a goal that transforms invention into a discovery of and adherence to the protocols established by the experts. Students perceive agency as a double mastery: mastery of a formula and mastery of the execution of the formula. Therefore, rhetorical education becomes a search for formulas and linear, logical writing procedures. An attentive search for the best formula characterized Gloria's initial approach to learning in my class. To be agentive for her meant mapping out the precise dimensions of any assignment, finding the recipe for producing correct writing in response to that assignment, and following the recipe lockstep. And so, encouraged by like-minded classmates, Gloria insistently asked for a list of ingredients and measurements: the number of words, the number of pages, the number of quotes, and the number of source materials.

Ably assisted in her search for the perfect recipe by her fellow classmates who were anxious for the same recipe, Gloria perceived writing as discovering and following the expert's blueprints, following the expertise of others because she did not believe in the existence nor could she imagine the value of her own experiences. In her journal response to the first assignment, Gloria wrote in protest, "I just don't know what you want from me," asking me to help her figure out what this assignment "looks like." She followed up this journal with an office visit, asking me to model a successful assignment, suggesting that I might be able to provide her with an outline or a scaffold of the assignment to serve as a guideline for her. As she looks for the specifications of agency, Gloria simultaneously signals her desire for agency and her belief that agency consists of obedience to the power of the status quo (or the professor). Within the parameters of rhetorical compliance, she seeks to enact agency as an algorithm, carefully delineated and exactly executed.

Even the hybrid class—one that combined fiction, creative writing, and traditional academic discourse, designed in part to make formulaic writing and formulaic writing processes problematic—evoked calls for recipes. Gloria and her supportive classmates demanded a precise delineation (numerical if possible) of the structural and content specifications of all writing assignments, traditional to nontraditional. In spite of assignment prompts, in-class discussions, and the reassurance of multiple drafts, in spite of collaboratively working on grading criteria for each assignment, and in spite of classroom sessions on point, purpose, audience, and exigence, Gloria and many of her classmates felt hampered without an explicit blueprint for success. In addition, the demands for specifications rose exponentially with the introduction of nontraditional writing assignments because such assignments did not lend themselves to recipes. Class members perceived these nontraditional assignments, as well as my efforts to turn responsibility for such decision making over to them, as an assault on their agency, on their ability to perform successfully in the writing classroom. Informal midterm responses from that semester reveal the desire among the majority of students for less freedom of choice, less space for play, and more meticulous descriptions of my expectations. They believed that by failing to provide algorithms, I deprived them of the chance to be agentive because I deprived them of the chance to mimic the formulas of the "experts."

The third limitation of rhetorical compliance that Gloria struggled to honor concerned the illusion of false unity A fundamental law of spectacle, Debord argues, is captured by the aphorism "If it exists, there's no need to talk about it'" because everyone shares an unproblematic reality (*Comments* 5). The cultural barrage of mass-mediated images and words presents reality as complete, one to which we contribute nothing except our quiescent attention. The illusion of false unity persuades us that we coexist without disjuncture, without difference. Thus, because writing and reading are predicated on the visceral belief that we are divided, a state that can be rectified by rhetoric (even as it was created in part by rhetoric), false unity persuades us that we have no division to bridge through language. In Kenneth Burke's terms, a false sense of unity makes us all already consubstantial. As a result, false unity truncates dialogue by convincing individuals they have nothing significant to say and no reason to say it. For example, Debord argues that "spectacle proves its argument simply by going around in circles: by coming back to the start, by repetition, by constant reaffirmation in the only space left where anything can be publicly affirmed, and believed, precisely because that is the only thing to which everyone is witness" (*Comments* 19). Like spectacle, rhetorical compliance renders communication a monologue in which we comply rather than a dialogue in which we respond.

Evidence of this monologic orientation erupts in the writing classroom repeatedly as we listen each semester to our students telling us with panicked sincerity that they have nothing to say. Students perceive themselves having no part in the monologue of experts. The teacher's job is to lecture and to require obedience. The student's job is to bank knowledge and to submit. The dynamic at play here is more than a problem with self-esteem, that is, "*I* have nothing to say that anyone would be interested in reading," although, without a doubt, self-confidence is a factor. At play here, as well, is the disappearance of gaps within which writer and readers may lodge themselves in order to disrupt the flow of images and words surrounding them. The suture marks between life lived and life represented provides a space for marshalling a resistance to representation, a resistance to an imposed silence (Gramsci). However, rhetorical compliance like spectacle persuades the writer that no disjuncture exists: the image and the text are the reality, so individuals embrace both as reality. Because "[i]mages can tolerate anything and everything," juxtaposing all things without contradiction (Debord, *Comments* 27), a writer cannot locate a point at which to turn around and examine a text as separate from self or reality; a writer cannot locate a point at which to turn around and produce a statement necessary for the well-being of another. As a result, students with complete conviction can protest that they simply have nothing to say because they do not believe their contributions have value.

Rhetorical compliance constitutes the "uninterrupted monologue" of the ruling order (Debord, *Society* 19), discouraging any instinct to "talk back." Thus, rhetorical compliance short-circuits dialogue, construing agency as an act of obedient listening rather than an act of engaged speaking. Bereft of the dynamics of dialogue and of the power to speak, listen, and reply, how can a writer grapple with the demands of creating a reader, an intensely dialogic process? Gloria's struggle with conceptualizing a reader stemmed in part from her efforts to shape her writing agency separate from the give-and-take of conversation. "Who are you writing for?" I asked in the margins of her writing journal and during our conferences. "Well, you," she consistently responded. For her, the teacher, as the institutionally designated expert, was always the reader, the sole audience. And she had nothing to say to me as teacher because I was the fountainhead of one-way communication, the person to whom she listened attentively and obediently. Caught within the monologue of rhetorical compliance, attempting to construe her agency by means of rhetorical compliance, Gloria had difficulty constructing an audience interested in dialogue; she could not believe that she could be a part of that dialogue.

Marked by immediacy, erased expertise, and false unity, rhetorical compliance invites the construction of a simulated agency, an attenuated agency that, regardless of its limitations, may function as a crucial middle step between the passivity of spectacle and active engagement in the world. A goal of a writing classroom, then, resides with inviting students to redirect their attentions from rhetorical compliance to risk taking, imagination, and creativity, for that redirection provides a foundation for an enriched, inventive agency. Gloria's work at the end of the semester points to the rewards of that difficult transition.

Like Obama's belief in agency, like his dream of change, Gloria's story, too, is remarkable because her tenacious efforts to craft agency moved beyond the middle step of rhetorical compliance, moved beyond her conviction that she could not write. Her final paper with its accompanying self-assessment reveals a writer inventing her agency through resistance to the precepts of immediacy, erased expertise, and false unity. Gloria's last essay, unique in its experimental format and nonformulaic organization, stands in contrast to her body of work for my class. She interwove a short story dealing with child abuse with the conventions of the traditional academic research paper. Moving confidently back and forth between a story of abuse and her argument about adult responsibility, Gloria stretched her rhetorical wings, concluding a strong paper with the devastating and poignant observation that "not only is the person committing the abuse guilty of a crime. The person who has evidence of the abuse and does not report it is guilty as well." As she exercised her agency, she wrote a paper that simultaneously highlights her belief in agency for herself and her audience.

In addition to the experimental format of the paper, a significant move for her, noteworthy about this paper was a dramatic shift in Gloria's belief about herself as a writer and about the potential of her right to affect the world around her. After a semester in which she consistently resisted evaluating her own papers because, she complained, she could not find anything positive to say, Gloria forthrightly states the paper deserves a B–/C+. She suggests the C+ not because she didn't know what she wanted to do but because she lacked sufficient time to do what she wanted to do. As she notes, she simply ran out of the time needed to "put her thoughts into words" once she discovered what she wanted to say. She lacked neither thoughts nor words, just time, a significant sea change in her belief in her right to speak. Finally, Gloria notes in her assessment the importance, the significance, of what she writes. Her paper, she believes, has direct and explicit value for persuading people to report child abuse, for both the abuser and the adult who turns a blind eye to the abuse are criminals. At this moment, for this paper, Gloria has tempered her doubts about her rhetorical agency and ability to write an essay that she believes will have an impact on a problem. She sees herself and her world differently, and she acts on that changed vision.

Understanding Gloria's fight for agency as connected to both visual and rhetorical habits expands our understanding of the obstacles to agency our students face and the strategies they devise to surmount those obstacles. Rhetorical compliance may be one such strategy, an important middle space between the passivity of spectacle and the activism of agency. Here students rehearse a form of agency that can potentially serve as a prelude for a belief in an agency, a first step to conceiving of agency as something other than a simulation. However, in this middle space, the possibility also exists for students to configure agency according to compliance and remain mired in passivity. Inviting students to tip toward resistance rather than acquiescence depends in part on the constitution of the writing classroom. Crucial to breaking the ties of the spectacle-rhetorical compliance interface is place, the last loop in the symbiotic knot of silence. Hope for agency wanes when place reinforces the bonds between spectacle and rhetorical compliance in a symbiotic knot of silence.

Thread 3: Monologic Classrooms and Consuming Writing

Gloria provides just one story of a struggle that many of our students experience, and that story is told from the perspective of a single place: the academic classroom. Too many students slip into our classrooms already inclined to embrace spectacle and rhetorical compliance. They are reluctant to write, reluctant to share, reluctant to speak *in that place*. As an official, credentializing, and institutionalized location, the classroom exists for many students as a sphere of spectacle, not a sphere of participation. Smith points out that illegeracy is a "problem arising from a simultaneous and intertwined failure of the systems of *mass media and education*" (200; emphasis added). The way we as teachers construct the writing classroom can be crucial for encouraging resistance and discouraging acquiescence, a point that Fox confirms with his advocacy of active intervention. The praxis we deploy can intertwine with spectacle and rhetorical compliance in ways that either reinforce or disrupt a symbiotic knot of silence.

As explained in chapter 1, social action emerges from the dynamic of a symbiotic knot: it is not solely the result of a visual habit or a rhetorical habit. Rather, the triad of visual habit, rhetorical habit, and place influences an individual's ability to believe in agency and imagine acting in the world. Place contributes to that dynamic through its linkages with visual and rhetorical habits. When the feedback loops joining visual and rhetorical habit foster social relationships and actions stifling dialogue, then a monologic place evolves. As Debord points out, spectacle erases places, such as the agora, salons, cafés, and so forth, where dialogue flourishes:

> [T]here is no place left where people can discuss the realities which concern them, because they can never lastingly free themselves from the crushing presence of media discourse. The spectator is simply supposed to know nothing, and deserve nothing. Those who are always watching to see what happens next will never act: such must be the spectator's condition. (*Comments* 22)

As spectacle, rhetorical compliance, and monologic places reinforce each other, the power of the symbiotic knot to predispose individuals to choose silence—to believe they have no agency—increases.

A monologic place has significant implications for a writing classroom. When teachers for whatever reason rely on relationships and activities inflected by spectacle, the classroom tends to become monologic; students, instead of acting, "are always watching to see what happens next" (Debord, *Comments* 22). They constitute themselves as passive recipients, not active constructors of knowledge. A monologic classroom neither invites nor supports the emergence of agency and social action. Garoian in *Performing Pedagogy* articulates this warning: "Spectacle methodologies consist of historically and socially constructed performances, reified, prescriptive procedures and techniques defined in advance that are closed to contextual circumstances" (70). Such methodologies, he cautions, diminish personal and political agency for students (2).

In this section, I map three pedagogical practices that through an array of relationships and activities configure the writing classroom as a monologic place, tightening a knot of silence. These three practices include a remediated presentational format, which focuses attention on the teacher as a giver of knowledge in the immediate moment; arhetorical writing assignments, which reduce students' confidence in their own expertise; and prescriptive style, which homogenizes the classroom by dismissing alternative discourses as socially and intellectually inept.[10] Infiltrating classrooms kindergarten through postsecondary, these three practices align with the three key characteristics of spectacle: immediacy, erasure of expertise, and imposition of false unity. As a result, they work with a symbiotic knot to erode students' belief in and desire for agency. I begin my exploration of monologic classrooms with a remediated presentational format, highlighting its focus on immediacy and the elimination of dialogue.

When a remediated presentational format couples with arhetorical writing assignments, a student's sense of expertise is undercut. Finally, the interweaving of remediated presentational format and arhetorical writing assignments with a master style produces a false sense of unity that truncates opportunities for dialogue.

Seemingly a relic of a bygone era and associated with large-lecture-hall teaching, presentational pedagogy is undergoing a renaissance effected by the explosion of digital technologies, resulting in a remediated presentational pedagogy. In his 1986 *Research in Written Composition*, George Hillocks defines a presentational pedagogy as a praxis characterized by lectures, teacher-led discussions, imitation of models, and teacher feedback solely on final drafts (116–17). Based on his meta-analysis of over 120 experimental studies, Hillocks concludes that this was the least effective, although the most "ubiquitous," means of teaching writing at that time (201). While the process and postprocess movements have eroded the dominance in writing classrooms of the presentational mode, the rise of digital technologies has provided new sites for the flourishing of a remediated presentational pedagogy, especially through PowerPoint presentations and Web-based online teaching.

Although no national survey data currently exist to establish the extent to which composition teachers rely on PowerPoint presentations, the growing popularity of PowerPoint as a medium for student projects—taught by teachers proficient with PowerPoint—suggests that PowerPoint constitutes a common tool for many writing students and teachers. Multimedia presentations for college composition students (Hocks), for graduate multilingual students (Tardy), and for high-school English students (Perry) all attest to the attraction of PowerPoint as a pedagogical instrument. Doubtless PowerPoint affords numerous benefits for the creators. For instance, Alan E. Perry describes the value of linking PowerPoint presentations with written research projects in a high-school English classroom. He claims that his students accrue at least one of five benefits by integrating the two activities, from honing their presentation skills to enhancing their technological literacies. The benefits, however, are accrued by the producers of the PowerPoint presentations. Nowhere does Perry discuss the benefits to the students *watching* the PowerPoints. Designed to convey information efficiently so that an audience can process that information equally efficiently, PowerPoint teeters on the edge of a presentational pedagogy revised for a digital era. Whether created by students or teachers, PowerPoint invites the audience to take on the role of spectator, to derive pleasure from passive consumption of knowledge produced and disseminated by others.

In addition, a presentational pedagogy remediates itself through Web-based online writing classes, creating a virtual monologic site for composition teaching. Kate Kiefer details the risks of online writing classes, claiming that online classes frequently fail the students in part because the platforms supporting Web-based online teaching, such as WebCT and Blackboard, invite lecture-style teaching through their design (143). Both platforms provide various strategies for posting lecture material—readings, lecture notes, PowerPoints, and so forth—that students can access on their own. In these cases, WebCT and Blackboard deliver information in isolated chucks, failing to facilitate conversation or collaboration among students (143). As a result of design issues, Kiefer notes that students can "write a paper without engaging other students in the course in any sustained or significant conversation" (144). Even the discussion features of both platforms fail to support interaction. Because lecture-modeled support software was not designed "for groups of students interacting about texts . . . [it] can make student dialog or other textual interactions needlessly difficult," Kiefer points out (144). Craig Stroupe confirms this difficulty. An instructional developer as well as a composition teacher, Stroupe describes a problem in an online course he helped design and produce. At the midterm, students in the online class complained to the instructor that they did not want to participate in the asynchronous discussion board. As Stroupe explains, "they saw the professor as the one with the knowledge they needed," so they considered dialogue with classmates a waste of time ("Making Distance Presence" 256). While Stroupe and the teacher envisioned this collaborative space as an opportunity to share ideas, experiences, and learning, the students saw it as "Styrofoam peanuts around the educational goods" (256).

The proliferation of PowerPoints and Web-based online composition teaching resurrects presentational pedagogy, tightening the threads of a symbiotic knot of silence by inviting students to consume information passively in the classroom. First, remediated presentation pedagogy reinforces a knot of silence by focusing students' attention on the immediate moment. Teachers perform; students watch. Consider the implications of Perry's description of his efforts to model good presentational techniques.

> I demonstrated good presentation techniques, with emphasis on speaking clearly and loudly and discussing the subject matter rather than reading text from slides. Using a laptop computer and television monitor, I demonstrated how to create text and change the font style, size, and color; insert pictures from files; make transitions; and format backgrounds. (65)

The students sit and watch, citizens of Debord's empire of passivity. As they watch a PowerPoint or take lecture notes, students live in the moment. They stay in that moment if not encouraged to do anything active with those notes (dialectical notebooks, group discussion, or some other application). Instead, the act of taking notes—the act of consuming the information in the lecture—constitutes learning, As Hillocks describes, students might be able to define and identify a thesis statement after presentational instruction, but they are unable to craft a thesis statement themselves based solely on information conveyed in a lecture (or a PowerPoint).

Second, a remediated presentational pedagogy fosters a monologic classroom by erasing students' sense of expertise. The "instructional voice," which Stroupe identifies as that which drives "the practice of much current instructional design," demonstrates the degree to which digital technologies potentially reinforce spectacle's power. Drawing on Mikhail Bakhtin, Stroupe defines the instructional voice as the voice of the expert or master who is the ultimate source of static truths that "the novice must learn, accept, and rehearse" ("Making Distance Presence" 259). As the shaping force behind instructional design, the instructional voice assigns to the student the role of apprentice who learns through imitation. As a result, discussion disappears (or fails to appear) because students perceive "themselves getting their money's worth not by chatting about information with other novices at a distance, but by getting close to the mind and even the heart of the expert who could share her professional vision" ("Making Distance Presence" 258). The instructional voice, like PowerPoint presentations, focuses on the creator's mastery of the material, closing off opportunities for students to contribute to the conversation, sending the subtle message that the audience has nothing of value to contribute. Like a lecture course, designed to give students information (which they then consume), the instructional voice, whether online or in PowerPoint presentations, fosters the intellectual growth of the creator while inviting the audience to serve as passive recipients of the display. Buoyed by a history of lecturing in the writing classroom with teacher as the sole voice of authority and the sole visual focus of the class, a remediated presentational pedagogy reinforces all of the vices of spectacle. If the goal of literacy teaching is "a class of students actively aware and participant, a class that does not 'swallow' the 'teacher's' remarks but *considers* them" (Deemer 123; emphasis in original), then a remediated presentational praxis cannot be effective. It evokes spectacle, smothering dialogue and agency.

Although PowerPoint presentations and Web-based online teaching lend themselves to a remediated presentational format, crafting as they do a monologic classroom, they do not dictate such an approach. Teachers and students make choices about how they use technology, just as they make choices about how they respond to television. Thus, technology need not invite and reinforce a monologic classroom. Nancy A. Myers highlights this. In "Acting On or Acting With," she warns that technology offers itself as a sophisticated information-delivery system, tempting teachers to use it as a sophisticated information-delivery system. By evolving praxis based on that orientation, teachers act on students, habituating students toward passivity through pedagogical choices that implicitly confirm passivity as the correct, the expected stance.

However, acting *on* students is not inevitable. Teachers can act *with* students via technology, and the first step consists of approaching technology warily, resisting its traditional configuration as an information-delivery system. Rather than requiring students to use particular digital tools, teachers need to invite students to create with, choose from, and critique those digital tools. Sensitive to the historical and social positioning of technology, teachers can then create praxis that disrupts a remediated presentational format and the student passivity it invites.

Stroupe concurs. Technology does not dictate a remediated presentational format. He details the possibilities of a "compositional voice" for crafting effective Web-based teaching that resists monologic virtual classrooms. Characterized by its rejection of the authoritative voice of the expert, compositional voice fosters "a structure that internally enables languages of different social contexts to speak to and reveal one another" ("Making Distance Presence" 259). It illustrates that teaching online can be guided by something other than the vision of digital technologies as an information-delivery system. In conjunction with other "voices," the compositional voice can contribute to effective Web-based composition teaching, eliciting more than shallow online chatter ("Making Distance Presence" 260). Like Myers, Stroupe advocates a technologically mediated pedagogy that acts with students rather than on students.[11] However, nurturing collaborative, interactive, dialogic classrooms, whether virtual or face-to-face, requires conscientious attention to undermining monologic tendencies, a process that requires carefully crafting the invitations to write that teachers issue to students.

The writing invitations a teacher extends can work with a remediated presentational pedagogy to reinforce a symbiotic knot of silence. Writing assignments form the backbone and set the tone for a writing course, revealing the teacher-student dynamic that the teacher values. In a benchmark essay, Richard L. Larson emphasizes the importance of carefully conceptualizing writing assignments so that they foster the kinds of learning important for the student. Pedagogical essay collections designed for novice composition teachers further affirm the importance of fashioning effective writing assignments.[12] Kiefer emphasizes as well the necessity of inviting writing that serves one of several nonacademic goals: personal expression, social awareness, critical literacy, lifelong learning, or professional advancement. Although different productive ways of creating an assignment exist, a central tenet of inventing a writing assignment consists of what *not* to do. In the midst of a cornucopia of options, a teacher must not craft what James Britton calls the *dummy run*.

A dummy run is an arhetorical pseudo-assignment designed solely to demonstrate to a teacher that the student has mastered a particular skill set: a mastery of modes, a clarity of organization, a consistency of address. Richard

A. Lanham in *The Economics of {Attention}* refers to dummy runs as "forced performances," something he spent a lifetime requiring in face-to-face class-rooms (234). Dummy runs erase a student's belief in her or his expertise as a writer because they are creations produced for assessment with the audience consisting of the teacher as evaluator (235). The text does not evolve out of a writer's sense of dissonance or recognition of disjunctures between reality lived and reality represented. Instead, students merely jump through a hoop (235). A dummy run exists for no other reason than to demonstrate to the teacher that the student can reproduce a specified kind of discourse, and, as Kiefer points out, "Our history in the last 50 years has emphasized the importance of engaging students in more than individual, iterated practice of formulaic academic responses" (143). However, in the wake of high-stakes testing and through the rise of Web-based online teaching, dummy runs, like presentational pedagogy, are creeping back into the classroom.[13]

A dummy run merely replicates texts without inviting students to grapple with what Smith contends is the dialectic necessary to combat illegeracy: the back and forth between the timeless great issues (ethics, history, politics, and the like) and particular, topical problems (abortion, poverty, police violence, and the like). Pseudo-assignments prevent people from recognizing "the systems they're enmeshed in and . . . the real choices available to them" (210). Instead, they directly reinforce a knot of silence by denying the student choices and by truncating the dialogue between writer and audience. The writer does not engage in discovering an insight important to both self and other, in "reading between the lines," as Smith urges, or reading the invisible. The assignment suggests, in fact, that no insight (or critical vision) is possible. Choice closes off rather than opens up. Students lose belief in their expertise because they make only minor decisions: how to devise a content that will neatly fit the prescribed assignment pattern.

Arhetorical pseudowriting links to and reinforces the third characteristic of a spectacle-dominated praxis: prescriptive style, an approach to teaching writing that confirms spectacle's false unity. Style, Thomas O. Sloane writes in a long entry in his *Encyclopedia of Rhetoric*, is responsible for the "manifestation of text as text. It is style that brings the text into linguistic expression" (745); thus, style constitutes an essential of rhetoric. However, style becomes problematic when separated from the content, the substance, of the text, something that happens all too frequently in spectacle. Stuart Ewen writes, "In a contemporary world, where the mass media serve as increasingly powerful arbiters of *reality*, the primacy of style over substance has become the normative consciousness" (2; emphasis in original). Through the homogenizing influence of spectacle, the primacy of style over substance quickly becomes the primacy of *one* style. In the writing classroom, this manifests itself as adherence to what Lanham refers to as the clarity-brevity-sincerity, or "C-B-S," model (*Style; Economics of {Attention}* 137–43), one that demands students genuflect to plain English, a habituation that undermines diversity and dialogue.

The fruitful and robust exchange of many styles, many Englishes, disappears from a writing classroom governed by a single style. The false unity of one style impoverishes all students' belief in their right to choose because it shrinks their pool of options. Diverse voices—diverse ways of using language, thus diverse styles—create tension, struggle, and conflict; individuals actively make decisions about communication (and miscommunication) amidst this diversity. Through such struggles, people come to new understandings and enrich their stylistic repertoires. In "Ideological Becoming," Sarah Warshauer Freedman and Arnetha F. Ball argue that, according to Bakhtin, "the coming together of voices of the different individuals . . . is essential to a person's growth" (6). By immersing themselves in the false unity of a single privileged style, students assimilate fewer words and fewer styles, subsequently decreasing their opportunities for learning and for action. Because they are barred from the discourses that are most meaningful for them, they begin to perceive their life as bereft of choice, one consequence of which is passivity in the face of social inequities.

The Symbiotic Knot of Silence: A Counterspectacle Strategy

If a pedagogy comprising a remediated presentational format, arhetorical assignments, and master style evokes a monologic classroom, then a pedagogy comprising counterspectacle strategies might evoke a dialogic classroom. If a symbiotic knot of silence actively cultivates passivity, then we can certainly shape a pedagogy that actively cultivates resistance. Obama and the eight parents demonstrate that agency and social action even in an era of disengagement occur. By aggressively seeking out educational opportunities, Gloria also illustrates the possibilities of agentive action. As teachers, we, too, can choose to shape pedagogies that untie the threads holding this symbiotic knot so tightly together.

This last section briefly describes a counterspectacle pedagogy, one that structured the writing class I shared with Gloria. Drawing from Britton's concept of spectator and participant roles in language, I created a course that combined speculative fiction with critical writing, image work with textual work. The vision of a dialogic classroom motivated my choices, one in which students participated actively in the creation of images and discursive texts, talking, complaining, protesting, sharing as they did so. While I do not claim that my class caused Gloria to develop into a more poised and confident writer—pedagogy is no more deterministic than technology, woven as it is out of visual habits, rhetorical habits, and place—I do believe that my class provided opportunities that invited her to extend her agency beyond the boundaries of rhetorical compliance; active engagement with both images and words served to oppose spectacle, harness her energies, and yoke them to a belief in change and the possibility of agency. Britton's work directly influenced the design and sequencing of these counterspectacle strategies, particularly his ideas concerning the active making/doing/reflecting abilities of language.

According to Britton, language users shuttle on a continuum between two language roles: participant and spectator. On the one hand, language in the role of participant involves language focusing on getting something done in the world: selling a car, negotiating a loan, explaining how to make sugar cookies, defending a weekend curfew (arguing against a weekend curfew), and so forth. Language in the role of participant consists of doing-with-others language. Here, the language user actively engages in the immediate situation and with the performance of doing. On the other hand, language in the role of spectator consists of language focused on making *and* reflecting. Drawing on D. W. Harding, Britton explains that individuals invent a narrative of an event or experience—they create a verbal artifact—to share with another, thereby reflecting on that artifact through subsequent dialogue. Language in the role of spectator makes and then seeks responses from other people to determine the validity, ethicality, and worth of the made experience. We use language so that we may share as a means to confirm or disconfirm what Fox calls our "internal symbol system" (194). Both language roles—participant and spectator—are essential to the richness of the other. One must do/act in the world to have the raw material necessary for the making and reflecting. But one's doing/acting is impoverished without the reciprocal enrichment of making/reflecting.

Primarily concerned with active engagement with language, Britton does not spin out the implications of his theory of language for visuality. I extended in my composition class the participant/spectator reciprocity to include engagement with images: active seeing requires the same doing/acting and making/reflecting dynamic. By inviting students to negotiate dynamic seeing and speaking, I also invited them to resist the three processes—immediacy, erased expertise, and false unity—by which spectacle, rhetorical compliance, and monologic place cohere as a symbiotic knot of silence. So, during the spring semester Gloria and I worked together, I requested my students to shift constantly along the participation-spectator continuum textually *and* imagistically. First, let me provide a brief overview of the course, and then I will describe the students' final assignment, a culmination of the image-language work they had done through our sixteen weeks together.

The course combined three kinds of texts: speculative fiction, specifically an array of award-winning science-fiction short stories and a fantasy novel; critical essays related to social issues, the genre of science fiction, and sci-fi art; and Ridley Scott's 1992 director's cut version of *Blade Runner*, a dystopian vision of the future loosely based on Philip K. Dick's novella *Do Androids Dream of Electric Sheep?* I chose these texts because of science fiction's imaginative focus on the future. Dealing with issues requiring sociological, ecological, and critical attention, science fiction at its best spins out the implications of the past and the present for the future. It emphasizes repeatedly the importance of the past and the future in the present moment, challenging spectacle's privileging of immediacy. In addition to the readings, the course consisted of four separate writing units with different kinds of assignments built within each unit. The four major units started with a critical analysis of the short stories, proceeded to an assignment that combined various critical voices responding to a fantasy novel. The third unit involved an exploration of a social issue derived from *Blade Runner* that incorporated research (loosely defined) relevant to that issue. Each of these assignments led to students' final unit: a research paper, which I defined as an argument in a range of genres incorporating different kinds of primary and secondary sources.

Each unit was supported by a number of complementary short assignments, including creating avatars for a sci-fi online world, book covers for essay collections, storyboards for in-progress essays, proposals for a videogame with an audience analysis, letters to the editor, book blurbs for different audiences, annotated bibliographies, and so forth. Students completed all the assignments, regularly received peer and instructor feedback, and organized the entire array in an assignment portfolio that they submitted, with a reflective essay commenting on the contents, at the end of the unit. Two common features marked the assignment array embedded in each of the four units. The mini-assignments began with an informal exploratory narrative in which students forged personal connections with the reading material. In addition, the mini-assignments involved the production and/or critique of imagery. Finally, I kept a finger on the pulse of the class through their regular class journals and conferences.

The choice for the focal texts, the design of the major assignments, and the shuttling between production of text and images within each major assignment aimed in different ways to confound a symbiotic knot of silence, unwinding the threads of spectacle, rhetorical compliance, and monologic place. The dynamic I attempted to create by the sequencing of the larger units and the textual/visual mini-assignments resembled the doing/making/reflecting Britton advocates, to which I added active seeing. The last unit of the semester offers a more detailed picture of the possibilities of participant-spectator continuum for disrupting passivity.

As required by the writing program at my institution, the final paper in all second-semester writing classes consisted of a formal research paper. However, individual instructors were empowered to interpret that requirement in various ways. For this class, I configured unit four as a six- to eight-page paper incorporating secondary sources that illuminated and supported the author's argument concerning a social issue suggested either directly or indirectly by the texts read throughout the class, a fairly traditional approach. A culmination of the preceding three units, the research project, like all the previous units, encompassed a series of nested mini-assignments. Through these embedded activities, I aimed to take and redirect the conventional research paper in ways that invited agency.

My mini-assignment sequence began with ekphrasis, a verbal description that combined elements of image and text. The ekphrasis assignment began with a narrative. I asked students to re-create a sense-soaked, vivid, verbal description of an instance—either fictional or real—of social injustice that might serve as the focus of their final paper. They had to describe it as if they were seeing it or experiencing it in real time. I chose this activity as my starting for their final project with the hope it would begin the process of shifting them from rhetorical compliance. The descriptive activity invited two specific outcomes, each of which opposes rhetorical compliance in different ways. First, to create the description, students had to draw on their own life experiences, observations, or acquired knowledge. With its roots in the spectator role in which students use language to make an account of the world and reflect on it, ekphrasis engages students in both shaping the world and reshaping it to share with others. Through spectator language, students take ownership of their own lives, becoming the voice of authority in those lives. Gloria chose to combine the elements of a science-fiction short story focused on child abuse with personal witnessing, interweaving fiction and reality in a vivid account of adult indifference in the face of a child's suffering. For the first time in the semester, she drew on texts written by others (the "experts") and experiences in her life, finding in the union of the two a new authority. By humanizing a particular social issue she wanted to explore, connecting it to her life, and reflecting on her own investment in that issue, Gloria constituted herself an expert on that issue.

Second, ekphrasis interfered with students' belief in false unity, providing an opening within which to initiate dialogue. To disrupt spectacle's passive consumption, Fox warns, children must develop internal systems of imagery and language that provide an alternative perspective by which they can be critical consumers of the language and images presented to them by the mass media. Ekphrasis facilitated the move from monologue to dialogue. To describe an instance of injustice, my students had to perceive the existence of social injustice; they had to recognize moments when their experiences or observations of life veered from the dominant narrative of life promulgated by mass media. Thus, ekphrasis invited dialogue, soliciting student participation in concrete discussions and explorations of what they saw and how what they saw connected to their lives, families, and communities. Recognizing the illusion of false unity constitutes the first move toward talking about change, a necessary prelude to evolving action to effect change.

Ekphrasis invited students to challenge rhetorical compliance. To challenge spectacle, I included as my second mini-assignment storyboarding, a tactic designed to engage students in the active production of images. Important not only as a means to underscore the visual but also as a means to create a new visual habit, one that supports active agency in the world, the storyboarding assignment asked students to map out their accumulating ideas for their research project in a sequence of pictures. If we ask our students to consume critically the images produced for them, then a logical extension of that agency is a reflective production of their own images. The pictures, like a storyboard for a film or television drama, had to tell a story, with a rising action, climax, falling action, and resolution. I timed the activity to occur in the midst of classroom discussions concerning effective research strategies, visits to the library for work with research librarians, talk about good sources versus bad sources, and efforts of students to work back and forth between their initial sense of the paper and the wealth of material they were collecting.

When I initially envisioned the storyboarding assignment, I had three optimistic outcomes in mind, each aiming to disrupt spectacle in different ways: an opportunity for reflecting on their research project's focal argument and the audience's reactions, a strategy for organizing the rich data they were collecting, and a chance to discover disjunctures and gaps as a prelude for dialogue. In theory, the storyboarding offered students a chance to perceive the drama of the argument they were building by imagining a rich backstory for their topic, engaging them emotionally as well as intellectually. It required my students to create a history for their ideas and envision a future for those ideas, both of which directly challenge the static immediacy of spectacle. In addition, storyboarding confirmed students' status as experts, for they decided which elements of their research to include in the storyboard based on their vision of their evolving story. Finally, the nontraditional storyboarding assignment continually disordered the illusion of unity. By translating their nascent linguistic sense of their paper into visual form, students had to tackle the uneven match between word and image. They had to reflect on the differences circulating through their research and act on those differences. However, my vision of storyboarding and students' interpretations diverged in provocative ways.

Students' responses to the storyboarding assignment, or, more precisely, their revision of that assignment to suit their own needs, indicate the extent to which they operated as active agents beyond rhetorical compliance. While I provided examples of storyboarding and assured them that drawing stick figures or cutting-pasting magazine images was perfectly acceptable, students took off in their own directions. Some did, in fact, work through the storyboarding with interesting results; others, however, modified the assignment to fit their material and their interests. For instance, Katie, a biology major, designed an evolutionary chart that recorded through images the phylogenetic development of an imagery animal: the unicorn. Her paper explored the scientific possibilities and ethical implications of creating a unicorn through genetic manipulation. Her modification of the storyboard mini-assignment enabled her to expand her original vision of her research paper from its purely biological roots to a speculative paper that addressed the knotty social questions and moral quandaries tied into genetic manipulation. She moved from the question "Can we create a unicorn?" to "Should we create a unicorn?" Gloria, who struggled with a dialogic sense of the audience through the previous weeks of the semester, chose also to modify the storyboarding mini-assignment. Instead of focusing on her research materials, she created a montage of readers. She took photographs, raided magazines, or drew sketches to come up with images of people that she organized in a "before reading my paper" and "after reading my paper" montage. To address proactively the concept of a dialogic audience, Gloria used the montage as a lodestone, guiding her as she shaped a paper designed to change people's perception of and responses to child abuse.

Pushing beyond writer's block and beyond writer's fear, Gloria countered the passivity of rhetorical compliance to speak with conviction and authority in her final paper (described above). She fought her way through a symbiotic knot of silence to believe in her agency and imagine herself as an agent of change. Similarly, Obama and his cohort of concerned citizens found a way to believe in agency and act on that belief. Understanding how literacy is conceived and grasped as a culturally inflected image-oriented dynamic provides us with a more profound understanding of resistance enacted by Gloria, Obama, and the eight Altgeld Gardens parents. It is not just habits of language, discourse communities, cognitive styles, writing apprehension, and gender, race, class, and age that trouble our students and our own literacies (although it is all of this). It is also a symbiotic knot of silence evolved from lives lived within a culture of mass-mediated images that insists on passivity in the face of an eternal present, erased expertise, and false unity.

As Anne Haas Dyson points out in her ethnographic study of first graders, "learning to write involves work of the imagination on the part of both children and teachers. . . . A child must say some version of, 'Yes, I imagine I can do this.' And a teacher must also view the present child as competent and on that basis imagine new possibilities" (397). By imagining new possibilities, by envisioning alternative ways to help our students break a silence enforced by immediacy, erased history, and the false sense of unity in a society of spectacle, we can simultaneously envision alternative ways to help our students configure agentive identities and participate in social action. Perhaps we, too, like Obama, can transform a crisis of faith into an affirmation of faith and teach with audacious hope.

3. A KNOT OF BODIES
Visual Animation and Corporeal Rhetoric in Empathic Social Action

> Nonviolence is the language of the heart and the gut.
> —Tom H. Hastings, foreword, *Peaceful Persuasion*

> In an age of (multi)media, we can no longer
> ignore the embodied nature of discourse.
> —Jenn Fishman, Andrea Lunsford, Beth McGregor, and
> Mark Otuteye, "Performing Writing, Performing Literacy"

In August 2002, members of the Women in Black Art Project joined with supporters on the corner of Seventeenth and Constitution in Washington, D.C., to walk in a "solemn procession" to the offices of the Organization of American States Commission on Human Rights ("Action"). At the end of their march, the women presented a letter to the commission chairperson, protesting the disappearance and murder of hundreds of women over the past decade, most of whom were workers in *maquiladoras*, low-wage assembly-line factories located in the border regions of northern Mexico. The letter urged the commission to declare those murders and disappearances crimes against humanity.[1] Integral to the silent march were the efforts on the part of the Women in Black Art Project to evoke visually the ghosts of these women and their grieving mothers through two strategies. First, in conjunction with the group's goal to "enhance the visualization and building of peace," the participants dressed in costumes that resembled those worn by female *maquiladora* employees or in costumes patterned after the black garb worn by the victims' mothers who demonstrated for justice in northern Mexico ("Women"). Each marcher also carried a picture of one of the victims, metaphorically carrying the dead themselves onto Seventeenth and Constitution. Second, in concert with the slow and quiet procession down a D.C. city street, telecommunications media artist Adriene Jenik initiated a parallel protest in the virtual world. Synchronized with the real-world street action, Jenik "marched" through an online visual chat room by inserting stylized images she created of the Women in Black Art Project participants, bringing to the digital site reminders of the lost, murdered women ("Action"). As a result of these two strategies, the living activists embodied the presence of the missing and the dead in two separate but related spheres. Thus, the August 2002 protest constituted a multifaceted social action that operated on and across the real and virtual worlds through the interface of images and bodies. Empowered by embodied agency, the street marchers cum digital disrupters enacted empathic social action, a compassionate means to a compassionate end that emerges from a symbiotic knot of bodies.

A symbiotic knot of bodies, which consists of the interweaving of visual animation, corporeal rhetoric, and lively places, possesses value for individuals concerned with social action in and out of the classroom. In the classroom, a knot of bodies serves as a deterrent to a knot of silence described in chapter 2. A knot of silence with its intertwining threads of spectacle, rhetorical compliance, and monologic classrooms predisposes individuals and communities to disengage from social action. Especially when tightly intertwined with gender, class, and race, a knot of silence undermines belief in one's ability to effect change in life on either micro or macro levels. Shaped by spectacle, people experience difficulty imagining a change and imagining themselves as agents of change. Therefore, lulled into passivity, they resist writing, limit speaking, and avoid acting. However, a symbiotic knot of bodies challenges the silencing of spectacle and rhetorical compliance by providing a counterspectacle strategy, defined in chapter 2 as contextually responsive actions that resist entrenched beliefs and conventions, particularly those habituated by spectacle (Garoian 70). More specifically, through the intersection of bodies and sign, a knot of bodies invites foundational changes in composition praxis. Pedagogy shaped in accordance with a knot of bodies goes beyond paper topics that concern social violence or injustice, beyond analysis or a cultural studies critique of production, circulation, and consumption. A knot of bodies calls for an epistemological change, a way of learning and living grounded in the body. That change, in turn, invites teachers and students to envision themselves as embodied agents of systemic empathic change.

Integral to the epistemological changes in the classroom invited by a knot of bodies are the seismic changes out of the classroom fostered by a knot of bodies. The nexus of visual animation, corporeal rhetoric, and lively places addresses a central challenge posed by social action: How do people know what constitutes compassionate living—the desired end for social action—and how do they know that a tool of social action—a particular rhetorical option—is also compassionate? These are not small questions because, as Martha C. Nussbaum points out, compassion is at the heart of social justice and social action. Without it, community members cannot bring about humane change. She argues that compassion consists of an emotional response jointly comprising situational assessments and vulnerability to the pain of another (297, 321). Motivated and guided by this emotion, community members use various symbol systems to alter situations that cause others deep distress. Central to this process is the reciprocity of means and ends. According to Nussbaum, the how affects the what. Therefore, the tools people use to bring about compassionate change must also be compassionate. Mahatma Gandhi puts this conviction at the center of his philosophy and practice of nonviolence, an ontology that later influenced the civil rights movement in the United States through such proponents as Martin Luther King Jr. Gandhi argues that because "there is no wall of separation between means and end," the method by which one fights for an objective is intrinsic to that objective (81). Every move toward a desired goal shapes the character of that goal; therefore, the actions one takes to bring about a change must resonate with the character of that goal (Parekh 54). The process and the product both need to be compassionate. Actor and act cannot be separated from the end result, so, to bring about compassionate living, actor and act must be compassionate.

Successful social action, then, requires discerning compassionate ends and devising compassionate means to those ends. But how do we do this, and, more specifically, how do we do this in the writing classroom? Those questions possess no easy answers. For instance, on one level, the emergence of *maquiladoras* in post-NAFTA Mexico constitutes a necessary element of compassionate living: employment opportunities, particularly for women, in a country rife with poverty. But the reality and the results of these low-wage assembly plants have been anything but compassionate: starvation pay, hazardous working conditions, and rising environmental pollution. Focusing on the global sex trade and protest videos used to mobilize action, Wendy S. Hesford offers another example of the means-end conundrum. Advocacy videos distributed by various international organizations aim to empower women bought and sold for the sex trade so that they might have access to justice and victim services. This is a laudable and compassionate agenda. But the means of accomplishing that end—narratives of victimization and naiveté—result in increased local and international surveillance and control that seek to restrict women in the name of protecting women (149). Hesford argues that activists "need to become more attuned to advocates' strategic and effective mobilization of victimization narratives, as well as the uncritical uses of such narratives in ways that may re-victimize women and support repressive cultural and political agendas" (148). Determining what constitutes compassionate living and establishing how to work toward that vision in ways that support the goal involve difficult decisions.

A symbiotic knot of bodies offers one robust response to these critical decisions in and out of the classroom, because an individual's humanity, her or his corporeal existence, interweaves with the threads comprising this knot. Both Nussbaum and Gandhi working from different philosophical starting points arrive at a similar emphasis on the importance of emotions and bodies in acting for change. Nussbaum maintains that an essential criterion of compassion is vulnerability to the pain of the other's suffering, a vulnerability that opens up one person to another (300).[2] Her position aligns with Gandhi's *satyagraha*, a surgery of the soul that unlocks the mind and heart, which Gandhi considers a necessary starting point for dialogue (Parekh 54). The various loops making up a symbiotic knot of bodies puts bodies—especially their vulnerability and their openness to others—at the center of compassionate living, fostering the emergence of empathic social change and embodied agency. Here, then, lies the logic behind the online and real-world modes of social action chosen by the participants in Women in Black Art Project, for these women transformed their bodies into tools of protest by blurring the distinctions between their bodies, those of the victims, and those of the mothers mourning their lost daughters. In deliberately making themselves vulnerable to and a conduit for another's pain, they invited passers-by to experience a similar vulnerability, a parallel permeability in which the boundaries between one's own body and another's become porous. These permeable boundaries allow the pain of victims to be experienced by passersby and serve as an invitation to remediate the injustices connected to that pain.

As philosopher and peace activist Tom H. Hastings points out, "nonviolence is the language of the heart and the gut" (xix), and a symbiotic knot of bodies weaves itself out of heart and gut. Such an insight is important in a postmodern age and a postmodern classroom where flesh has been stripped from the bones of language and vision. Naomi Schemann in *Engenderings* argues the need for an embodied agency in a conceptual universe that has no foundations. She asserts that "by putting flesh back on our bones, it would allow us to be responsible while acknowledging that there is nothing beyond ourselves [no transcendental reality/truth] to be responsible to" (192). A symbiotic knot of bodies puts bodies back in vision, language, and places; it puts bodies back into writing pedagogy and social action. By doing so, it connects the goal of social action—compassionate living—with compassionate means for achieving that goal. Through a knot of animation, corporeal rhetoric, and lively places, we do not abandon bodies; rather we live, learn, and teach in ways that are generous to those bodies.

This chapter traces the interwoven threads of a symbiotic knot of bodies to map the emergence of empathic social action and the exercise of embodied agency in and out of the writing classroom (see fig. 3.1). I begin with visual animation, describing its two characteristics and mapping its connection to performing literacies. Interweaving corporeal rhetoric with animation in the second section, I illustrate this rhetorical habit through the activities of the Women in Black (WiB), the parent organization for the Women in Black Art Project. Established in 1988, WiB is a worldwide association of women who use their bodies as language to protest violence against women. The third section integrates the writing classroom, advocating a lively, performance-based writing pedagogy as a means of offering students an invitation to exercise embodied agency as a prelude to empathic social action. Finally, I examine the impact of the entire symbiotic knot of bodies, highlighting threats to its formation and its sustainability.

Thread 1: Visual Animation and Embodying Change

The visual habit of animation exists as an integral part of a symbiotic knot of bodies and empathic social action. *Animation* is a rich, complex term particularly apt for the embodied and permeable visual practice explored in this section. First, according to *The Oxford English Dictionary, animation*, as the "action of imparting life, vitality, or (as the sign of life) motion," connects with a physical existence of blood circulating and lungs breathing. Animation and material life intertwine. Second, *animation* links to imagery and technologies. It refers to the process by which still pictures acquire motion and the illusion of life,

Figure 3.1

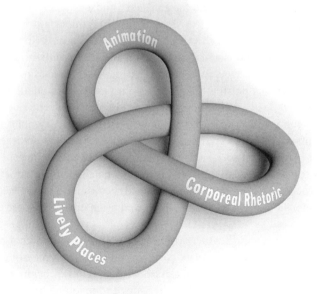

Empathic Social Action

A Symbiotic Knot of Bodies

tying the term to what the *OED* calls the perception or "representation of things as alive," which again highlights the importance of corporeality in this way of seeing. Finally, *animation* evokes the boundary blending of interinanimation, a term I. A. Richards borrows from John Donne to name the dynamic by which language obtains meaning through the mutual infusion—interinanimation—of words and context.[3] For instance, the word *dog* gains meaning in part from its linguistic context: its relationship with other words in a sentence, paragraph, text, and so forth. However, *dog* also gains meaning from experiential contexts: the array of situations involving dogs that an individual experiences. The meaning of the word *dog* borrows from linguistic and experiential contexts. Words and life permeate each other; without that mutual blending, meaning would not exist. *Animation* resonates to that infusion. These three layers—vitality, enlivened images, and porous borders—coalesce in animation and circulate throughout the two dominant conventions that characterize this way of seeing.

Two practices differentiate visual animation from other ways of seeing and serve to organize this symbiotic knot. The first practice consists of embodiment: the fusion of image, object represented, and perceiver so that image becomes an incarnate sign of that which it signifies. The roots of embodied vision are sunk in the physiology of human perception. In *The Power of Images*, art historian David Freedberg engages in a wide-ranging and careful analysis of human perception and response to images, both the "high" images of art and the "low" images of quotidian life. He argues that reactions to imagery, regardless of historical moment or culture, are organized by *animism*, "the degree of life or liveliness believed to inhere in an image" (32). The beholder perceives an image not as a representation—that is, not as an artifact standing in the place of or referring to something else—but as infused with the presence of that which is represented. Freedberg refers to this movement between image and object as the oscillation between representation and presentation, between "seeing a token of the Virgin to seeing her there" (28). Embodiment in visual animation—the shuttling between representation and presentation—transforms an image into a living manifestation of that which it signifies and then back into an image.

An example of this practice in visual animation can be found in the strategies employed by the Women in Black Art Project. During the August 2002 march, these protestors sought to blend various images—the pictures of the lost women, the clothing many of them might have been wearing at the moment of their attack, and the specter of the mothers left behind to mourn their daughters—with their own bodies. The protestors signified in material terms the immensity of past and present violence in northern Mexico. Unlike other protests that included photographs or representations of the murdered women, social action, as defined by the Women in Black Art Project, involved presentation: creating an unforgettable corporeal image—lines of women dressed in black, marching silently—that brought to the fore the deaths in Juarez and Tijuana. The protestors did not only stand in for the murdered women (representation); they were also the murdered women themselves (presentation). By shuttling between representation and presentation, the marchers became a living embodiment of the lost women and the grieving mothers.

The second convention of visual animation consists of boundary blurring: visual animation obscures the separations among actor, act, and audience. Through animation, the actor is simultaneously act and audience. While the convention of embodiment in animation is rooted in the physiology of perception, the convention of boundary blurring aligns with the rise of interactive digital imagery. As Richard A. Lanham in the now-classic *The Electronic Word* notes, the increase in digitization brings with it a new porosity, which, in turn, requires "a rhetoric of the arts like none seen before" (4).[4] In interactive digital media, Lanham argues, the user acts as reader, writer, designer, and respondent simultaneously. Thus, the separations among actor, act, and audience are always mutually constitutive in this new mode of expression. He refers to these unstable boundaries as the bistable decorum of oscillation in which a user constantly shuttles between looking at and looking through a verbal or visual expression (*Electronic World* 5, 14). This new way of acting, being, and seeing in the world involves the individual looking at an object with acute sensitivity to the dynamic interaction among object, maker, viewer, reality, and motive; it includes as well looking through the object with total disregard for the medium of expression. Thus, at this particular historical juncture, the development and widespread dissemination of interactive imagery, especially interactive digital imagery through new-media technologies, take the phenomenon of boundary porosity and make it an intrinsic element of a new way of seeing. As Lanham argues, "looking through experience and at it, first one and then the other, comes to seem a natural way of seeing, a habit of perception. Such an oscillation will constitute [an individual's] characteristic way of looking at the world" (*Economics* 26).[5]

Elements of this dynamic aspect of animation circulate through the August 2002 march, particularly in Jenik's online action: inserting stylized images, or avatars, of the Women in Black into digital chat rooms. Jenik takes her inspiration for this mode of social action from her work with the Desktop Theater, a phenomenon that she codeveloped with Lisa Brenneis and one that deliberately invites boundary blurring. Desktop Theater aims to create real-time theatrical performances within a series of visual electronic chat rooms provided by Palace, free, 2-D, visual-chat-room software with robust cross-platform capability.[6] Drawn to a space "where the barrier between artist and audience has not yet been built," Jenik and Brenneis began in 1997 to create scripts, design avatar/characters, and block out action for performances in a specific Palace room . Actor-avatars, created to align visually with roles in plays, such as Samuel Beckett's *Waiting for Godot*, perform the scripts within a populated online social space where fictional characters and chatters (members of the chat rooms) interact. The chatters are literally in the middle of the play. Throughout this venture, then, the actors, who are themselves chatters, and the scripted actions they perform are subject to interruptions/contributions from other chatters not formally enlisted in the project. Jenik notes that such collaborative performances "provoked a deeply empathetic response" among the viewers as the demarcation among act, actors, and audience blurred ("Desktop Theater" 99).

Jenik adapted this boundary blurring approach for her contribution to the 2002 D.C. march. She created three silhouetted, shrouded, two-dimensional characters (graphical cartoons) that served in the visual chat rooms as avatars for the Women in Black (see fig. 3.2). Like the Desktop Theater, this mode of protest relies on obscuring the boundaries among actor, act, and audience characteristic of visual animation, for, within this environment, chatters are actors (the ones who protest), actions (the avatars), and audience (those who respond to the images). Jenik explains that the avatars "slowly and silently moved through the spaces," interacting with other chatters and "evoking a variety of responses, as would such a procession on 'real' streets" ("Re: 2002 DC March"). In addition, Jenik created a series of small props, such as signs that read "No War" or that provided information about world violence. These props, along with olive leaves the avatars carried, were left in the various chat rooms to provoke empathic responses after the avatars disappeared, opening up chatters to the possibility of their own social action.

As enacted by the 2002 march, visual animation, with its twin protocols of embodiment and boundary blurring, constitutes a participatory, constructive, and enlivening process of perception. Students similarly rely on this way of seeing to organize and deploy a participatory, constructive, and enlivening literacy, one that underscores the corporeal ethos of language and the dynamic relationships among author, reader, and text. Performing literacy, "grounded in the body" and "always involving the body and performance," provides an example of a literacy infused with visual animation (Fishman et al. 228). Based on preliminary results of their longitudinal study of the writing practices of Stanford undergraduates in and out of the classroom, Jenn Fishman and Andrea A. Lunsford, with Beth McGregor and Mark Otuteye, find that "students' live enactment of their own writing" figured prominently in their literacy practices. These dramatic changes in literacy are the result of equally dramatic changes in digital technologies, which "have brought rhetoric's performing bodies 'back to life,'" they argue (Fishman et al. 229).[7] Therefore, "in an age of multi-media," Fishman and Lunsford believe that "we can no longer ignore the embodied nature of discourse" (Fishman et al. 229). Performance "helps us look toward

Figure 3.2. Women in Black avatars (Desktop Theater screen capture by Adriene Jenik. Performers include Lisa Brenneis, Adriene Jenik, and Connie Samaras. Used with permission.)

the future and the great range of self-aware, media-savvy moves that are coming to signal full literacy, indeed, the multiliteracies that present-day college writers must strive to achieve" (Fishman et al. 229).[8]

First, performing literacy, like visual animation, is characterized by embodiment: beholder, image, and object are mutually infused. In visual animation, the beholder breathes life into the image, shuttling between perceiving the image as a representation of an object and as the object itself. This confusion of representation and presentation erupts in the emerging twenty-first century literacy that Fishman and Lunsford describe. They theorize the "slippery ideas of 'performing'" through performance studies, which enables them to define performing as "both medium and act, noun and verb" (Fishman et al. 227). This definition provides a necessary flexibility because, as they explain, their entry into this discussion of performativity comes at "the intersection of body, rhetoric, and writing" (Fishman et al. 228), an intersection that teeters on the edge between representation and presentation.

Beth McGregor's performance reveals the organizing force of embodiment in her literacy. For McGregor, an undergraduate drama major, writing is intimately involved with the internal dialogues she scripts and performs mentally. The actors in her mental drama include herself, her Creative Content Editor (the CCE who wears the face of Jenn Fishman) and her Grammar and Flow Editor (the GFE who wears the face of another teacher, Roland Hsu). McGregor performs a sample of a drama she created—My Performance Text, she calls it—to demonstrate the way she negotiates their advice in writing. Through an internal dialogue peopled with real/not real characters crucial to the production of external text *and* her performance of that technique, McGregor oscillates between representation and presentation. McGregor's "adopted character" is both herself and an image of herself. Her internal CCE and GFE are and are not Fishman and Hsu. Presentation and representation merge. Without the dynamic of embodiment in visual animation, McGregor could not have scripted and enacted her dramatic dialogue, a technique integral to her literacy.

Second, performing literacies relies on visual animation's boundary blurring among actor, act, and audience. For instance, in visual animation, the actor is the act; in fact, in visual animation, it is difficult to determine the points at which the actor is and is not the act, a dynamic process replicated in performing literacies. Fishman and Lunsford claim that writing is an activity—"an act always involving the body and performance"—and the actor becomes a writer in that activity. The actor impinges on the nature of the act; but the performance of that act in turn structures the actor. Writer and writing are fused in the performance, each affecting and affected by the other. Mark Otuteye exemplifies that actor-act blurring in both his textual performance in the pages of *College Composition and Communication* and in his digital performance available through the *CCC* Online Archive.

"I'm a poet and a lover of words, and I'm here to show you how experience with performance can improve your students' writing" (Fishman et al. 238), Otuteye boldly announces in his paper. Cofounder of the Stanford Spoken Word Collective, "a community of poets that meets regularly to write, collaborate on, and perform spoken-word poetry," Otuteye performs two different versions of his poem "I'm Daaaaaaaat Nigga!!" to demonstrate his argument about performance and writing (Fishman et al. 238). The first reading of the poem is a simple recitation; the second one, however, releases "the vast amount of nonwritten music that actually lives in me, the performer, and not on the page" (Fishman et al. 240). With self-performed texts, Otuteye argues, "the lyrics (the what) cannot be separated from the music (the how). . . . Rather, the performer creates the how dynamically and on the fly as the performance is occurring" (Fishman et al. 239). The writer is most intensely alive as a writer in the act of performing the writing, an act grounded in the body and reliant on the actions of the body. As Otuteye explains, in performing literacies, "the music of the poem lives in the performer" (Fishman et al. 239). At the moment of performance, the music, the poem, and the performer fuse, like Yeats's dancer and dance.

Otuteye's performance also blurs the boundary between actor and audience, a separation that visual animation renders porous in two ways. The first kind of permeability occurs when the audience literally participates in the performance. In visual animation, the actor is not engaged in a solitary display, a type of spectacle; rather, the actor is involved in a community whose members at any moment can join the performance. Actors watch in order to perform, which is exactly what Otuteye enacts. His performing literacy evolves within the context of "a community of poets that meets regularly to write, collaborate, and perform spoken-word poetry" (Fishman et al. 238). The audience, then, of Otuteye's performance poetry consists of fellow poets, watching and listening as participants who at any moment can become actors. In addition, Otuteye's use of direct address throughout his presentation to an audience of 4Cs academics signals his efforts to help his audience self-identify as participants, not spectators. He liberally salts his talk with the second person pronoun—"When you work with self-performed texts," "a text that you are writing," "you've probably experienced," and other similar references—to draw and even to lure the audience into the performance as participants. Finally, the writing students Otuteye envisions are both actors and audience. He says, "One of the ways to get students to a place where they truly understand the importance of 'how words are said' is to work with self-performed texts in which this distinction is literally embodied and personified" (Fishman et al. 239). Otuteye advocates that students perform *and* watch as potential performers, blurring the demarcation between actor and audience simultaneously.

As the work of Fishman, Lunsford, McGregor, and Otuteye illustrates, visual habit, new-media technologies, and literacy flow back and forth, reinforcing shared characteristics and maintaining each other's stability:

> Performance is a dynamic form of literacy expression that is both fun and deeply serious. Immediate and face-to-face, performance encourages active participation and collaboration, and thus it models many of the qualities that we value most in real-time new-media writing, while at the same time it brings renewed attention to talk and scripted forms of oral communication. (226–27)

Visual habit, imagery artifact, and language practice knot together, and, in that (con)fusion of acts, actors, audience, words, images, and bodies, a stage is set for corporeal rhetoric and empathic social action. Fishman and Lunsford allude to the possibilities of performing literacy for social action. The muddle of embodiment and blurred boundaries can become "a catalyst to personal and social transformation," an invitation to social action, because "through the dramatization or embodiment of symbolic forms," the confusion of image and presence fosters "alternative arrangements" to reality (Jon McKensie qtd. in Fishman et al. 232). These alternative arrangements serve as a foundation for visualizing change, a step necessary in agency, for people must be able to envision change before they can act on that vision. The process by which people move from vision to strategies for social action is the subject of the next section.

Thread 2: Corporeal Rhetoric and Empathic Social Action

The interface between visual animation and performing literacy highlights the reciprocity between the way people see their worlds and the way people use language to make sense of their worlds. Visual animation also links with the way people use language to bring about change in the world. Visual animation coevolves with a *corporeal rhetoric*, a rhetoric that, to quote Margaret Atwood, operates "At the point where language falls away . . . / . . . & the body/itself becomes a mouth" (1299). The interface of corporeal rhetoric and visual animation—that is, the performance of corporeal rhetoric perceived through visual animation—provides a matrix for the emergence of empathic social action, where means and ends are both compassionate. In this section, I first trace the processes of embodiment and boundary blurring in corporeal rhetoric and use as my exemplar WiB. Then, by teasing out the necessary contribution of visual animation and corporeal rhetoric to the experience of empathy, I highlight the way in which a knot of bodies provides a tool by which activists can determine what constitutes compassionate means and compassionate ends.

Corporeal rhetoric reinforces and relies on visual animation, sharing the characteristics of embodiment (the shuttling between representation and presentation) and boundary blurring (the porosity of act, actor, and audience) that characterize this way of seeing. Through corporeal rhetoric, the body shapes itself into an image that becomes a word, and that image-word seeks to change some aspect of reality. Corporeal rhetoric is literally a physical rhetoric, a "rhetoric of love," to quote Jim Corder, where "argument is not something *to present* or *to display*. It is something *to be*. It is what we *are*" (26; emphasis in original). This mode of persuasion is exemplified in the rhetorical practices of the Women in Black, who use the body as a message. An international network of women, WiB is "committed to peace with justice and actively opposed to injustice, war, militarism, and other forms of violence" ("About WIB"). All people—whether victims, perpetrators, or observers—are part of world violence. WiB attempts to evoke that realization of one's membership in a world community through its corporeal rhetoric. According to the Women in Black Web site, the group is not an organization per se but a "means of mobilization and a formula for action." Typically, protest takes the form of women in casual, black clothing congregating in a public place and standing there silently. A rule of the organization is that while standing vigil, the women must be silent and remain silent. They cannot respond to threatening or derogatory heckling of passersby because the protestors do not wish to force or frighten others into action. Rather, by means of their joint vulnerability, the women hope to persuade by calling forth a shared experience of the cost of violence. They perform their rhetoric through their voluntary silence, an agentive silence that speaks volumes when reinforced by the physical presence of their black-clothed bodies gathered on street corners. By speaking only through silence and their mourning clothes, the protestors' bodies are literally on the line, defenseless together. Concerned like WiB with the threat to women posed by a violently reactive society, Nancy Welch asks, "What might we lose in vulnerability and what might we gain in power through becoming visible *together*?" ("Who's Afraid of Politics" 350; emphasis in original). WiB participants gain an option for social action that emphasizes the necessity for compassionate living, because all bodies—even those acting together—are at risk.

Candace Walworth, a Buddhist activist, highlights the qualities of embodiment and boundary blurring in WiB's corporeal rhetoric. Driving home from work, she describes her first sight of WiB: "an unexpected silence and stillness," on the "corner of Canyon and Broadway in front of the Boulder Municipal Building" (20). Dressed in black, eighty to a hundred women were assembled at a street corner simply standing. With "no petitions to sign. No candidates to promote. No initiatives. No money to raise," this was a "feast for the eyes, not ears," Walworth writes, in which "the customary signifiers of social action were strikingly absent" (20). Touched by this silent vigil, this interruption of "grief and sadness with a huge silence," Walworth joins these women and their protest, positioning herself on what she calls the "permeable boundary between 'actors' and 'audience,'" a boundary that provided a site for Walworth the Buddhist activist and Walworth the Buddhist practitioner (20, 21).

The two conventions of visual animation—embodiment and boundary blurring—circulate through the rhetoric that Walworth witnesses and then later enacts herself. First, the poignancy of WiB derives from the activists' reliance on embodiment, their existence as an interinanimation of image, object, and perceiver. They deliberately structure their protest according to the fusion of image, object, and perceiver, and that protest then invites from passersby an oscillation between representation (the symbol of the women as protests against violence) and the presentation (the women as victims of violence). WiB participants allow their protesting bodies (the image) and the victims' suffering bodies (the object) to infuse the other until one is indecipherable from the other. Representation shifts into presentation. Such corporeal rhetoric invites visual animation from passersby. As a perceiver who is taken by that oscillation, Walworth joins the permeable line of WiB activists. *Because* of that shuttling, Walworth offers her own body as a site of suffering and protest, becoming a part of WiB's corporeal rhetoric.

Second, like visual animation, corporeal rhetoric blurs the distinction among actor, act, and audience, emphasizing the necessity of shaping the *how* of action so that it aligns with the *who* and the *what* of action. For instance, WiB articulates an agenda for its international organization that implicitly reveals the group's commitment to actor-act permeability. In a speech to the 2003 annual general meeting of the Women's International League for Peace and Freedom, British sociologist Cynthia Cockburn argues for the importance of a feminist framework, because such a framework would, first, highlight the permeability between actor and act, and, second, provide a philosophical rationale for uniting actor and act. She says, "We are looking for a rationale for what we [WiB] do. One good reason for getting it clear is that it might shape our strategies for action and our choice of words," implicitly affirming the necessity of aligning means (strategies/words) and ends because actor cannot be separated from act. Choices for action evolve out of the blurring of actor and act. The protestor is herself the protest. Who, what, where, how, and why are inextricable, meaning that one's rhetorical choices must, logically, also be part of who one is and what one aims to do.

In addition to actor-act reciprocity, WiB also highlights the blurring of actor-audience. For WiB, actor and audience constitute fluid, reciprocal identities. As Walworth notes, the line constituting WiB continually reshapes itself as passersby stop and take a position within the group. The decision of audience members, such as Walworth herself, to join that quiet vigil on the corner of Canyon and Broadway in Boulder, Colorado, is likewise the result of the porosity between actor and audience, which enables audience members to envision themselves as actors, as WiB activists. It also enables them to identify with the victims of violence and injustice whom the Women in Black mourn. Edie, a member of the Gulf Coast WiB, explains her participation similarly: "I only changed myself, because I once saw someone else doing something and went and found out about it. So maybe someone could ask, seeing me there [in silent vigil]: what is it to be non-violent?" ("Women in Black Art Project" 5). The blurring of the actor-audience boundary emphasizes the participatory quality of community in corporeal rhetoric. As protestors physically invest in the performance itself, they also invest in ameliorating the ills they protest.

Finally, the corporeal rhetoric of the WiB relies for its persuasive power on the fusion of word, image, and body. Like visual animation, corporeal rhetoric constitutes a means of persuasion that clings to the body: it is performed with and through the body in defiance of the culturally entrenched separation of body and mind dominant in the West since the Enlightenment. Corporeal rhetoric returns persuasion to the body. To illustrate, Cockburn, in her profile of the Gulf Coast WiB, recounts a rhetorical tactic employed by the group when protesting outside the fence of MacDill Air Force Base, Florida. WiB protestors were allowed five minutes at the microphone to articulate their protest. When the women took their place in front of the massed protestors, they chose a five-minute silence "that startles, that wins attention. That models rather than teaches" (5). That silence, within which bodies, individually and collectively, "spoke," became the vehicle of persuasion. Deliberate silence, inseparable from the bodies, highlights those bodies as the site of the violence being protested and as the coin—the corporeal capital—used to pay for that violence.

Important in this description of corporeal rhetoric, and, perhaps, indivisible from it, is the nature of the social action that emerges from the confluence of embodiment and boundary blurring. The knotting of visual animation with corporeal rhetoric bids protestors to configure themselves—to act—as citizens in particular ways. Visual animation joins with corporeal rhetoric to serve as a foundation—or, in Cockburn's words, a framework—for a social action that fosters a joint responsibility for redressing the world's ills. The visual animation–corporeal rhetoric interface invites an empathic social action that possesses the "same inviolable connexion between the means and the end as there is between the seed and the tree" (Gandhi 82). In other words, linked through embodiment and boundary blurring, visual animation and corporeal rhetoric open up the individual, both actor and audience member, to empathy, the basis of social justice and social change.

To determine what constitutes compassionate means and compassionate ends, to determine how to devise protests that maintain the integrity of means and ends, an activist relies on empathy. A variety of scholars from a range of disciplines have connected social action and empathy, arguing that empathy motivates and sustains social activism.[9] For instance, psychologist Martin L. Hoffman, who has traced the developmental path of empathy from the phenomenon of the synchronized crying of newborns in hospital nurseries to the more sophisticated language-mediated empathy of adulthood, considers empathy intrinsic to what he calls prosocial activism: the "sustained action in the service of improving another person's or group's life condition either by working with them or by trying to change society on their behalf" ("Empathy and Prosocial Activism" 65). Hoffman defines empathy as a vicarious emotional response to another person's situation in which the observer's feelings resonate with those of the model ("Interaction" 103). The emotional response, particularly empathic distress or anger, impels the observer to alleviate the victim's suffering by changing the situation causing the misery ("Empathy and Prosocial Activism" 71). Then, once engaged, the activist is sustained by empathy. Gandhi identifies a similar belief at the heart of his social protest, contending that every human resonates to the distress of another. However, Gandhi explains, some people have a very small empathy circle: a small cadre of others with whom they empathize. The goal, then, is to expand the circumference of that empathy circle so that more rather than fewer people are potentially subjects of compassion (Parekh 56). As the circumference increases, so does the scope of social action. How, then, do we expand the circumference of an individual's empathy circle? The answer to that crucial question relies on the dynamism and sensuality of embodiment and boundary blurring.

To see empathically and to act empathically require living according to the twin protocols of embodiment and boundary blurring. Empathy, Hoffman explains, involves people subordinating awareness of their own situation by imagining themselves in another's place, a process that intrinsically taps an individual's ability to shuttle between representation and presentation and to blend boundaries. For example, according to Hoffman, role-taking involves two major forms: other focus and self-focus. Both techniques depend on the oscillation of representation and presentation, a process that enables one person to be vulnerable to the pain of another.[10] The first role-taking strategy—that of focusing on the victim—involves imagining how the victim is feeling, visualizing the sufferer's behavioral responses so that missing nonverbal cues are provided, and responding to the images as if the situation were physically perceivable. It is a way of seeing—of imagining—that animates the physical and emotional situation of the other. The second strategy, that of focusing on self—or identification—is one in which the individual pictures himself or herself in the victim's position instead of just imagining the sufferer's feelings. Perceivers immerse their values, drives, and behavioral patterns in those of the victim, merging identities. Here, the actor, image, and body meld, confusing the point at which one is separate from the other. By inhabiting the position of the other, the perceiver empathizes with the other's pain and distress. Important to my argument is that empathy initiates and sustains compassionate modes of social action aimed at alleviating the suffering of the other.

WiB illustrates the complex network of feedback loops by which empathy taps the double protocols of embodiment and boundary blurring, both relying on and infusing visual animation and corporeal rhetoric. From the activists who experience empathy for the silenced victims of injustice, to the passersby like Walworth whom the activists seek to persuade through nonviolent strategies, empathy serves as both means and end in their social action. WiB protestors create a visual tableau that invites role-playing from those they hope will join them in their silent vigil or enact some other form of nonviolent protest. Caught up in the vision of the women mourning silently, Walworth identifies with the protestors, with the grief they embody, and through that identification, she joins their vigil. She, too, puts her body on the line, making it a sign for herself and for others. The WiB activists shape a corporeal rhetoric that guided by empathy invites empathic responses. Seeing through visual animation, passersby identify with both means and end, motivated to engage with the protest and sustain the action. Thus, through the intertwining of visual animation and corporeal rhetoric, WiB places bodies at the center of nonviolent social change and engage in empathic activism, expanding a community's empathy circle. This empathic activism also points to the importance of the writing classroom, for a teacher's pedagogical choices contribute to the contraction or expansion of a student's empathy circle.

Thread 3: A Lively Classroom

What we teach and how we teach our writing students affect their options and strategies for social action. I emphasized this point in chapter 2 by detailing the reciprocity among monologic classrooms, spectacle, and rhetorical compliance. The resurgence of a remediated presentational format, especially evident in the use of PowerPoint presentations and the information-delivery design of much Web-based online teaching, acts on students in ways that reinforce the passivity of spectacle. Coupled with arhetorical writing assignments, which dismiss student's expertise, and an insistence on a single master style, which closes down dialogue, a remediated presentational format creates a monologic classroom, tangling students in a knot of silence. The problems presented by a monologic classroom require that we as teachers seek out pedagogical practices that resist spectacle and move students beyond rhetorical compliance or simulated agency. A symbiotic knot of bodies offers one option. Through our teaching choices, we can structure classroom activities that nurture animation and corporeal rhetoric, providing an atmosphere that invites students to engage empathically in and out of the classroom. We can challenge spectacle's hold with a praxis that resonates to the protocols of embodiment and boundary blurring. By doing so, we can potentially configure the classroom as a safe space within which strategies for "peaceful persuasion" may emerge (Gorsevski).[11]

In this section, I explore two options for creating a lively classroom with our writing students: live drama and multimodal assignments. My goal is to demonstrate different ways of organizing a syllabus guided by the double processes of embodiment and boundary blurring. With these processes as a backbone, the classes become hospitable to visual animation and corporeal rhetoric, offering an invitation for students to enlarge their empathy circles and act on that empathy. These two different pedagogical approaches enact a performance-based approach to writing. Each approach creates a lively classroom that supports habits integral to empathic social change. Thus, my fine-grained analysis of a community-outreach program and a multimodal-assignment sequence provides insight into what teachers can do to draw from their students an embodied agency: acting in the classroom and the world as a corporeal being answerable to one's own and others' bodies. As embodied agents in the classroom, students not only create interesting responses to assignments but they also shift the terms of the learning so that they become their own teachers. They embody their learning. While a praxis founded on embodiment and boundary blurring does not guarantee that students will pursue an agenda of empathic social action outside the classroom, it opens up space for such behavior.

The first pedagogy for fostering a lively writing classroom involves live drama. Integral to the performance art of activists like Jenik and the Women in Black Art Project, live drama relies on a corporeal imagery that fuses image, object, and viewer and blurs the boundaries among actors, act, and audience. Christopher Worthman's two-year ethnography of TeenStreet, a Chicago-based community-theater ensemble for inner-city teenagers, spins out in more detail the connections between live drama in the classroom and a knot of bodies. An after-school residency outreach program, TeenStreet features an annual project with a rotating group of students who apply for admission.[12] Between fifteen and twenty participants work together to write, produce, and perform a play. Integrating writing, music, and bodywork, TeenStreet seeks to develop literacy and agency. At the same time, it seeks to link both literacy and agency with empathic action. Two core strategies—imaginal interactions and dialogic perspective-taking—form the backbone of the project, and both engage the protocols of embodiment and boundary blurring necessary for the cohesion of a symbiotic knot of bodies.

Imaginal interactions consist of visual and somatic performances of individual life stories that depend on students shuttling between representation and presentation. The outreach project stipulated that the play TeenStreeters wrote and performed evolve out of students' life experiences. So participants used imaginal interactions as their predominant means of creating a source pool of raw material. However, beyond the pleasures of creating and performing a jointly scripted play, students benefited in other ways from the imaginal interactions. The payoff for their visual and somatic performances, Worthman contends, consisted of developing a proactive embodied agency and literacy "grounded in each participant's physicality or place and time in the world" (1). Imaginal interactions begin with basic emotional and physical responsiveness to one another. One exercise, which the students called the Watusi, involved TeenStreeters interacting only through physical, nonverbal reactions. Designed to help students better understand the need to act in conjunction with others, the activity required students to fuse image, object, and perceiver. It began with

TeenStreeters standing in a circle. Using only peripheral vision, the participants had to imitate each other's movements, but no one could voluntarily initiate the first movement. So TeenStreeters had to watch each other as both image (the representation to be imitated) and the object (the person who would make the first move) simultaneously. So the students stood with their bodies, not their eyes, intensely focused on the others, sensitive to the least movement and poised on the edge of representation and presentation. Then, at the first sign of an involuntary twitch, the mimicry began, gradually swelling until everyone moved by imitating others' movements.

The Watusi activity focused action on the corporeal level, restricting options for physical action to those movements that responded harmoniously to the movement of other bodies. The activity taught not only the importance of acting in concert with others but also the importance of attending to others when deciding how to act (Worthman 25–26). Acting required acting with. A second example of representation and presentation in imaginal interactions consisted of dynamic, multimedia role-playing that unfolded in two parts. To begin, author-actors created dramatic "imaginative retellings" of their personal experiences, enacting those retellings via visual somatic imagery. Then, other members of the cohort had to answer those performances with reflective interpretations expressed through "writing, improvisation, movement, drama, and music" (Worthman 10). Both aspects of imaginative retellings relied on the protocol of embodiment so central to a knot of bodies and both aspects of imaginative retellings fostered embodied agency and empathy. To retell a life story through dramatic somatic imagery, teens had to use their bodies as a sign, as both representation and presentation. Then, to interpret another's retelling, TeenStreeters, first, had to engage emotionally with a classmate's performance by identifying with it (presentation) and, second, had to cast that engagement in some corporeal form that could be shared with others (representation). Imaginative retellings asked students to open themselves—to make themselves vulnerable—to classmates; interpretations asked them to take their own vulnerability and use it to structure their responses. Both invitations situated their bodies at the point of action and reaction in embodiment.

Quoting James Britton, Worthman calls the teenage participants "meaning weavers," with their bodies as the loom (86). "At TeenStreet," Worthman bluntly states, "meaning-making arises from an intense focus on one's body in time and space through visual imagery" (112). Such somatic imagery, Worthman concludes, serves as the foundation of all language use outside as well as inside TeenStreet, a realization he finds transformative: "[T]he guiding principle of my research evolved to where I realized that we are individual body and blood first and that others, too, are individuals, bodies and blood; that everything we do prepares us for using language and not vice versa, even as the two—language and experience—converged into reciprocity" (32). Beyond the pleasures of creating and performing a jointly scripted play, then, the rewards for these teens consisted of developing the habit of acting through and with the body. Both agency and literacy blossomed from each participant's unique physical embodiment in the world.[13]

Operating according to the protocol of embodiment, imaginal interactions emphasize the importance of acting in the world as bodies sensitive to and responsible for other bodies. The second strategy—dialogic perspective-taking— emphasizes the importance of imagining a world of options through blending boundaries, the second process important to a knot of bodies. The TeenStreet activity of dialogic perspective-taking deliberately confuses the separation between self and others, self and world, and self and word. Essentially, this strategy requires students to inhabit the perspective of another: to take on another's role. The dialogic dynamic between seeing oneself as others do *and* by seeing oneself as self constitutes the key to perspective-taking. Worthman explains that exercises in perspective-taking were designed so that teens would inhabit competing and contradictory viewpoints; they did not focus on one particular experience but on a multitude of experiences: "The TeenStreet creative process is about getting at the essence and interrelatedness of experiences and moving beyond them by taking those experiences and creatively imagining how they might have been and can be different" (54).

One version of dialogic perspective-taking involves the activity of shadowing, which nurtures the possibility of an empathic social action through blurring actor-audience boundaries. Shadowing consists of choosing a phrase or line from a writing and then doing a quick free writing on that phrase or line. Crucial to such work was relooking: "Shadowing one's own writing was an effort to get at one's thoughts and feelings by reflecting on how one sees one's writing being seen by others. It is re-looking at what one wrote" through the imagined eyes of another (Worthman 50). The individual self finds in those linkages different configurations of identity, different options for actions. Consequently, deciding which of those newly possible identities to pursue in the world requires first deciding how those identities affect others. The configuration of the self-in-action cannot be separated from the perspective of others-in-perception because self arises in dialogue with another.

Another version of dialogic perspective—polyphonic story—blurs the distinction among actor, act, audience, and world, thereby nurturing alternative options for action that link a means to an end. The cohort, including Worthman as participant-observer, created textual music out of an *exquisite corpse*: "a group story, with each member contributing a line or two and passing it to the next writer, who contributes a line or two and so on" (42). Students enriched this text by contributing narratives about a transforming experience. Then, small groups created out of these texts a musical ensemble. TeenStreeters performed their pieces as if the words were music. Worthman describes the experience:

> With one person in each group acting as conductor, the rest of the group took directions, starting and stopping their reading, increasing or decreasing the volume of the reading, at the conductor's behest, who also read from her piece. Each group member, when given the floor by the conductor, could read any part of her piece she wished, repeating parts, jumping around, or reading from beginning to end. Everyone could be reading at once, one person could be reading, or any variation of people within the group. (42–43)

As the group performed their texts, Worthman reports that Ron, the director, urged them to draw on their ongoing work with improvisation: the teens were to "listen and respond to one's own words, using intonation, volume, rhythm, and repetition" (43) in ways that complemented their group members' words, intonations, volumes, rhythms, and repetitions. What resulted, Worthman says, was "a symphony of voices. I heard my story meet with others' as if they were responses to mine" (43).

The polyphonic story not only confirmed the importance of each TeenStreeter's individual story but also invited TeenStreeters to experience alternative lives and realities. Intensely introspective and intensely communal at the same time, dialogic perspective-taking through the polyphonic stories fashioned a world out of relationships between actor and act and actor and other. It offered opportunities to imagine multiple realities, multiple options for change because the performance of writing gained significance, meaning, and power *in conjunction with* the performance of another's response. Life, as well as the story of a life, depends on an other who listens deeply and responds compassionately. Stories live, people live, in interaction with others, Worthman notes (54). As a result of this blending between self and other, self and act, self and world, the teenagers experienced alternative possibilities for the same events, leading them to the discovery that life has options (49). Thus, "we have an obligation to listen," Worthman contends, "if only because our own agency, our own stories, depends on our listening to others and their stories" (55).

Through its implicit advocacy of seeing the other as part of the self and through its emphasis on one's own bodily position as "the anchor from which one acts" (122), TeenStreet's dramatic, multimediative orientation provides a milieu where agency through embodiment and boundary blurring may flourish. Embodied agency, then, opens the door to embodied action through corporeal rhetoric, a theme that circulates implicitly throughout Worthman's ethnography. As Worthman explains, TeenStreet was established for "creative and agentive reasons" (44). Throughout their time together, participants wrote, explored, and expanded on stories as a means "to invigorate possibilities for each teenager" (44). By discovering options—invigorating possibilities—teens grew to believe in their individual ability to make choices about their lives. "In believing one has possibilities and in pursuing them," Worthman points out, "one becomes an agent in the world. It is knowing that what *has* happened is not necessarily what had to happen, or that what is going to happen is never preordained" (39; emphasis in original). The fledgling actors, writers, artists, and musicians learned that they could act in their own lives to control the direction of those lives. They could make choices because they could imagine those choices into existence.

Furthermore, TeenStreet helped students imagine themselves as embodied agents of compassionate change outside of the classroom. TeenStreet's dramatic orientation and focus on imaginal interactions offered a powerful strategy for moving students from classroom to street. As Worthman emphasizes, Teen-Street encompassed more than exercises and scriptwriting. It helped "teenagers reconceptualize themselves not only as writers and artists but also as agents in the world" (130). Infused with multiple voices, that agency arose out of interacting with and exploring possible existences (130). As a result, the participants become "effective instigators of change" beyond the boundaries of a nine-month outreach program (130). And as they became agents of change, they also began to imagine themselves as agents of empathic action. The embodiment of imaginal interactions and the boundary blurring of dialogic perspective-taking yield rich, empathic engagement, Worthman points out. Shuttling between body and sign, creating moments when representation and presentation infuse, these two strategies "fostered engagement with and empathy for others' experiences, enriching one's own perspective-taking and voice" (10). Thus, the live drama at the center of this performance-based pedagogy served to expand each student's empathy circle and enlarge the participants' options for social action.

TeenStreet's imaginal interactions and dialogic perspective-taking offer intriguing options for evoking a lively classroom. The program's experimental, creative approaches based on the extensive and regular bodywork of live drama resonate with the nontraditional orientations that characterized composition in the 1960s and 1970s, a productive "kookiness" of which we, as writing teachers, have, to our detriment, seemingly "purged ourselves" (Sirc 7). However, the powerful duo of embodiment and boundary crossing through imaginal interactions and dialogic perspective-taking need not be limited to a program of music, improvisation, and exquisite corpses. Instead, a symbiotic knot of bodies can be fostered in a lively classroom organized according to a second performance-based strategy: a multimodal approach to writing. Multimodal composing can encourage visual animation and corporeal rhetoric to coalesce, thus providing an invitation for embodied agency and empathic social action.

Jody Shipka in "A Multimodal Task-based Framework for Composing" provides a second way to structure a lively writing classroom based on embodiment and boundary blurring. Concerned with rethinking composition's "semiotic and productive potentials" and the exclusion of "the wide variety of sign systems and technologies students routinely engage," Shipka asks how might the "purposeful uptake, transformation, incorporation, combination, juxtaposition, and even three-dimensional layering of words and visuals—as well as textures, sounds, scents, and even tastes—provide us with still other ways of imagining the work students might produce for the composition course?" (278). It is not enough to "add and stir" multimedia to the composition classroom, she says. Such an approach "will not, in and of itself, lead to a greater awareness of the ways systems of delivery, reception, and circulation shape (and take shape from) the means and modes of production" (278). Instead, when students tap rich semiotic repertoires and deliberately structure the delivery and reception of language for a specific purpose of their own making, they shape "new ways of thinking, acting, and working within and beyond the spaces of the first-year composition classroom" (279).[14] Let me offer a quick orientation to her course before addressing the specifics of embodiment and boundary crossing.

To begin, Shipka places the dictum "students learn by doing" at the core of her approach (291). She advocates structuring assignments where students determine a specific goal of a project, the steps for accomplishing that goal, and the means of delivering the artifacts related to that goal. In addition, students learn by doing with a wide variety of materials. In her class, Shipka explains, students "engineer" their rhetorical events using *"any number or combinations of things"* (300; emphasis in original), from digital to analog technologies. Shipka's *OED* assignment provides an apt and entertaining illustration of the possibilities of a multimodal, performance-based approach for nurturing visual animation and corporeal rhetoric.

Used in the fourth week of a first-year composition course, the *OED* assignment asks students to research the etymology of any word they choose using the online resources of the *OED*. One student, Prakas Itarut, designed a multifaceted experience of the word *scare*. It included a paper, an unlabeled floppy disk, and a set of instructions that listed the sequence of activities the reader should follow as well as the setting—alone at night—for performing those activities. If the reader follows the instructions, he or she would slowly read aloud a scary short story in the middle of night with frightening sounds and images erupting unexpectedly on the screen. Understanding the word *scare* requires experiencing the word *scare*, and Itarut designed an "essay" that would evoke exactly that experience.

According to Shipka, when teachers require students to shape their own objectives and "to structure the production, delivery, and reception of the work," they accomplish three curricular goals: greater sensitivity to what various media allow (and disallow) a writer to communicate; greater proficiency at "contextualizing, structuring, and realizing the production, representation, distribution, and delivery, and reception of their work; and better negotiators of various communication contexts, both academic and everyday" (283–84). These are all laudable pedagogical ends for a first-year writing classroom. However, this approach also addresses other, equally important pedagogical goals. Identifiable within this project and others in Shipka's classroom are the elements that are key to fostering a symbiotic knot of bodies: embodiment and boundary blurring.

First, like Worthman's imaginal interactions, Shipka's pedagogy privileges embodiment in which students shuttle in multiple ways between representation and presentation. That oscillation manifests itself particularly in terms of the reader's experience of the text and the designer's experience of reality. As Shipka points out, students "decide *how, why, where,* and even *when* that argument based on specific readings will be experienced by its recipient(s)" (286; emphasis in original). To answer these questions about the participant's experience, the students have to explore their own experiences as potential representations that become, for readers, presentations. For instance, Karen Rust created out of the *OED* assignment a "Mirror IQ Test," a project deliberately designed to evoke in her audience the same confusion she felt in responding to the assignment (293). As she writes in her "heads up statement" (a postproduction reflection), "I wanted the participant to feel the pressure of completing the test in a given amount of time much like how I felt pressure trying to complete the assignment in the amount of time I had" (294). To achieve this end, Rust asks her "readers" to engage in imaginal interactions. Unlike Itarut, who asks his "readers" to engage in his experience in a specific place and at a specific time, Rust instructs her "readers" to imagine a particular setting in which the participant is to take her "Mirror IQ Test." Because both Itarut and Rust stage-manage their "readers'" experiences, Shipka claims that this work is more akin to that of choreographers and engineers than to conventional/traditional writers (300). Students produced a script, even if informally, that aimed to evoke their readers' embodiment of an experience, a goal that involved a "complex orchestration" of bodies, images, and words fluctuating between representation and presentation.

These embodied experiences invite embodied agency, particularly as enacted on the border between sign and medium. Shipka argues:

> By refusing to hand students a list of nonnegotiable steps that must be accomplished in order to satisfy a specific course objective, the framework asks students to consider how fairly simple, straightforward, relatively familiar communicative objectives might be accomplished in any number of ways, depending upon how they decide to *contextualize, frame,* or *situate* their response to these objectives. (286; emphasis in original)

Here, the media themselves increase students' possible options for corporeal action. The materiality of the communication medium itself invites students to conceive of medium as tool and experience, representation and presentation, expanding their pool of possible choices that they as agents can make. In addition, because the students decide how to contextualize, frame, and situate their activity, they have to navigate among the medium's *potential* as tool and experience. They engage in what Shipka calls "innovative choosing" and, in the process, expand their composition repertoire to include possibilities in "modes, materials, and methodologies" (300).

Second, like Worthman's live drama, Shipka's multimodal approach blurs boundaries among actor, act, and audience, emphasizing the importance of relationships for guiding actions. The multimodal assignment is all about interrelationships. In negotiating the complex tasks, students "began forging important connections between the classroom and other lived spaces" (293). The heads-up statement serves as a vehicle for such forging. In this written assignment, students explain their decisions and their rationale for those decisions. These statements ask students to grapple with the relationships artifact, creative process, and intended readers. "Requiring students to produce these statements underscores the importance of being able to speak to goals and choices in a way that highlights *how, when, why,* and *for whom* those goals and choices afford and constrain different potentials for knowing, acting, and interacting," Shipka explains (288; emphasis in original). Thus, students not only created conceptual, methodological, and human connections but also developed a metacognitive sensitivity to those interrelations, increasing their ability to create those interrelations in contexts beyond the classroom.

Unlike the participants in TeenStreet, Shipka's students did not rehearse movement or improvisation; they did not create Zen-like spaces or exquisite corpses. But they did create projects that relied on and fostered the embodiment and boundary blurring so crucial to a symbiotic knot of bodies. Thus, both TeenStreet and multimodal composition invite students to engage in and with the world through a symbiotic knot of bodies. Both performance-based approaches encourage the linkages between visual animation and corporeal rhetoric, inviting students to experience embodied agency and envision responsible acting in the world. Both demonstrate that teachers, through their pedagogical choices, can support an environment within which empathy becomes a central part of composing. Here, I believe, lies the most significant contribution each approach makes to empathic social action.

TeenStreet and multimodal composition as organized by Shipka highlight the importance of answerability and the importance of taking responsibility for the ends of actions. A symbiotic knot of bodies suggests that we determine ends and means on the basis of our answerability to each other and to our joint material existence. Arguing for the importance of a Bakhtinian "ethics of answerability" in the development of students as moral agents, Mary Juzwik characterizes answerability as the "unique responsibility that characterizes the individual's responses to others in everyday interaction and in textual production" (538). How one answers/addresses another affects both individual and communal realities; therefore, everyone is responsible for acting in ways sensitive to each other's unique, incarnated specificity and to the web of language that ties people together. Answerability intertwines with each thread of a knot of bodies, providing a means to determine compassionate means and ends.

Answerability figures into Worthman's experiences at TeenStreet, particularly through visual animation. Only when Worthman begins to participate with the TeenStreeters—to practice visual animation as his preferred way of seeing—does he discover the importance of bodies in language and in change. For instance, Worthman confesses that he did not initially join the activities of TeenStreet (16). Instead, he watched from the sideline, recording the actions of others. He detached himself visually and spatially from the teens. Shedding that detached vision and becoming a part of, a member of, the community allowed Worthman to learn the importance of embodiment and blended boundaries. As he explains, he came to Bakhtin's conviction that there is "no alibi in existence." Focusing on the intense, immersive nature of imaginal interactions and dialogic perspective-taking, he notes:

> Participation carries with it more than opportunities for literacy development; participation offers other mediational tools, such as mental and somatic signs and gestural and musical expression, that augment language use and voice development. Participation also brings with it responsibility, responsibility that rings with M. M. Bakhtin's (1993) notion that there is no alibi in existence, that we are responsible for responding to others from our own place and time. We are responsible for honing our own voices. (34)

Answerability intertwines with a symbiotic knot of bodies through a way of seeing that oscillates between one's own and another's embodied existence.

Second, answerability interweaves with corporeal rhetoric—a way of speaking and listening—throughout these approaches. From the perspective of a symbiotic knot of bodies, community members cannot take or advocate an action for others that they are not willing to live through themselves or that they are not willing to require a loved one to live through. Becoming answerable for what we learn how to see thus entwines with becoming answerable for what we learn how to say or hear or do. A symbiotic knot of bodies highlights the material realities of the choices people make rhetorically and visually. Shipka emphasizes the quality of corporeal-material answerability in her multimodal, task-based approach to composition teaching. She says that these kinds of assignments demand "that students both think and act more flexibly as they assume responsibility for determining what needs to be done along with how it might possibly be achieved" (292). Students decide; they act on their own agency in that place. In the process, they are asked to accept the responsibility that ensues from such agency. A symbiotic knot of bodies fosters and is founded on an ethic of joint responsibility for one's vision, one's rhetoric, and one's actions in the world.

Finally, a lively place in a symbiotic knot of bodies possesses its own answerability. Places evolve not only out of the material characteristics and design of particular sites but also out of dynamic relationships and actions within those sites (Stewart). Places themselves can be answerable to the vision of their design. TeenStreet itself illustrates such answerability, for it functions as its own empathic social action: a place that persuades those within it to explore their lives, discovering options for agency that respect the possibilities of life for themselves and those around them. TeenStreet exists as a rejoinder to its own goals of literacy and empathic social agency. The quality of answerability, reinforced by the interweaving of visual animation, corporeal rhetoric, and lively place, thus provides a response to the key questions concerning compassionate means and ends that drive this chapter.

Although nothing guarantees that a knot of bodies will evolve in a writing classroom, even a lively classroom, the possibilities of fostering empathic social action increase when teachers make pedagogical choices informed by embodiment and boundary blending. Performance-based praxis, through live drama or multimodal assignments, constitutes one powerful option. Performance, Fishman and Lunsford point out, "encourages active participation and collaboration, and thus it models many of the qualities that we value most in real-time new-media writing, while at the same time it brings renewed attention to talk and scripted forms of oral communication" (226–27). TeenStreet's dramatic orientation and Shipka's multimodal, task-based structure each works to shift students from the passive consumers of images created by others to lively empathic enactors of their own and others' images. Both pedagogical approaches increase students' empathy circles.

Symbiotic Knot of Bodies: Refusing the Invitation

If we as teachers are interested in using the classroom to cultivate an orientation sensitive to empathic social action, then we need to consider the threads of a symbiotic knot separately, as I have done throughout this chapter, and as a whole, which I address next. Empathic social action does not emerge from animation or corporeal rhetoric or lively classrooms. It emerges from the entire symbiotic knot propelled by embodied agency. A variety of factors can disrupt that emergence. This section, then, addresses the conditional nature—the "if" quality—of empathic social action. Crucial to animation, corporeal rhetoric, and lively places are the individual agents who decide how to see and how to act on what they see. Donna J. Haraway claims that we must "insist on the embodied nature of all vision, and so reclaim the sensory system that has been used to signify a leap out of the marked body and into a conquering gaze from nowhere" (*Simians, Cyborgs, and Women* 188). By so doing, we become "answerable for what we learn how to see" (190). What happens, though, when individuals respond to another's corporeal rhetoric by deploying something other than answerable, somatic visual animation?

Worthman's detached way of seeing that he deployed during his first months at TeenStreet illustrates the fragility of a symbiotic knot of bodies. Only when he engages in visual animation does he begin to understand the power of imaginal interactions and dialogic perspective-taking for agency and empathic action. Likewise, struck by the permeable line of WiB activists, Candace Walworth joins the women standing silent vigil on a street corner in Boulder, Colorado, *because* she sees through the twin processes of embodiment and boundary destabilization. She perceives the WiB tableau as an invitation to join a protest against violence and responds in ways that are answerable to her perception. Without trusting to visual animation, neither Worthman nor Walworth would have engaged empathically with the invitations offered them. However, seeing WiB protestors, seeing the TeenStreeters, or seeing any student through something other than animation results in different effects, ones that undercut the compassion and answerability circulating through a knot of bodies.

As Linda Martín Alcoff points out, "there is no perception of the visible that is not already embued with value" (272), which means ideology—systems of values, beliefs, attitudes, and convictions—flows throughout every visual habit. Particularly important to the formation and sustainability of a symbiotic knot of bodies are ideologies operating on and through the body. N. Katherine Hayles helpfully describes the interaction between ideology and bodies. On the one hand, she identifies the *body* as an ideological construct, an invention of the dominant culture consisting of a normative network of biosocial information. Thus, the images of bodies published in textbooks, the generalizations made about bodies in legal discourse, the popular conceptions about bodies disseminated through the mass media all reflect the ideology of the dominant culture. The body constitutes the touchstone that individuals use as they shape their own and others' identities, whether they acquiesce, negotiate, or resist those cultural definitions. On the other hand, *embodiment* differs from the cultural body in that it consists of individual enactments of or experiences in a body, occurring in and shifting with different times and places. These enactments frequently contradict the teachings of the dominant ideology. While body exists as a social construct, reinforced through language and image, embodiment exists as an ongoing creation arising out of an individual's unique incarnate experiences in the world. Both the culturally normative body and individually experienced embodiment connect reciprocally, constraining and informing the other ("Materiality of Informatics" 154). Moments of embodiment—one's own or another's—are continually juxtaposed and measured against the culturally privileged body, resulting in a hierarchy of bodies, a sliding scale in which some bodies have more value, credibility, and visibility than others.

If perception of the visible is always imbued with value, as Alcoff says, then the perception of visible bodies is always imbued with value. Individuals choose to perceive an instance of corporeal rhetoric, such as the 2002 D.C. march, guided by their cultural training and predispositions. Because individuals learn how to embody themselves based on their socialization, their choice, even their unconscious choice, to perceive through one visual habit rather than another, arises to a large degree out of the nexus point of body and embodiment dominant in that moment, in that place. Sexism and racism constituted two ideologies especially devastating to the stability of a symbiotic knot of bodies. Both intertwine with vision to privilege a particular way of seeing that unravels a knot of bodies. Arising out of sexism, scopophilia consists of a way of seeing that devalues the female body, undercutting the emergence of empathic social action. Arising out of racism, racial invisibility consists of a way of *not* seeing that devalues the bodies of women of color, similarly eroding empathic social action. Both visual habits undercut a knot of bodies.

A Freudian concept reclaimed by Laura Mulvey in a groundbreaking 1975 essay on cinema, gender, and the male gaze and later nuanced in a 1981 essay, scopophilia consists of a visual habit deeply infused with patriarchal attitudes and orientations to the female body.[15] Through scopophilia, the male gaze objectifies the female body, reducing it to a passive array of discrete and unrelated parts designed for male viewing pleasure. The value of the parts is in direct ratio to the erotic appeal of the parts. Scopophilia severs the viewer from the viewed so that the female body becomes a thing without sensibility or subjectivity and therefore exempt from answerability. The male agent does not need to act in ways responsible to the woman's body because that body is not valued as a body; it is an object to be owned, used, and discarded. Tied to voyeurism and fetishism, scopophilia skews embodiment and truncates the vulnerability of boundary blurring. Rather than evoking the compassion and empathy of visual animation, scopophilia evokes violence against women.

When individuals through the lens of scopophilia perceive instances of corporeal rhetoric, especially as practiced by women, a symbiotic knot of bodies unravels. First, scopophilia shifts embodiment from representation and presentation to a one-way eroticism where the viewer derives pleasure from seeing without responsibility for that seeing. Perception, then, becomes an occasion to consume, not an occasion to identify, which is so necessary for answerability. The identity and value of women derive from the degree to which women possess erotic visual appeal. From the perspective of scopophilia, then, instances of corporeal rhetoric become invitations to enact a male-marked way of seeing: embodiment ceases to be a protocol for social action but an opportunity to reconfirm a status quo in which women's bodies gain and retain value based on the pleasure they afford.

Ron, TeenStreet's director during Worthman's two-year ethnography, attempts to nip in the bud any tendency on the part of participants to see each other through the lens of scopophilia by designing an exercise that undermines objectification. Early in Worthman's first year, students gathered for a Saturday rehearsal, and Ron introduced them to a "contact improvisation exercise" in which one student—the "water"—had to mimic water by using both hands to stay in contact with a partner, moving those hands over the partner's body like water. The partner was instructed to move around the room, dipping and swaying in unexpected patterns, either pushing against or pulling away from the "water." The "water" had to keep pace with those improvised movements. Ron explained to the students that they could see this as sexual and they could take it as sexual, but by doing so they would inhibit themselves and their movements (23). If, however, they could "see this as a way of connecting with others and letting go of some of [their] inhibitions," then they might learn the way in which communication is embodied, welling up from touching and watching one's partner (25).

Scopophilia also undermines the compassion of a symbiotic knot of bodies because it avoids boundary blurring: act, actor, and action remain discrete categories. As a result, scopophilia lends itself not to compassion but to sexual violence.[16] Activists involved in WiB grapple with the threat of scopophilia's policed boundaries. They acknowledge the possibility of antagonistic responses to their vigils through an organizational policy that stipulates silence in the face of catcalls, jeers, and other forms of verbal heckling. As their statement of principle reads, they stand in deliberate silence "for the silenced ones who cannot speak for themselves" (Cockburn, "Women in Black" 5). Such a policy reflects not only the organization's commitment to silence as a rhetorical strategy but also, and perhaps more important, it reflects the organization's realization that women's bodies will elicit uninvited responses. By rehearsing and committing to nonviolent, nonverbal reactions, the women who stand silent vigil implicitly acknowledge the possibility that passersby will perceive their mode of social action through scopophilia or alternative modes of seeing, ones that close down the boundary blurring necessary for empathy.

By valuing male and female bodies differently, sexism supports a way of seeing that threatens the formation and sustainability of a symbiotic knot of bodies. By valuing *female* bodies differently, racism supports a way of seeing that also threatens a symbiotic knot of bodies. *Which* female bodies stand silent vigil on a street corner matters because some bodies will be seen; others will not. If White women's bodies have value only according to their pleasure quotient, then female bodies of color, perceived only through racial invisibility, have no value at all. As a racist way of seeing, racial invisibility erases women of color from the perceptual field. Robert Bernasconi describes the phenomenon of racial invisibility, one that involves both men and women of color: "The refusal of Whites to see Blacks was predicated on the fact that they knew who was there to be seen and sought to control them by choosing not to see them" (287). Racial invisibility constitutes a culturally privileged way of *not* seeing people of color. But its effects are even more heinous when gender enters into the equation, for this way of seeing is practiced by both men and women. Using as her example domestics during second-wave feminism in the 1960s, bell hooks points directly to the invisibility of women of color. She argues that middle- and upper-class White women crossed out of their homes and into professional careers on the backs of domestics—predominantly working-class women of color—who cleaned those homes and cared for the children (*Killing Rage*). To these White women, domestics of color were simply invisible. Alice Walker concurs, contending that Black women are perceived as the "mules of the world," carrying the burdens that "everyone else—*everyone* else—refused to carry" (237). Again, hooks articulates this hierarchy of female bodies: "In a white supremacist sexist society all women's bodies are devalued, but white women's bodies are more valued than those of women of color" (*Yearning* 62).[17] This differential valuation of bodies erases the possibility of empathic engagement through embodiment because it disrupts the oscillation between representation and presentation. Operating according to the perceptual habit of racial invisibility, the gaze that abuses (hooks, "Oppositional Gaze" 315), White men and women witness women of color enacting corporeal rhetoric without engaging the protocol of embodiment because they choose not to perceive any bodies of value.

Evidence is rampant of the power of racial invisibility to dissolve a symbiotic knot of bodies by rendering invisible women of color, whether victims of injustice or protestors of injustice. First, the lack of empathy in local, national, and international reactions to violence perpetrated against women of color manifest this invisibility. For instance, the 2007 controversy following the Patrick Kennedy case, which involved a Louisiana man who received the death penalty for raping his eight-year-old stepdaughter, highlights the invisibility of women of color within the U.S. legal system in two ways. To begin, statistics over the last five decades indicate that of the 455 men put to death for rape, 405 were Black men convicted of raping White women (Sothern). Statistics over the same time span reveal that no White man has ever been executed in the United States for the nonhomicide rape of a Black woman or child (Totenberg). The bodies of women of color disappear, cancelled out as insignificant. Because they are invisible, they cannot be the subject of either embodiment or boundary crossing. Subsequently, they initiate no empathic social action.

Next, the lack of empathy in local responses to protestors who are women of color also underscores their invisibility. Mothers of murdered or disappeared *maquiladora* workers in northern Mexico have publicly and collectively protested the failure of local authorities in Tijuana and Juarez to investigate the crimes and arrest the perpetrators. The march in Washington, D. C., described at the beginning of this chapter, occurred in part as a response to the past and ongoing violence against young women and girls in these border towns. But it also occurred because of the failure of the mothers' collective action to move the local governments to address the violence. Feminists involved in the action ask whether the deaths and disappearances of hundreds of *White* women would have received the same national and international inattention. They could as well ask whether the protests of hundreds of *White* mothers would have received the same national and international inattention. Without bodies, neither victims nor protestors can effect any sort of change in systems of injustice.

Sexism and racism, individually and jointly, conspire to shape visual habits antagonistic to the embodiment and boundary blurring so essential for the formation of a symbiotic knot of bodies. Scopophilia disrupts embodiment and boundary blending by transforming women into objects of pleasure. Racism disrupts both protocols by rendering women of color invisible. Vulnerable to ways of seeing that devalue bodies and truncate boundary blending, a symbiotic knot of bodies cannot sustain itself and cannot retain its stability. Thus, the dilemma posed by these entrenched ways of seeing suggests that we as teachers have to do more than cultivate practices in and out of the classroom that nurture embodiment and boundary blending. While TeenStreet and Shipka's multimodal, task-based assignments provide a start for transforming praxis, something more is needed, something that moves individuals out of the injurious ways of seeing that disrupt empathic social action.

In "Speaking in Tongues," Gloria Anzaldúa urges all women of color to "shock yourself into new ways of perceiving the world; shock your readers into the same" (172). Resist the censors "who snuff out the spark"; tear away the "gags that muffle your voice"; and "write with your eyes like painters, with your ears like musicians, with your feet like dancers. . . . Write with your tongues of fire (173). Through a corporeal rhetoric of "blood and pus and sweat," Anzaldúa evokes the double dynamic of embodiment and boundary blending in a symbiotic knot of bodies (173). She implicitly highlights the potential contribution of a knot of bodies to communal health and to empathic social action. But she underscores as well the importance of developing strategies to challenge and change the ingrained ways of seeing that continue to erode the rhetorical power of women of color. Our students need more than a knot of bodies. They need to develop ways of seeing and being in the world that provide protocols for sabotaging harmful systems that support sexism and racism. The symbiotic knot of contradictions, which I address in the next chapter, provides options for subversion, options for shocking self and other into new ways of seeing.

4. A KNOT OF CONTRADICTIONS
Antinomy and Digressive Rhetoric
in Subversive Social Action

> The classroom remains the most radical
> space of possibility in the academy.
> —bell hooks, *Teaching to Transgress*

In *Outlaw Culture*, bell hooks briefly describes her struggle to escape a "horrible, bittersweet relationship" (237). Given her past abusive family dynamic where she was "routinely tortured and emotionally persecuted," it was hard, she writes, to "even imagine a space in which I wasn't involved with people who seduce and betray" (*Outlaw Culture* 238). Her struggle to escape her matrix of abuse aligned with her struggle to imagine a different space, a different reality, in which pain did not trap her in the role of victim. She found that space in performance art, which enabled her to invent a character who could speak for her; this art constituted an "important *location of recovery*" within which she began to heal (*Outlaw Culture* 238; emphasis in original). An imaginary and intensely visual space where hooks invented new self-representations and new realities as means to counter mistreatment, a location of recovery serves as an important element of this cultural critic's social action and individual well-being. Only by carving out a protected imaginary space through her writing, her art, and her imagination was hooks able to transform herself from family and romantic scapegoat into an intellectual activist committed to dismantling sexist, racist, and imperialist institutions.

The process of imagining and working toward new personal and public realities constitutes the subject of this chapter. Integral to locations of recovery is a symbiotic knot of contradictions, a combination of antinomy, digressive rhetoric, and radical places from which subversive social action emerges (see fig. 4.1). Unlike a symbiotic knot of bodies, which provides a matrix for empathic social action, a symbiotic knot of contradictions offers protocols by which community members can imagine new, innovative realities. As argued in chapter 3, a knot of bodies serves as an important counterspectacle strategy because it recalibrates the tools and options of the dominant culture to serve compassionate social agendas, becoming expressions of and conduits for change. However, a knot of bodies does not help address the means by which community members develop novel modes of social action. In addition, a knot of bodies remains vulnerable to visual habits infused with sexist and racist ideologies. Thus, a key conundrum posed by social action concerns hooks's location of recovery and her subversive invention in that space: how does a member of a culture, immersed in the visual and discursive regimes of that culture, imagine a different reality and a different selfhood in ways that do not replicate the old matrices of abuse and the subjectivity of victim (or victimizer)? How might a community member devise rhetorical strategies that disrupt established and taken-for-granted ways of seeing and speaking? A symbiotic knot of contradictions provides a response to those questions. With its interwoven threads of antinomy, digressive rhetoric, and radical places, a knot of contradictions offers insight into the complexities of discursive and material transformation, moments when writers alter the patterns by which they think, compose meaning, and orient themselves in the world. Through a knot of contradictions, community members can begin on both micro and macro levels to alter matrices of abuse by imagining different subjectivities and realities.

As emphasized in chapter 1 and highlighted in chapter 2, agency involves an act of both imagination and faith; people must be able to imagine and believe in themselves as agents before acting as agents. Performance artist Charles R. Garoian underscores the imaginative and creative possibilities in contradictions. He discovered in his studio that "contradictory and conflicting ideas, images, and actions" help to "expose and transform the conflicting discourse into a social praxis that would enable me to create new ideas, images, and actions based on my own cultural perspective" (3). This aesthetic discovery then moves Garoian to a pedagogical transformation in which "contrary ideas, images, and actions introduced in the classroom" serve as an invitation to "personal/political agency" for his students (1–2). A symbiotic knot of contradictions holds similar possibilities for writing teachers and students interested in cultivating social action, issuing an invitation to antinomian agency.

This chapter explores the potential of a knot of contradictions for antinomian agency and subversive social action. Beginning with the visual habit of antinomy and the literacy it fosters, I examine three key processes in antinomy: bricolage, paradox, and agenic invention. Through these perceptual activities, antinomy continually dismantles and then reinvents visual order, doing so in concert with the barrage of different images that characterize our culture. The second section explores the linkages between antinomy and the rhetorical habit of *digressio*, which challenges the status quo through fragmentation and misdi-

Figure 4.1

Subversive Social Action

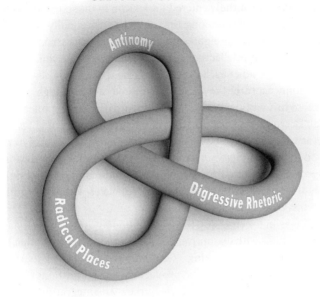

A Symbiotic Knot of Contradictions

rection. To illustrate the antinomy-*digressio* interface, I focus on the growing phenomenon of hacktivism, a subversive form of social action. Focused on an antinomian approach to revision, the third section attends to the composition classroom, to the *radical* composition classroom, where a symbiotic knot of contradictions can be reinforced by deliberate attention to bricolage, paradox, and agenic invention. The conclusion examines the entire knot of contradictions, which invites new options for change. However, like a knot of bodies, a knot of contradictions also poses a danger. Antinomy, *digressio*, and radical place can become so tightly intertwined that the pleasure of fragmentation and the seduction of lawlessness become ends in themselves. The knotting, then, leads not to new order but to the constant play of disorder, a threat that truncates both invention and subversion, offering no location of recovery. The key to a productive knot of contradiction rests on maintaining a fruitful balance between chaos and stable locations of recovery.

Thread 1: Antinomy, Literacy, and the Poetics of Change

As a way of seeing that privileges change, antinomy—*anti*, or against, plus *nomos*, or lawfulness, thus *against lawfulness*—highlights the constant play of contradiction. I choose the term *antinomy* for this visual habit for four reasons.

First, the word has historically referred to contradiction and paradox. According to the *OED*, *antinomy* initially entered the lexicon in the sixteenth century as a way to refer to legal contradictions: the conflict of two equally binding laws or authorities. Later, in the late eighteenth century, it became associated, through Immanuel Kant, with intellectual paradoxes, as when two conclusions, both equally logical, contradict each other. Thus, the traditional usage and definition of antinomy captures the sense of disrupted order through paradox that is so central to this visual habit. Second, the word *antinomy* connects to rhetoric. The Greek word *nomos* means laws of man, unlike laws of kings (*thesmos*) or laws of nature (*physis*). The Sophists, through their teachings in rhetoric, contributed to the rise of *nomos*, from which arose democracy: the formation of laws developed out of cultural agreements and maintained through joint commitment (Herrick 40). Thus, antinomy resonates with the beginnings of rhetoric in the West.

My third reason for choosing the word *antinomy* for this visual habit concerns its associations with disruptiveness. *Antinomy* also refers to what Kenneth Burke calls "verbal 'atom cracking'" (*Attitudes toward History* 308), a process of "perspective by incongruity" that produces new classifications (*Permanence and Change* 90–93). Verbal antinomy—Burke's "disintegrating art" (Crusius 26)—highlights the impossibility of imposing anything more than a temporary meaning on the fluid boundaries of our realities. Burke advocates a deliberate courting of antinomy as a habit of mind necessary for individual and cultural health, preventing us from becoming too committed to or persuaded by one meaning, one value. Fourth, again through Burke, the word *antinomy* carries with it echoes of transformation. For Burke, invention—making something new—arises out of dialectic, a process of negotiating tensions implicit in all meaning. Because words are defined within the context of what they are not, paradox is intrinsic to meaning: "To tell what a thing is you place it in terms of something else," he argues, thus producing an "antinomy that must endow the concept of substance [meaning] with unresolvable ambiguity" (*Grammar of Motives* 23, 24). Individuals' efforts to resolve ambiguity produce new orders that then are subject to further resolution. Thus, the paradox intrinsic to meaning creates an alchemical—or transformative—moment. Antinomy helps individuals cut "across the bias" so that they come to have a "new angle of vision" (*Permanence and Change* 154n1); thus, through antinomy, people invent and subvert through that invention, potentially engaging in a social action that reshapes harmful subjectivities and realities.

The word *antinomy*, then, engages a network of associations—order, disorder, invention, and transformation—associations that are at the heart of visual antinomy. Composed of bricolage, paradox, and agenic invention, visual antinomy juggles the ongoing tensions between contradictory images and words; it juxtaposes fragments of images and words so that they both create an order—a lawfulness—and simultaneously retain the power to disrupt that order, thus opening up a space for invention and subversion. Visual antinomy constitutes a new way of imagining particularly apt for this postmodern moment. Unlike spectacle and animation, which both coevolve with specific visual artifacts—television in the former case and interactive images in the latter—visual antinomy develops in conjunction with the barrage of images produced and circulated through disparate media. The intensely destabilizing, frustrating fragmentation of postmodern life invites the emergence of antinomy. Citing Achille Mbembe, visual critic Nicholas Mirzoeff argues that to be comprehensible, the radical breakdowns in everyday postmodern life require new forms of imaging. Without these new forms, a population has no way to imagine its identity in the midst of chaos. Through bricolage, paradox, and agenic invention, antinomy constitutes an important new way of seeing, one that enables the perception of new subjectivities and realities.

First, antinomy makes sense of the visual world via bricolage. A French term, *bricolage* refers to the process of creating something new by cobbling together bits and pieces of the old. Initially associated with artistic or literary practices, the term has been used to characterize theory formation in the sciences of primitive societies (Lévi-Strauss), learning in children (Papert), and online-identity construction (Turkle). It has also been used to describe the means by which subcultures, like punk, differentiate themselves from the dominant culture by taking fragments of that dominant culture (safety pins, hair styles, clothing) and creating a style that undercuts the *nomos* of the ambient culture (Hebdige).

Bricolage provides a mechanism by which Westerners can order their world of visual excess. We in the West are subject to a visual barrage on a daily basis. For example, consider the kaleidoscopic visual reality we inhabit as we cruise through a busy urban center. Bits and pieces of billboards flit by jumbled in our visual field with bits and pieces of shop displays. Glimpses of decorations, political posters, window displays, and graffiti impinge on the eye. This imagistic bombardment is rendered even more chaotic by the mental images we conjure as we whiz through the urban fun house. Because images, like words, carry traces of their previous locations, people tow into the urban chaos visual snippets of television shows, movies, commercials, and music videos. These outer and inner video streams are further disrupted by radio.[1] If we switch from cruising downtown to cruising the Internet (or try to do both via cell phones), the degree of visual fragmentation becomes even more apparent. Making sense out of the West's visual excess requires piecing together a crazy quilt of constantly shifting bits and pieces. Irit Rogoff argues that "individuals create unexpected visual narratives in everyday life from 'the scraps of an image [which] connect with a sequence of a film and with the corner of a bill board or the window display of a shop we have passed by'" (qtd. in Mirzoeff 29). They engage in bricolage, stitching together a visual reality out of a ragbag of images.

Second, visual antinomy relies on the process of paradox, an element of antinomy particularly important to subversion. Through bricolage, people quilt together fragments to shape meaningful perceptions, but bricolage does not in and of itself disrupt the status quo. Paradox in conjunction with bricolage opens up the possibility of disruption because it creates a visual crisis, a Burkean alchemical moment. A visual crisis opens the door for subversion because it calls into question the specious unity of the status quo. Paradox operates on three interlaced levels in antinomy: within the visual narrative itself, between constellated images, and between image and word.

To begin, neither verbal nor visual narratives are intrinsically orderly. Rather, each is cobbled together out of competing and frequently contradictory elements. Consider, for example, the conflicting elements in Mattel's Barbie doll mythos. Cindy Jackson, the human Barbie doll, finds in the Mattel toy an inspirational narrative of physical possibility, one that leads her to transform herself via plastic surgery into the physical image of Barbie. However, other women and men, such as the participants in the Barbie-in-a-Blender Day art project, have found in the Barbie mythos an opportunity for subverting the narrative Jackson finds so seductive (Jackson; "National"). They have created artifacts featuring Barbie dolls in situations and with technologies that challenge the cultural narrative privileging female beauty—and White standards of female beauty—as the criterion by which women judge their self-worth. The first level of paradox in visual antinomy exposes the gaps in visual narratives and requires the active construal of visual meaning, a construal that opens up moments for new meaning.

The second level of paradox in visual antinomy consists of contradictions among images themselves. Images do not always agree with or reinforce each other; this disjuncture provides an opportunity for exploring the social and cultural factors that value one image over another. For instance, the self-portraits created by Korean American photographer Nikki S. Lee deliberately highlight contradictions among images, moving the viewer to a visual crisis. To illustrate, with the help of meticulous research and individuals in various subcultures or social groups—yuppie stockbrokers, lesbians, drag queens, and hip-hoppers—Lee reconfigures herself physically to match members of the subgroup and then photographs herself disappearing into that group identity. Thus, in one photograph from *The Hispanic Project*, Lee poses with and as a member of a group of young Hispanic women on a crowded urban street. The women smile for the camera as if recording a holiday outing or an unauthorized escape from school. Lee blends in, visually indistinguishable from the other young women in the photo. Through this technique, Lee creates what Jennifer Dalton calls the "Where's Waldo?" effect in which the snapshot-like photographs call the viewer to decode the masquerade (47). Lee aims to create a paradox in her self-portraits by juxtaposing the ostensible goal of self-representation (identity) and the material results of her photography (invisibility). These paradoxical self-portraits, Dalton argues, bring fresh energy and insights to the serious debates concerning assimilation and passing, processes by which immigrants and marginalized members of a culture gain entry into the dominant culture (47). By deliberately courting imagistic paradox, Lee brings into view "the intricate visual markings and broader social functions of our cultural boundaries" (47).

The third level of paradox in visual antinomy involves the contradictions between images and words. As chapter 1 details, because images and words are not the same, they both complement and contradict each other, sometimes at the same time from different angles. As image and word tug against each other, they call into question the stable meaning of the other, creating a moment of visual crisis. Ella Shohat highlights the power of this level of paradox to reveal fissures in reality through her historical examination of Cleopatra and the discursive struggles over her visual image. Shohat argues that "each age and each culture seems to project its own Cleopatra, visualizing her in a new way" (196), shaping her according to its own needs and desires. In her fine-grained analysis, Shohat carefully tracks texts, contexts, and images, revealing in uncanny ways the discursive and visual systems that swirl around Cleopatra during any given historical moment and within any given geographical place. "Each 'take' on Cleopatra," Shohat concludes, "unmasks not only a facet of Cleopatra, but also a facet of the representer, and, more important, reveals the nature of the prisms through which Cleopatra has been seen and imagined" (196). The contradictions among diverse visual representations of Cleopatra and discursive accounts validating the correctness of one representation over another move the perceiver into a visual predicament, the resolution of which can potentially open up a new understanding about race, self, other, and cultural fantasies.

These three levels of paradox—within the visual narrative, between images, and between images and words—serve to create moments of chaos, moments of visual crisis, which, in turn, invite moments of transformation. Through paradox, perceivers become intensely aware of the constructive nature of vision and of their participation in that vision. Barbara Maria Stafford argues that membership in a heavily fragmented visual culture invites an active vision that capitalizes on puzzlement and pattern making.[2] Perception "does not necessarily entail deception nor . . . must it be a subjugating instrument of unification forcing diverse phenomena into an unreal fusion," Stafford argues (*Good Looking* 71). Instead, perception can and does invite a partnership with the perceiver. Paradox in visual antinomy constitutes one aspect of that perceiver-perception partnership, a powerful process that helps reveal the existence of the status quo and opportunities for subverting that status quo.

Finally, in addition to bricolage and paradox, visual antinomy relies on the process of agenic invention, which Susan Zaeske defines as the means by which "rhetors/subjects/agents formulate rhetorical strategies to break free from dominant subjectivities." Zaeske argues that agenic invention, "loiter[ing] at the sites of discursive tension," provides individuals and groups with "the rhetorical resources to struggle for change, to subvert subjectivities." Agenic invention also loiters at the site of visual tensions. It situates the perceiver as an active inventor of vision, not merely as active participant in vision. Through agenic invention, individuals develop a new vision—a new image—of what can be or should be, thus impelling people to action. For example, hooks demonstrates the importance of visual agenic invention for subverting abusive realities. Struggling to cope with a dysfunctional romantic relationship, she confesses that she needed a therapist, some "apparatus for understanding" at a time when she had none. So she "invented" this figure, creating, when necessary, an "improvisational performance on this persona" (*Outlaw Culture* 238).[3] As a result of creating and interacting with an imaginary person, hooks realizes that she can invent a subversive strategy and a space for exercising that strategy (*Outlaw Culture* 238). Agenic invention, then, contributes to the perceiver's ability to break free of injurious subjectivities and realities, both as victim and as victimizer.

The qualities of bricolage, paradox, and agenic invention combine to shape the visual habit of antinomy. Antinomy also interweaves with language to foster a complementary form of literacy. Just as spectacle combines with illegeracy (see chapter 2) and animation with performing literacy (see chapter 3), antinomy aligns with a specific kind of language use. Antinomy predisposes individuals to engage in popular literacy: the self-sponsored, nonacademic acts of meaning making that can be used to resist dominant constructions of reality.

Popular literacy, John Trimbur maintains, consists of acts of meaning making that tap "the available means of communication" to serve the individual's personal agenda (3). Operating according to its own poetics, Trimbur says that popular literacy "is caught in shifting relations of forces between the periphery and the center" (4). While popular literacy is a phenomenon present throughout all historical eras, the means—the poetics—by which it is produced and disseminated are shaped by the ambient culture. As Trimbur describes it, the modes of production, or poetics, of twenty-first-century popular literacy include "cut-and-paste, recycling, and recombinant practices associated with a knowing and ironic postmodernism" (9). These "unauthorized" literate acts include an array of products—graffiti, placards, T-shirt logos, 'zines, underground comics, scrapbooking, and quilting—all "popular" in the sense that they are created by means of symbol systems and materials that are also part of the creator's everyday life. Twenty-first-century popular literacy organizes itself according to the perceptual processes of visual animation. To demonstrate the connections between visual animation and popular literacy, I turn to one of my daughters and her creation of a ninety-six-page cartoon saga she called *The Mutt's Dark Side* (*MDS*).

A maverick who from preschool bucked the pressure of her classmates to conform to community expectations in both dress and behavior, my younger daughter Lindsey fought to forge and reforge an identity in the white-hot intensity of middle-school peer wars. The results of her efforts to cling to a unique, offbeat identity charmed her teachers but alienated many of her peers who subjected her to a troubling barrage of verbal and physical bullying on a daily basis. As author and illustrator, Lindsey used *MDS* to grapple with social trauma and imagine a reality free from mistreatment. In the chaos of colliding fragments of images and words, Lindsey developed and exercised a visual practice that enabled her to shape a space apart—a location of recovery—where she possessed power, where she was not victim but defender of victims. Using the imaginary space of *MDS*, she envisioned new realities and launched her efforts to bring those realities into being by sharing the cartoon with interested acquaintances, who subsequently became friends. Gradually, *MDS* became Lindsey's passport into community, serving as an expression of that group's pain and altering in small ways the social fabric of her middle-school world.

A close analysis of *MDS* provides insight into the poetics of antinomy operating in millennial popular literacy. The third installment serves as a vivid illustration of Lindsey's evocation of alternative realities and powerful subjectivities. In *The Mutt's Dark Side III*, "Attack of the Killer Bones," the first frame features a peaceful house and a moonlit night with what appears to be a comet lighting up the sky (see fig. 4.2). The second frame explodes this peacefulness with a tremendous "BOOOM" that fills the entire square. From this volatile opening and throughout the four-page narrative, the puppy protagonist experiences a variety of adventures, beginning with her discovery that her dreams become reality. "I think I'm pychich," she tells her companion, Anna Fish, because she keeps "having dreams that come true," dreams in which she wins a bone contest and receives spinach bones. The bones that she wins, however, are the vanguard of an invasion of aliens who had come streaking to Earth on a spaceship in the opening frame.

To battle the aliens, the puppy treks with Anna Fish through the desert searching for a fabled ninja suit that will help her fight the aliens (see fig. 4.3). With the suit, the puppy transforms into "Ninja Dog," gains a mighty sword, battles the invading bones, and sends the aliens away. A twist of the narrative, though, is that Ninja Dog and puppy, while the same, also are two separate characters. So, at the end of the narrative, puppy and Ninja Dog face each other,

Figure 4.2. Opening page, "Attack of the Killer Bones," installment 3, *MDS III* (by Lindsey Fleckenstein. Used with permission.)

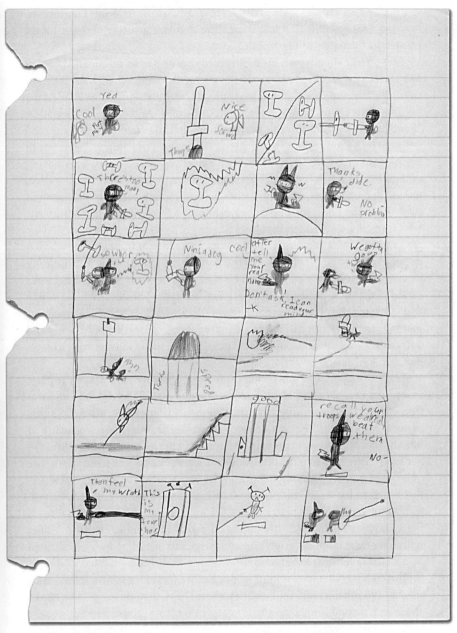

Figure 4.3. *MDS III* quest (by Lindsey Fleckenstein. Used with permission)

and puppy asks Ninja Dog to "take your mask off." However, Ninja Dog refuses, replying, "At the credits I'll take it off." The credits, consisting of the last eight frames, immediately follow this promise.

These frames begin with Lindsey identifying herself as author and illustrator. Then in four sequential frames, she offers her thanks . . . with a significant twist. She first says "speacil thanks Anna" with a drawing of Anna Fish. At the bottom of the frame, however, under the drawing of Anna Fish, Lindsey adds, "For being me." The next frame is a thanks to Molly (the puppy) "for being me," followed by a frame giving "spealcal thank Lindsey For being me" and one to her sister (Anna) "For being me too." The next-to-the-last frame is a drawing of the alien ship with "I'm Leaving Good" written in, suggesting that the alien, too, is Lindsey. Finally, Lindsey reaches the last frame, where, clustered around the words "The End," she draws the major characters, erasing the distinctions among enemy, victim, and hero.

As a representative sample of the larger category of literate acts included in popular literacy, *MDS* attests to the importance of antinomy for inventing locations of recovery that can then become sites of subversion. Just as hooks creates a therapist persona and a performance space within which she works through her painful realities, episode 3 of *MDS*, as well as the seven other segments, functions similarly. It serves Lindsey as both a location of recovery and a strategy for subversion, doing so through the poetics of antinomy: bricolage, paradox, and agenic invention.

Transformation and subversion begin with bricolage, a remix of the parts and pieces of reality. Bricolage provides the raw materials for Lindsey's location of recovery, beginning with the fragments hidden beneath *MDS*'s tidy surface. Lurking under the narrative's ostensible seamlessness is a wealth of bits and pieces: Lindsey's two years in karate and her love of manga and animé; her family life including the family dog, Molly, her sister, and her mother. The quest theme in all eight segments and her construction of the hero position owe much to her experiences with online gaming in RuneScape and her affection for Link, the character in the *Zelda* video games who always rescues the eponymous princess. Although *MDS* contains no audio element, it does reflect her taste in music, from importing lyrics to including music (indicated by musical notations) as her hero sings.

Through her juxtaposition of words and images, Lindsey imagines, constructs, and inhabits different realities where she is, first, no longer a victim of abuse and, second, someone who liberates others from abuse. Lindsey creates a subjectivity where she is an agent for change, not a helpless victim of change, a first but necessary step for any kind of social action. For instance, in *MDS III* described above, she confronts aliens, journeys to find a sword (and identity) that will provide the power to battle the aliens (or their robot minions), and then returns to combat the danger, discovering in the process that she and the aliens are the same. A similar narrative, cobbled together from bits and pieces, appears in *MDS II*, in which she receives a crown of power that allows her to survive underwater. There she rescues her mother, who, worried about her absence, has followed her into the sea. She battles villains, and with her puppy protagonist singing "I've got the power," she returns home safely with her mother in tow, taking pleasure in rescuing the rescuer. Fiddling with these fragments of images, words, and inchoate experiences, Lindsey builds a space within which she liberates and thus, through that act, is liberated. However, piecing together fragments does not in and of itself promise subversion.

Out of chaos, out of fragmentation arises the possibility of new order, the possibility of creating a location of recovery. More than just "fiddling," more than just ordering disordered fragments occurs in *MDS* and other acts of popular literacy. If *antinomy* were just a synonym for *bricolage*, then there would be no possibility of Burke's alchemical moment, no possibility of transformation in this location of recovery, no possibility of a social action that aims to change injurious realities. As Trimbur and other cultural theorists have pointed out, expressions of popular culture need not be resistant; they can, in fact, reaffirm the values and agendas of the dominant culture. Diana George in her analysis of visual representations of poverty, especially the videos of Habitat for Humanity, underscores our ability to reinvent the status quo from visual fragments. What is necessary for subversive invention is the quality of paradox intrinsic to antinomy, a paradox that elicits a visual crisis ("Changing the Face of Poverty").[4] Antinomy's paradox functions on three interlocking levels in *MDS*: within the visual narrative itself, between constellated images, and between image and word.

Contradiction erupts within the visual narrative because any narrative—verbal or visual—is sewn together out of bits and pieces of images, a process that disrupts the specious coherence of chronological order. We cannot include all images, all words, or all events, in a narrative. We sift through a bewildering kaleidoscope of images, picking and choosing what to attend to and how to respond to those selected images. Thus, a visual narrative obtains a sense of order and rightness because we actively endow it with such. However, all those bits and pieces we leave out press for attention. They put pressure on the tenuous narrative unity so that disorder and incoherence erupt. *MDS* and similar expressions of popular literacy reveal this narrative agitation. *MDS*, in fact, derives much of its power from what is not there. That which is absent clamors for attention almost as insistently as that which is present. Perhaps the most persistent absence is that of authority: the rules of reality itself are suspended (the puppy breathes underwater in *MDS II*); social authority—from parental to institutional—is missing. Peer authority, particularly, is also in abeyance. And, yet, all of those authority "holes" press against the visual narrative, disrupting the ostensible unity of the narrative by underscoring the need for the narrative. The abusive milieu within which Lindsey spent eight hours a day, five days a week tests the narrative unity, tugging attention to what is not there because of what is there.

In addition, a visual narrative is potentially paradoxical because it joins the linearity of chronological order with the spatiality of visual images.[5] Postmodern geographer Edward W. Soja argues that the cross-fertilization of space and time creates not narrative but *lateral narrative*, a story split into alternate lines— into simultaneities—a process that disrupts the specious "ever-accumulating history marching straight forward in plot and denouement" (22–23). Stretched along the vertical dimensions of space and the horizontal dimensions of time, the visual narrative out of which we construct our realities and subjectivities is itself fraught with contradiction and multiplicity (15).

Such contradictory alternative lines are evident in *MDS*. The frames of the cartoon invite digressions into different story lines, as when the puppy Molly travels to the desert to retrieve the sword and armor necessary for her to fight the robot army. The interactions with Anna Fish similarly disrupt the "straight march" into denouement. In fact, if there is one feature of Lindsey's *MDS* that is consistent, it is the way in which she invests, through the interface of images and words, a wealth of stories within a single narrative. She enriches her options for recovery in this location through this narrative richness, through the cheerful disruption of networked story lines all agitating for attention.

The second level of contradiction occurs when images current within a culture contradict each other, a phenomenon people experience on a daily basis, demonstrated in American culture through such images as police brutality coupled with images of police beneficence, captured by the words "To serve and to protect." Another devastating contradiction consists of the image of a Catholic parish priest, handcuffed and arrested for multiple acts of child molestation, jostling an image of Pope Benedict conducting mass for forty thousand celebrants in a Washington, D.C., baseball stadium. Such contradictions open up spaces for a critical response to those jostling images. *MDS* juggles similar paradoxes, especially evident in Lindsey's choice of a puppy protagonist named Molly. The puppy as persona is an interesting choice because the family pet has been to a large degree Lindsey's self-selected responsibility. Lindsey mothers Molly, assuming responsibility for the beagle's well-being as if Molly were her child. And, yet, Molly the puppy persona in each segment of the *MDS* gains power in some arcane way and performs actions that demonstrate her ability to care for others. The hero of the cartoon in each segment's narrative evolves out of the contradiction between dog as dependent recipient of care and puppy as independent giver of care.

Beyond juggling the contradictions within visual narratives and between images, paradox also functions on a third level: between image and word. Image and words operate according to different logics, logics, which, while not the same, exist only in conjunction with the other.[6] Because of this doubleness, images and words can contradict as well as complement each other simultaneously. This play of contradiction/complementarity is whimsically illustrated by Réne Magritte's famous *Ceçi n'est pas une pipe* ("This is not a pipe"), a Surrealist painting that calls into question both visual and verbal representation by placing the two in apparent conflict.[7] Popular forms of literacy, from graffiti to scrapbooks to quilts, reflect the potentially transformative power of image and word tugging against each other. Lindsey's choice of the cartoon form, a medium that depends on the juxtaposition of image and word, directly taps into that power.

In comics, pictures do not mimic or merely replicate words. Instead, as Mark James Estren in *A History of Underground Comics* notes, pictures in comics both complement and contend with words simultaneously; in fact, the effect is rather like a "McLuhanesque 'mosaic'" (8). Thus, *MDS* becomes its most interesting when the images and words within a single frame create a tension, a visual crisis that the author-illustrator invites the reader to resolve. Such a visual crisis is especially noteworthy in Lindsey's final frames of *MDS III* where she identifies herself with each character or group of characters, an explicit process for her sympathetic characters (Anna Fish, Molly, sister Anna) and an implied process for the aliens themselves. In the final frames of her adventure, she reaches for the very force she had battled throughout her ninety-six frames only to make the troubling discovery that she and the aliens may in fact be one and the same.

A location of recovery—a protected imaginary space within which to imagine new identities and realities—requires the dual action of bricolage and paradox in antinomy. Bricolage offers a rich pool of materials for constructing a location of recovery where the individual envisions self as agent in a different reality; paradox creates a visual crisis that invites transformation, the alchemical moment that transfigures old pain into a new reality. The moment of visual crisis opens the door to transformation, to inventing the new. But to walk through that door requires agency. The shift from inventing the new into inventing a *subversive* new is driven by agenic invention: the individual's design of a reality and subjectivity that challenges oppression. Agenic invention relies on active, participatory, critical perception: a visual "conversation" among what is, what can be, and what should be. It arises out of the conscious contribution of the perceiver to the perception so necessary to antinomy. Lindsey exercises agenic invention through her critical interpretation and reshaping of her middle-school realities and subjectivities. A central sticking point in Lindsey's struggles with the dominant peer group was her steadfast refusal to kowtow to either peer or institutional pressure to blend in. Although she might have easily translated this dilemma into an "us" and "them" dynamic, in which she re-creates the trench warfare of World War I on a middle-school battlefield, she instead perceives herself as engaged in a fight *for* her peers, for a reality in which aliens and heroes rescue each other.

In addition, Lindsey's choice of *MDS* as, initially, her outlet and then later the zeitgeist for her growing group of both marginalized and mainstream friends, invites in return agenic invention *from her readers*, an essential part of *MDS* as nascent social action. Marshall McLuhan argues that "comics provide very little data about any particular moment in time or aspect of space, of an object. The viewer, or reader, is compelled to participate in completing and interpreting the few hints provided by the bounding lines. . . . Comics . . . are a highly participational form of expression" (qtd. in Estren 8). Her classmates had to read themselves into Lindsey's patchwork narrative, into her world where puppies have power, and aliens are defeated. They had to experience actively and critically the suture points where aliens—feared and defeated—were also the classmates themselves. Without such a process, they could not have cohered as a supportive group nor reached out to other members of their middle-school milieu, keeping the identity of the group fluid, egalitarian, and, to an unusual degree, nurturing.

With her marshalling of contradictory image and word fragments to create a story of self and community, Lindsey and other practitioners of popular literacy piece together narratives that disrupt conventional categories of identity and craft a different way of being in the world. They become agents of invention. For Lindsey, agenic invention involved dismantling the seemingly unassailable social categorizations of adolescent life that had classified her as other and then cobbling together word and image to narrate into existence a different classification. As social action on the micro level, *MDS* enabled Lindsey to create a location of recovery that subverted the painful play of dominance-victimage; it helped her create a community of agents who challenged in small but effective ways middle-school turf wars.

Lindsey invented *MDS* as an expression of and outlet for her subversion. Thus, *MDS* serves as personal and communal expression. But, like much popular literacy, it also serves as rhetorical expression, and the mode of rhetoric it enacts is that of *digressio*. Lindsey could assail directly neither the dominant peer group nor the administration that barred her from deliberately displaying her difference and directly challenging her victimizers through offbeat clothing choices. Instead, she had to tackle them on the sly, shaping *MDS* into a mode of communication that helped her undermine the rigid peer structure in her middle school. Such sly rhetoric unites with antinomy to provide a matrix for subversive social action.

Thread 2: *Digressio*, Antinomy, and Subversive Social Action

Antinomy with its poetics of bricolage, paradox, and agenic invention constitutes a powerful resource for change, and this visual habit coexists with a complementary rhetoric. Hints of that rhetoric circulate throughout my description of *MDS* and illustrations of popular literacy, particularly evident in Zaeske's concept of agenic invention. As Trimbur points out and as George ("Changing the Face of Poverty") illustrates, expressions and formations of popular literacy can function rhetorically, as points of resistance, as subversions of the cultural order. This section explores the interface of antinomy and rhetoric; I claim that antinomy coevolves with a rhetoric of digression, a rhetoric of fragmentation and misdirection through which a rhetor can undermine the social foundations that support and are supported by various abusive structures. Out of this interface, subversive social action can emerge. I offer hacktivism, especially as practiced by postmodern artist-activists, as an example of a mode of protest shaped by the shared interplay of bricolage, paradox, and agenic invention.

Digressio, or the technique of interrupting the logical progression of an argument with what ostensibly appear to be non sequiturs, is a classical trope whose use dates back more than two thousand years. In *De Oratore*, Cicero advocates a judicious use of *digressio* as a powerful way to affect the feelings of the audience. Connecting *digressio* with the larger category of *amplificatio* (illustration) in *De Inventione*, Cicero uses an extended example of *digressio* in *Pro Archia*, a speech defending the right to Roman citizenship of the poet Archias. In *Pro Archia*, Cicero diverts the audience's attention from the technical elements of the case by arguing for the importance of literature, especially literature that takes as its subject matter the glory of Rome. This digression invites the audience to identify implicitly with Archias and invests Cicero's listeners emotionally in the poet's fate, an argument through indirection. H. V. Canter, in his study of *digressio* in Cicero's speeches, notes that while Cicero relies on a long digression in *Pro Archia* (three-quarters of the speech) and while Cicero uses digression frequently across his speeches, he also uses it sparingly within his speeches: "he sowed his examples by the handful not by the sackful" (354). In short, *digressio*, if used judiciously, serves as a transformative rhetorical tactic.

Digressio erupts in different forms in other periods in Western history, implicitly reflecting changes in culture, including changes in visual culture. For instance, Anne Cotterill spins out the implications of *digressio* for a seventeenth-century British rhetoric, where the use of *digressio* for certain writers shifted from handfuls to sackfuls.[8] In an age remarkably different from Cicero's Rome, *digressio* becomes a major tactic for authors who perceived themselves marginalized politically and socially. Cotterill focuses on five seventeenth-century authors—Marvell, Donne, Browne, Milton, and Dryden—and their nondramatic texts to trace "the sweet liberty of digression" (1). These authors employed the unconventional strategy of *digressio* as a "veiled expression of political doubt and enmity" and as an "exploration of hidden or unruly or disturbing parts of the speaker's self" (2). Operating under the dual threat of politics and patronage, they "reflect on the dangers of being invaded and transformed or otherwise consumed and silenced by others' words" (2). Because these five perceived themselves to be exiled from the power base of their culture and, because of that exile, at risk socially and politically, they developed rhetorical tactics—namely, *digressio*—that allowed them to assail the status quo indirectly; they engaged, like Lindsey, in a sly rhetoric.

While inner-city graffiti and a middle schooler's offbeat cartoon may appear unrelated to Cicero and Milton and while the twenty-first-century visual culture may be distant from first-century Rome and Cromwell's England, I propose that both Lindsey and Milton, underground cartoons and seventeenth-century pamphlets, tap into the subversive power of *digressio*, using techniques informed by the visual culture dominant during each one's particular historical-cultural moment. As *MDS* and other acts of millennial popular literacy reveal, *digressio* interfaces with antinomy in unique ways, providing a wellspring for new forms of social action. A vivid example of twenty-first-century social action that depends on the linkages between *digressio* and antinomy is hacktivism.

Alexandra Samuel describes hacktivism "as the marriage of political activism and computer hacking" (1). More specifically, "hacktivism combines the transgressive politics of civil disobedience with the technologies and techniques of computer hackers" (1–2). It is "the nonviolent use of illegal or legally ambiguous digital tools in pursuit of political ends," a definition Samuel develops for this evolving phenomenon (2). Such electronic mischief includes Web-site defacements, Web redirects, denial-of-service attacks, information thefts, site parodies, virtual sit-ins, virtual sabotage, and software development. It exists in the shadowy region between legal and illegal, a region that cyber legalists are still struggling to define (Kreimer). Carolyn Guertin, who associates hacktivism with the social action of cyberfeminists, defines it in ways that resonate to Samuel's work: "It is a solution-oriented form of political action that inserts bodies and media-based dissent into real time material concerns."

The visual habit of antinomy and the rhetorical habit of *digressio* infuse postmodern (pomo) hacktivism, which takes the Internet as its venue for and its object of social action. Unlike cyberactivism, which uses the Internet as a medium to communicate political messages, hacktivism considers the Internet itself as the sphere of and for social action.[9] Two examples—virtual sit-ins, associated with the Electronic Disturbance Theater (EDT), and virtual picketing—illustrate the scope and strategies of pomo-left hacktivism. Inspired to harness the World Wide Web and Web browsers for social action, EDT, linked to Electronic Civil Disobedience, staged its first virtual sit-in in 1998. Developing and using

Flood Net software, EDT organized thousands of participants, who used their computers to lock down Mexican government Web sites, thus disrupting the services of those Web sites. Protestors engaged in a digital version of Gandhi's nonviolent noncompliance, drawing attention to the government's presence in the virtual world. The protestors aimed to interrupt service as a peaceful means of calling attention to unjust government policies. A second nonviolent pomo-left hacktion consists of virtual picketing, particularly Web site picketing. For example, in the year following EDT's first virtual sit-in, Web-based activism erupted in Indonesia, where rebels hacked into government websites to reconfigure HTML code so that the message "Free East Timor" scrolled across the screen of the official site, destabilizing the identity and institutional power of that site through digital picketing. As these examples illustrate, hacktivism moves beyond the use of the Internet as a means to communicate about social action in the real world. Instead, virtual sit-ins and digital picketing both emphasize the use of digital technologies to disorder political policy in the *virtual world*. This version of pomo hacktivism constitutes a form of subversive social action in which means functions peacefully to bring about a compassionate end.

The hacktivism of the postmodern left involves artist-activists who seek to effect change within the virtual sphere through disruptive but not malicious strategies.[10] The central tenets that anchor postmodern-left hacktivism, Samuel explains, include commitment to nonviolence, accountable action, and avoidance of transnational violent conflict because of pacifist convictions (36). For instance, pomo-left hacktivists publicly deplored the Virtual Monkeywrench 2001 political cracking because it lacked accountability. Motivated by two goals—to destabilize the annual meeting of the World Economic Forum by disrupting this "well oiled machine" and to oppose intellectual-property rights—the Virtual Monkeywrench group hacked into the database of the World Economic Forum and distributed employees' personal information, some of which was later published in a Swiss newspaper. The group labeled the cracking a "good sabotage" although the only thing freed was personal information, including e-mail addresses, credit-card numbers, cell and landline numbers, and so forth. However, pomo hacktivists condemned the action as cyberterrorism not hacktivism because the tool did not align with the goal. The distribution of personal information hurt individuals, not corporations. Publishing employee information disrupts a corporation's business as usual but does nothing to bring to the public eye corporate transgressions. Thus, it arouses no desire to change the reality of unsavory corporate practices.

At the same time hacktivists condemn the Virtual Monkeywrench incident, they support similar efforts to hack into corporate data banks to obtain and distribute sensitive information that reveals corporate misdeeds and cover ups.[11] Publishing evidence of corporate malfeasance provides impetus for change that corrects and establishes oversight of misdeeds. An example of such means-end reciprocity involves a hacktion designed to expose Dow Chemical's laggard response to the Bhopal tragedy. In 1984 in Bhopal, India, a Union Carbide plant, a subsidiary of Dow Chemical, accidentally leaked poisonous gas, killing thousands of individuals in the surrounding villages. The purpose of the hacking was to reveal unpublished corporate responses to the Bhopal tragedy and its aftermath, highlighting the extent to which Dow Chemical limited its accountability, reparations, and cleanup. Unlike the Virtual Monkeywrench hacktion, which hurt people, the Dow Chemical hacktion exposed corporate crimes and ethical bankruptcy.

Focusing on such wide-ranging issues as corporate malfeasance, World Trade Organization depredations, and Mexican politics, pomo hacktivists aim to disorder established regimes and through that disordering open up the possibilities for different actions and thus the possible emergence of different worlds. In addition, both Guertin and Samuel concur that a central trademark of pomo hacktivism, with its focus on the virtual public sphere of cyberspace, is its impact in the real world. As Guertin explains, "One of its trademark features is that the Web cannot contain hacktivism's flows, allowing it to spill out into the world in the form of political protest at WTO and G8 events, for example, and in books, pamphlets, net.art, and performance art." Thus, the political hackers who wrote the code that penetrated China's Internet firewall, designed to block citizens' use of the World Wide Web, directly influenced real-world access to the virtual public sphere. Artist-activists such as Coco Fusco and Guertin herself similarly straddle the real-virtual divide by taking their performances back to the street even as they devise canny new-media elements so that their performance art reaches a wider audience through the Internet. Through this wider reach, social protest has the potential of coalescing into transformation and change.

The power of pomo hacktivism to function as a mode of social action that disrupts what the practitioners perceive as matrices of abuse rests on the triad of qualities it derives from the antinomy-*digressio* interface: bricolage, paradox, and agenic invention. To begin, hacktivism relies on bricolage in two complementary ways. It shapes its hacktions by "fiddling" with bits and pieces of real-world, nonviolent protest strategies. Then, it takes those reworked strategies online to disrupt the specious order of political-economic oppression. As Samuel notes, postmodern-left hacktivism closely aligns itself with the performance art of street activism, a connection that Guertin emphasizes. Thus, hacktivism, a bricolage of real-world tactics, makes those tactics effective in the virtual world. Stephan Wray's description of EDT highlights the degree to which this organization's modus operandi for electronic civil disobedience derives from a bricolage of real-world procedures.

Growing out of the Zapatista movement and initially focused on supporting real-world change in Mexico, EDT connects its civil disobedience to the
history of civil disobedience in America. In 1998, Wray envisioned real-world
possibilities manifesting from EDT's social action:

> The same principles of traditional civil disobedience, like trespass and
> blockage, will still be applied, but more and more these acts will take
> place in electronic or digital form. The primary site for Electronic Civil
> Disobedience will be in cyberspace.
>
> In the next century, for example, we on the left will witness or be part
> of an increasing number of virtual sit-ins in which government and cor-
> porate web sites are blocked, preventing so-called legitimate usage. Just
> as the Vietnam War and the Gulf War brought thousands into the streets
> to disrupt the flow of normal business and governance—acting upon the
> physical infrastructure—future interventionist wars will be protested by
> the clogging or actual rupture of fiber optic cables and ISDN lines—acting
> upon the electronic and communications infrastructure. Just as massive
> non-violent civil disobedience has been used to shutdown or suspend
> governmental or corporate operations, massive non-violent email assaults
> will shutdown government or corporate computer servers.

EDT's primary strategy of the virtual sit-in enables individual users from multiple sites to slow or shut down access to targeted Web sites. By fiddling with a
real-world protocol for social action, EDT has created and deployed a virtual-
world protocol that interrupts the functioning of such Web sites as Mexican
financial institutions, government consulates, and international conferences,
including the 2006 G8+5 global Dialogue on Climate Change, as a means to
bring Internet attention to poverty and rebellion in Mexico.

In the hands of pomo-left hacktivists, bricolage consists of reworking bits
and pieces to invent new order, and it consists of disrupting narrative order.
A goal of hacktivism is to challenge and destabilize the realities established
and maintained by repressive regimes. It fragments into bits and pieces the
virtual presence of what protestors see as political and economic systems of
abuse. As David Ronfeldt and John Arquilla argue, social networks adhere by
creating and sharing a joint narrative; hacktivism aims at splintering this narrative through bricolage. Recognition of and respect for fragmentation are also
implicit in Samuel's choice of the term *postmodern left* for artist-activist hacking. Postmodernism, with its focus on disintegration, constant reorganization,
and surface play, emphasizes disruption. Hacktivism fiddles with a vengeance,
crafting experiences that require the Web-site surfer who stumbles on such
performances to engage in his or her own bricolage: fitting together these bits
and pieces of the disrupted virtual presence into a new order.

Paradox complements bricolage in hacktivism. Hacktions take the bits and pieces of bricolage and juxtapose them in contradictory ways, becoming transgressive through paradox. Through contradictory juxtapositions, hacktivists demonstrate alternative interpretations of reality and possible alternative actions. The construction of parodic Web sites illustrates hacktivism's reliance on deliberate contradiction to open up locations of recovery. Straddling the legal-illegal divides through their use of copyrighted Web-site domain names, Web-site parodies zero in on the Internet presence of repressive institutions (ranging from governments to corporations), attempting to destabilize the ethos created by those Web sites by juxtaposing Web sites with a contradictory ethos. For example, the Dow Chemical Company parody Web site "Hurt-halting Hires" (http://www.dowethics.com/) mimics the visual design and satirizes the content of Dow's corporate site (see fig. 4.4). The parody site features a disclaimer for the Bhopal disaster in modest font size and typeface on the right-hand side of the page, farthest from where we would normally start reading if guided by conventional Western reading practices. The disclaimer explains that worries about price share prevented Dow Chemical from acknowledging any responsibility for the actions of its subsidiary Union Carbide. The site then provides links to two other Web sites disclosing detailed information about the scope of that disaster, including a point-by-point exegesis of Dow Chemical's statements concerning Bhopal. The array of "news items" leads off with the attention-grabbing headline "Halt-hurting Hires." Announcing Dow Chemical's recruitment of Jacques Cousteau's son, this headline juxtaposes the ethos evoked by the Cousteau name with the corporation's flagrant and repeated environmental depredations. All elements on the Web site seek to disorder Dow's virtual corporate persona and challenge its ethical credibility through a subtle blend of visual identification and linguistic contradiction. The parody destabilizes because of this push-and-pull of similarity and difference.[12]

In concert with bricolage and paradox, hacktions cultivate transformation through agenic invention—critical and participatory seeing that disrupts selective blindness to expose inequality—evident in the activist-oriented performance art of many pomo-left hacktivists. One example of the agenic invention consists of the "identity correction" of the Yes Men, a hacktivist strategy that falls within gray legal waters. Engaging in a performance act that straddles both virtual and real worlds, Yes Men don the identity of corporate employees by literally impersonating them, transforming into yes men to inveigle themselves into corporate meetings and photo opportunities. Once in these situations, the performers disrupt "business as usual." Distinguishing identity correction from identity theft, the Yes Men Web site explains that identity correction consists of honest people impersonating "big-time criminals in order to publicly humiliate them." Their targets include leaders and international corporations "who put profits

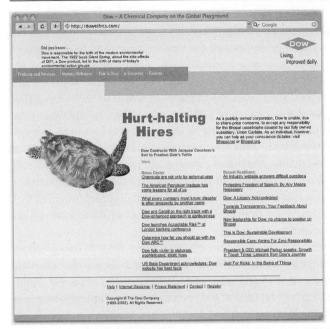

Figure 4.4. Dow Chemical hacktivist Web site

ahead of everything else." In addition, Yes Men ferret out information related to virtual presence and real-world actions of various corporations and governmental institutions, such as the World Trade Organization (WTO) and World Bank, disseminating that information to expose corporate misbehavior. The Yes Men's shenanigans both enact and invite agenic invention in that the participants devise their identity corrections through critical re-creations of targeted individuals; those critical recreations, in turn, shock audience members into their own critical, participatory seeing. Things are not, after all, as they seem.

The performative digital poetry of Annie Abrahams also illustrates the agenic invention of hacktivism, requiring a critical, participatory seeing from the reader (see fig. 4.5).[13] Abrahams's "karaoke" seeks to subvert matrices of abuse that sanction violence against women by using the cyberpoem as a location of recovery. Part of Abrahams's sprawling *being human* Web site, "karaoke" exposes and disrupts violence against women by luring the reader/viewer into participation in that violence. The cyberpoem features an image of a woman crouched on a kitchen floor in front of a refrigerator. As the viewer engages with the Web site, the figure flinches in and out of a fetal ball, her arms protecting her head and legs jackknifing into her body. Down the left side of the image float the letters *d*, *o*, and *n*, while on the right side of the image, up the screen floats *t*, and at the bottom, the word *close* sits encased in parentheses. Under image and word streams a series of phrases beginning with "I do agree, you are right, yes, I agree." As the image, words, and letters move on the screen, an eerie, pulsing soundtrack plays. Voices crying "don't," a series of loud, gunlike explosions and tapping noises assault the viewer. According to Abrahams's Web site explanation, the reader is supposed to "sing" along with the words scrolling at the bottom of the page, assuming the role of the abuse victim placating her attacker. The reader has to track the words to their conclusion before the images—the enactment of violence—disappear. In addition, if the reader clicks the parenthetical *close*, he or she is taken to an interactive site where participants can contribute their experiences, opinions, or fears about violence. These comments, Abrahams explains, are remediated into different creative pieces, all part of her effort to alter matrices of abuse. Throughout her Web site, Abrahams creates intensely participatory digital performances that function as agenic invention, drawing the viewer into active, critical interaction with images, texts, and words.

Like any digressive rhetoric, pomo hacktivism subverts through transgression: it attempts to change policy in part by circumventing policy, a characteristic it shares with Lindsey's *MDS* and other real-world strategies of protest. Pomo hacktivism seeks to expose repression and open up imaginary spaces—locations of recovery—within which victims and marginalized peoples can reconfigure themselves as agents with options for action. Subversive social action, social action that works on the bias, emerges from the rich interface of antinomy and digressive rhetoric. Through such subversive social action, people have the poten-

Figure 4.5. Participatory seeing in "karaoke" (screen capture of digital poem by Annie Abrahams, http://www.bram.org/karaoke/karaoke.htm. Used with permission.)

tial to transform their worlds by transforming their (and others') images of their place in the world. When antinomy fuses with rhetoric, it invites new nonviolent options for change that literally sap the foundations of repressive status quos.

As teachers as well as activists, we are confronted with the question of how a classroom might be configured to encourage the interface of antinomy and *digressio*. As artist-teacher Garoian discovered, students do not always automatically experience the powerful generative connection between antinomy and *digressio*; sometimes they need help. As he explains, he discovered the productive power of contradictions as he worked in his studio to juxtapose the space of the canvas against the space of his body. However, he acknowledges that his students, even with similar experiences and a similar immersion in a contradictory culture of images, do not always develop a parallel awareness of contradiction and thus harness the potential for social action. A visually fragmented and contradictory culture does not mechanically imprint antinomy and *digressio* on an individual; therefore, a child can grow to adulthood in a visually saturated culture without developing antinomy or *digressio*. Nor, once developed, is there an inevitable link between antinomy and digressive rhetoric, no guaranteed straight path from digressive rhetoric to subversive social action. The dynamic of coevolution might predispose an individual to shape a symbiotic knot of contradictions, but the individual negotiates those contradictions, retaining the power to accept or decline the invitation posed by the symbiotic knot. One way to tip students toward embracing a symbiotic knot of contradictions and its potential for subversive social action, as Garoian himself determines, consists of fashioning out of the classroom a radical place, a place encouraging the play of contradiction. By deliberately juxtaposing imagery and language, teachers can help students develop a contradictory orientation in writing, one that invites them to take an inventive, subversive approach to meaning, which, in turn, invites them to take an inventive, subversive approach to personal and social change.

Thread 3: The Radical Classroom and the Art of Revision

Change, personal and social, requires disorder from which a new order can evolve. Paulo Freire makes this very point in *Pedagogy of the Oppressed*. The radical, whom Freire defines as anyone committed to human liberation, cannot afford to "become the prisoner of a 'circle of certainty' within which he imprisons reality" (36). Change is predicated on breaking out of that circle. Jacqueline Jones Royster echoes Freire, pleading that composition scholars directly address our unfortunate tendency to lock ourselves "into the tunnels of our own vision and direct experiences" (615). Identifying the "circle of certainty" and tunnel vision with a belief in a transcendent "academic discourse," T. R. Johnson proposes a radical move in the classroom:

Instead of organizing ourselves around a central, transcendent "academic discourse" as that which names, masters, and controls reality, we need to sensitize ourselves and our students to the openings, cracks, and fissures in every discursive act. . . . Such a move would lead us beyond the "mirror stage" of our self-conception, in which we agonize over and do battle with questions about our own integrity and authority, and would release us into the mobility and strength of the symbolic, where all is constructed and negotiated in an ongoing process akin to the playing of a game. (638)

Breaking the "circle of certainty" requires designing a counterspectacle pedagogy around a symbiotic knot of contradictions, "releasing" ourselves and our students into "the mobility and strength of the symbolic" (638). An approach to writing structured according to bricolage, paradox, and agenic invention can be fruitfully and systematically enacted in the composition classroom; one focal point is revision, a powerful blend of invention and arrangement. Lainie, a student in my first-semester composition class, offers an example of the possibilities of contradiction for opening up space for radical change.

A tall, vivacious eighteen-year-old when she entered my class, Lainie displayed a self-confidence derived from highly successful high-school writing experiences, which she wanted to weave into a teaching career. A double major in English education and athletic training, Lainie quickly established herself as a student leader by volunteering her draft for a full-group response in the second week of class. She continued in her role as groundbreaker, risk taker, and spokesperson by being the first to wear floppy, fuzzy "leopard" slippers to class, the first to complain about the degree to which this particular writing class incorporated nontraditional methods, and the first to garner a following in the class as the preferred peer respondent. While she always took her work seriously, she was particularly invested in her second paper. Lainie's essay about father-daughter bonds highlights the transformative possibilities of a symbiotic knot of contradictions.

Lainie's essay and writing process relied on bricolage, paradox, and agenic invention to dismantle meaning and recraft it in new ways. Consider excerpts from three versions of Lainie's essay: combined, they illustrate the remarkable change that Lainie effected in her writing. These excerpts are taken from the introductory and concluding paragraphs of a workshop draft, a final assignment revision, and a final course-portfolio revision.

First Draft, First Paragraph
"What is your major?" "What are you going to be when you grow up?" "Have you picked a career?" These questions have grown to be similar to the questions, "How are you?" "How was school?" When you become a

junior in high school, suddenly these questions flow like water. Everyone wants to know what you plan on doing with your life and how you're going to go about doing just that. Some juniors in high school have the luxury of knowing at that point but most are still oblivious to the fact that they will be leaving high school in a matter of months.

Final Assignment Revision, First Paragraph
Throughout our lives, we are led to believe that our fathers are perfect. They can do no wrong, they are here to protect us and give us anything, after all, we're their little girls. But often times, the opposite is true. Fathers are not heroes, they are human. They too have faults, they too have feelings and sometimes they cannot handle their fatherly duties. But don't abandon your fathers completely, even if they abandon you. Although they cannot be a father, they can be a friend.

Final Course Portfolio Revision, First Paragraph
Throughout our lives, many of us are led to believe that our fathers are perfect. They can do no wrong, they are here to protect us and give us anything; after all, we're their little girls. But often, the opposite is true. Fathers are not heroes. They are flawed. They too have faults, they too have feelings, and sometimes, they cannot handle their fatherly duties. They abandon us. But this does not mean we must abandon them. In order to be happy though, we need to abandon the dream of them being our hero and start accepting them as the individual. Although he cannot be a father, he can be a part of our lives.

First Draft, Last Paragraph
Without having the opportunities that I had and the support of my family, I would not be one of those lucky people that can answer the questions about my future. As parents, you need to support your children. Although you might not like their decision at first, you have to help them reach the right choice and then support them living with it. Not every decision they make will be the right one but we learn from mistakes. Support is what helps us to be sure in ourselves. It is what makes me know that I will be an athletic trainer in a high school in a matter of a few short years.

Final Assignment Revision, Last Paragraph
Although I tried to return to the relationship I had once known with my father, I accepted the fact that I would never be his little princess again and this is what led me to preserve a relationship of any form with him. Just because you can't be "daddy's little girl" anymore doesn't mean you can't be "daddy's friend."

Final Course Portfolio Revision, Last Paragraph:
> "There is nothing so likely to produce peace as to be well prepared to meet the enemy," George Washington said. Realizing that a father is flawed is not easy. But the only way for us, as girls with fathers that are absent or distant, is to accept the flawed figure. If we do not come to terms with the man that cannot offer himself as a father, we will only remain unhappy. If we continue to hold our anger towards them in, we also remain unhappy. The only way to break through and find happiness is to accept what we can have, we shouldn't settle for anything less than we deserve but accept what they are willing to offer. When we understand the character that is flawed, when we are prepared to meet the enemy, we will be able to make peace within ourselves and within the relationship we have with our fathers.

In response to the broadly construed topic of *dilemma*, Lainie fashioned a first draft that focuses on a difficult decision she had to make during her freshman year of high school: she had to choose between pursuing a successful softball career and seizing the opportunity to work as an assistant athletic trainer. Central to her dilemma was her relationship with her divorced parents, especially her father, for her sole link to her father consisted of her ballplaying. Thus, Lainie's writing process begins with a competent but pedestrian argument about the importance of family support in making hard career choices. However, as these excerpts reveal, Lainie's essay and her position within a problematic family dynamic undergo a sea change. She transforms a predictable paper into an essay exploring the emotional choices daughters of absentee fathers must make to fashion lives unstained by disappointment and bitterness, an essay marked by its depth, dimension, and vigor.

The transformation in Lainie's essay—from family support to family dissolution and out of that dissolution renewal—was enabled in part by bricolage: fiddling with and remixing a montage of fragmentary, disjointed images. "This portfolio is hard to describe," Lainie writes in a metacommentary of the evolution of her second paper.

> I don't know where it came from really. It all started with a picture of a heart being separated by bold lines. It is cracked down the middle and on one side, I have volleyball and softball, on the other training. I have words to describe each. Volleyball and softball: love, skill, comfort, knowledge, unpredictable, disappointment. Training; new, security, unknown, fun, future, friends. This was my dilemma when I was a freshman. I didn't know which direction to go. That was where the whole process started. Seems completely unrelated to my current final draft.

As Lainie explains here, the image of a broken heart that began her writing process reflects her emotional state when she had to make a choice in high school between playing softball and serving as an apprentice athletic trainer. The choice pitted her against her divorced parents, placing her in the agonizing position of placating differing parental expectations while trying to steer a course that would help her fulfill her dreams. Her journal describes this experience, and her subsequent first draft, a product of both image and journal entry, essentially elaborated Lainie's dilemma in her first year of high school. For example, she writes:

> This [a decision to give up softball so that she might work as an assistant athletic trainer in high school] disappointed my dad. When I was two months old, he took me to my first baseball game. From that point on until even now, baseball is our bond. When I was six years old, he would take me to the park to practice my batting. We would go to Comiskey Park and sit outside the stadium in the park across the street. We would listen to the game on the radio and watch the fireworks afterward. This is where we knew each other. I took this bond away from him when I decided to be a trainer.[14]

Lainie's life and essay at this point seemingly consist of bits and pieces of images that will not cohere in a unified visual or discursive narrative. As she seeks to please a mother and father often at odds with each other and with her own vision of her future, her reality reflects an imagistic crisis that characterizes contemporary culture. Thus, Lainie comes to her visual predicament, struggling to image and imagine her constantly changing situation. As she shuttles among images, journal, and draft, she works to make sense of this difficult period in her life, one in which her career and life choices were tightly intertwined with the problematic family dynamics of a divorced home. At this alchemical moment, she creates new forms of imaging that invite new realities and subjectivities. Central to that transformation is paradox.

Lainie's alchemical moments rely on the paradoxes nascent in her representation of her family dynamic. For Lainie, paradox functions on three levels: that within the unexpected visual narrative; that between constellated images; and that between image and word. In response to a second round of peer and instructor comments, Lainie begins to identify and wrestle with the contradictions woven throughout her second draft. The initial contradictions evolve from her visual narrative, one disordered by multiple story lines, multiple orderings of space and time. She grapples with at least three different renderings of the same experiences: her mental images, her mother's verbal images, and her father's repeated injunction to see the past from his perspective: she "should not believe everything she is told," he protests. For instance, Lainie taps a visual scenario of her father abandoning the family when she was five, leaving in a recreational vehicle to wander around the United States. She contrasts the mental drama of his return two years later with the befuddlement of her younger sister who saw not her father but a threatening stranger. Lainie also seeks to piece together troubling images of the brief months she and her younger sister lived with her father, a time in which she was forced to assume responsibilities beyond her years as she coped with raising both herself and her sister. Into this uneasy visual-kinesthetic narrative, she attempts to weave her mother's verbal images, vivid anecdotes of violence, inconsistency, and irresponsibility. Finally, she is left with the meager, imagistically barren story line her father provides: the mother's account of abandonment and Lainie's memories of abandonment "weren't exactly like that."

The second level of contradiction occurs when images current within a culture contradict each other. Lainie directly grapples with conflicting meanings in daddy's little girl, which encompasses a reciprocal pair of images: daddy's little girl and a girl's (daughter's) hero. Promulgated by American culture, these ideal images conflict with the reality of Lainie's current life and with the swirling images of her childhood. As she notes in her first draft, softball served as her sole bond with her father during her growing years. Beyond that bond, he was remarkably absent from her life. Now, he indirectly finds her a job, he counsels her about her athletics, and he takes her to an occasional lunch. However, he rarely attends her sporting events, never appears at her special school activities, and can offer only awkward comfort at the death of her cousin. The ideal and the reality conflicted repeatedly throughout the evolving drafts and within any single draft as the shifts between Lainie's various conclusions reveal. When she factors her father's almost complete absence in her current life with his total absence during two years of her childhood, she is forced to deal with the paradox between images of what she might long for as a daughter and images of what she must accept and can count on.

Beyond juggling the contradictions within visual narratives and between images, Lainie also confronts the third level of contradiction: between image and word. Her final set of contradictions results from the misalignment of a central image—her father on a pedestal—and the language in the text suggesting that it is no longer possible for her to see her father as a hero. Instead, as her revision for her course portfolio reveals, he is an enemy for whom she must be prepared if she is ever to find peace. If she expects no more of him than the occasional lunch, social event, and contact, then she will be able to wend her way through bitterness into a kind of serenity. Out of this montage of fragmentary, contradictory images and words, Lainie knits together a different story, a different image, and a different father-daughter relationship. Her central graphic image morphs from broken heart to a heroic monument to a figure toppled from the pedestal. Her final portfolio revision constitutes the strongest essay that she wrote that semester, and it is one which she continues to revise so that she might submit it for publication as a nonfiction essay in the undergraduate literacy magazine. In addition, it has generated two poems, published electronically, that explore the emotional resonance of an injurious family dynamic.

To create new images that represent her relationship with her father and her identity, Lainie exercises agenic invention. As an agent with the power to recraft subjectivity and reality, Lainie labors to make sense of the fragmented images that comprise her experience, imagining new patterns of meaning. She notes in her portfolio narrative that revising this essay required her to confront a confusion of broken, unanchored mental images, a confusion that, until she rewrote this paper and shared it with her mother, she was never sure had any basis in a coherent reality: the mental snapshot of her father throwing a flowerpot at the car as her mother sped away from him with Lainie and her sister in the back seat; the scene in the police station where her mother, bruised and battered, huddled with Lainie and her sister seeking protection from their father's anger; the frozen image of her father stepping through the back door of Lainie's house after a two-year absence and her younger sister failing to recognize him. To make sense of these inchoate, paradoxical images, she must negotiate not only the past but also the present. The broken images of her father's past behavior had to be placed within the frame of her father's current behavior and her sense of a man who has "changed a lot since then. He no longer loses his temper, he doesn't abuse my stepmother, he doesn't drink as much." But even this assessment is leavened with tentativeness, for, as Lainie concedes, "He is a better person from what I can see. Then again, I don't live with them and I rarely go to their house." To reach this point, Lainie enacted a participatory interpretation in which perceiving was inextricable from interpreting, enabling her to wrestle with her broken images in productive ways.

The agenic invention implicit in Lainie's revision leads to far more than an absorbed investment in and interpretation of the bricolage of her life, important though those processes may be. Agenic invention also encourages the deliberative act of endowing significance to one's meaning and identity within the world. It encompasses both the intimate audience of self as well as the larger less-personal audience of unknown other, initiating for Lainie a radical shift in the focus of her second draft. Rather than refining the topic of career choices and family expectations, Lainie digs more deeply into the family that rendered this choice a dilemma in the first place, specifically exploring the conflicted father-daughter relationship. Her desire to please her father, to make decisions that will evoke his approval rather than his disappointment and thereby maintain the fragile bond between them, becomes the subject of inquiry by deliberate choice. Furthermore, by choosing to address as her audience other women contending with parallel experiences, Lainie connects her situation to the larger dynamic permeating the culture—the phenomenon of absentee fathers and the cultural myth of a daughter as daddy's girl—seeking to act on that personal and cultural tension.

A drawing, a visual enactment of Lainie's agency, accompanies the essay Lainie writes and rewrites. In an early sketch, Lainie had situated a figure of her father on the top of a pedestal, reflecting the hero role that daughters assign to their fathers. It was a drawing in which Lainie was entirely absent. In her revision of both text and sketch, however, the hero figure is toppled from the pedestal, and the agent of that action is Lainie's hand. For herself and as a stand in for other daughters, she dislodges the father from his pedestal, breaking what she sees as an injurious interaction wherein she can only be a princess if her father remains a hero. In dislodging her father, Lainie also takes herself out of the princess role, the role in which she does not act but is acted upon. She places herself, instead, in a proactive role, one in which, as she states in the conclusion of her revision for her course portfolio, she and other daughters can "break through and find happiness," making "peace within ourselves and within the relationship we have with our fathers."

Through a revision process marked by bricolage, paradox, and agenic invention, Lainie engages in transformation on a variety of levels, not all of them comfortable or comforting. As she continues to cope with residual bitterness and sadness, she recognizes that the results of this process reduced her mother to tears and simultaneously deepened their bond. In her end-of-the-semester reflection, Lainie writes:

> My second portfolio came from somewhere that I wasn't ready to deal with at the time but I think that dealing with it at that point, confronting it before I thought I was ready, was really therapeutic. I think [I] feel a lot more open to the whole situation and I think that I have found answers to things I have always questioned. I think that this was the best portfolio for me to write even though it was the hardest. I think that each step I took in revising and writing made me open my eyes a little bit more and in general helped me deal with what happened. I liked this portfolio by the end even though it was hard to get there. It's true that the hardest work pays off the most in the end. I see that with this portfolio.

The conjunction of agenic invention with bricolage and paradox invited Burke's alchemical moment, offering Lainie the opportunity to change vision—the way in which she sees and the angles of her perception—thus producing a different meaning and reality. In her essay, she achieved Burke's goals of a disintegrating art by "setting the mind off balance and allowing for all sorts of cognitive and perceptual processes not normally possible" (*Rhetoric of Motives* 167). Rather than merely being subject to images, emotions, and words, Lainie became an agent of change in her own life and in, she hopes, her readers' lives: young girls who struggle with the pain of an absent father. Her efforts to publish her essay and the poetry arising out of this new vision of reality and identity reflect her desire to change the social narratives that privilege the unreal hero in fathers and the unreal daddy's girl in daughters. Derived from immersion in a culture of disjointed, contradictory images colliding with bits and pieces of decontextualized words, the symbiotic knot of contradictions can be a powerful and productive force in our writing classrooms.[15]

A Symbiotic Knot of Contradiction: The Antinomian Threat

The poetics of antinomy circulates through such diverse social actions as art, popular literacy, Internet hacktivism, and a student essay that changes the writer and seeks to change the writer's world. The symbiotic knot of contradictions offers a powerful matrix for change, opening up locations of recovery within which people can imagine new possibilities for agency and action. However, despite the potential of antinomy, digressive rhetoric, and radical classrooms for creating opportunities for re-vision, I cannot conclude this chapter with the contention that a symbiotic knot of contradictions provides a surefire source of transformatory social action. When antinomy, digressive rhetoric, and radical places tightly intertwine, a symbiotic knot of contradictions can be dangerous; a knot can choke off change rather than foster it. As Burke warns, humans are "rotten with perfection"; we strive to achieve the best, most perfect representation of a role. For a symbiotic knot of contradictions, this admonition means that we sometimes aim to be as contradictory as possible. The contradictions become an end in themselves, not a step or a stage to change. When a symbiotic knot is rotten with perfection, the means to an end obliterates the end, blinding us to the change we seek in the first place and producing a subversion of matrices of abuse. Johnson alludes to this extremism in "School Sucks" by his references to "play," which resonate to Teresa Ebert's criticism of postmodern or ludic feminism. According to Ebert, ludic feminism takes as its ends the play of signs, a play with signs, and, as a result, fails to engage with signs to change systems of oppression. The means becomes the end.

A symbiotic knot of contradictions holds a similar threat. Freire warns that expression is merely verbalism. It is futile without action. Similarly, action without word results in action without teeth: mere motion and similarly futile. When tangled in a chokehold, the threads of a knot of contradictions invite expression—the play of signification—without attention to action. The symbiotic knot fragments for the pleasure of fragmentation, as an end in itself, keeping the individual on the surface of reality, an illusion of lawlessness with no accountability. Although the word *antinomy* entered the lexicon in the sixteenth century, that word was preceded by another related term, *antinomian*, a word used to describe a segment of early Christians who, through an extreme interpretation of

Paul's New Testament letters, believed that they were not subject to Mosaic law. Because, according to Paul, people were saved by grace and not by good works such as observing strict Mosaic laws, many early Christians believed that they were exempt from any law in the material world. Thus, *antinomian* became synonymous with lawlessness, and lawlessness imbues this symbiotic knot. The danger posed by a knot of contradictions manifests itself when fragmentation and contradiction become the goal: the individual is unable to create a location of recovery out of the chaos. In digressing, the rhetor becomes seduced by the pleasure of digression, forgetting the whole reason for—the need for—digression in the first place: to expose the matrices of abuse, evoke a location of recovery, and move from that location into social action.

We cannot live without boundaries and without order. We cannot move to action without deciding what needs to be changed and what can be changed. So we are charged not only to destroy boundaries but also to take pleasure in and responsibility for creating boundaries (Haraway, *Simians, Cyborgs, and Women* 150). To prevent the potential for chaos in a knot of contradictions, we must foster not one way of seeing, not one counterspectacle strategy, whether based on a knot of bodies or a knot of contradictions. We must foster many. This double charge is essential as well for a composition pedagogy aimed at encouraging personal and social action. A visually and rhetorically rich writing praxis that encourages many different ways of seeing and speaking in the world provides the greatest possibility of hope for our students, a possibility I address next.

CONCLUSION
The Possibility of Hope

> If you lose hope, somehow you lose the vitality that keeps life
> moving, you lose that courage to be, that quality that helps
> you go on in spite of it all. And so today I still have a dream.
> —Martin Luther King Jr., *The Trumpet of Conscience*

> There is power in looking.
> —bell hooks, "The Oppositional Gaze"

Intrinsic to social action is hope, a belief in the possibility of positive change, even in the face of contrary evidence. As Martha C. Nussbaum writes, "In hope oneself or what one loves is in some uncertainty but with a good chance for a good outcome" (28). Conviction in a good chance for a good outcome despite uncertainty motivates and sustains individual and collective efforts to change some aspect of a harmful reality. Nancy Welch acknowledges the necessity of hope in her own activism. In her opening chapter of *Living Room*, Welch recounts two stories of collective protest against U.S. involvement in Iraq during the 2003 Conference on College Composition and Communication in New York. One occurred in the evening, in the rain, with the police pushing back the protestors pressing against the barricades, leaving Welch awash in "helpless despair" and doubting the possibility of a good outcome. The second one, two days later, involved an afternoon march down Broadway to a sunny Washington Square. Protestors proceeded in a peaceful column forty blocks long, wending their way through Manhattan with minimum official interference. In contrast to the rain and police intransigence of the evening protest, Welch felt "buoyed along in an ocean of humanity whose intelligence and good sense surpassed that of Congress" (3), inspired with an "unrelenting hope" that ordinary people can seek and find ways to be heard despite "formidable constraints that convince most people that there's very little they can do" (4).

Hope, in the midst of uncertainly, drives the arguments presented in *Vision, Rhetoric, and Social Action in the Composition Classroom*, hope that, in spite of formidable constraints, ordinary people have a good chance of finding ways of speaking *and* ways of seeing that bring about a good outcome. Throughout this book, I have argued that any approach to social action, individual and collective, micro to macro, depends on rich repertoires of ways of speaking and ways of seeing, both of which coalesce to open up (and sometimes curtail) options for intervention in particular places. A symbiotic knot offers invitations to ordinary people, who negotiate among the threads, choosing to engage (or disengage) with the world in ways that increase human dignity, value, and quality of life. From Coco Fusco's raw protest play *The Incredible Disappearing Woman* to Barack Obama's community activism, from a cohort of women dressed in black standing silent vigil on a street corner to one woman struggling to voice in a composition classroom, from hacktivists challenging Dow Chemical's corporate ethos to an adolescent creating a subversive location of recovery, *Vision, Rhetoric, and Social Action in the Composition Classroom* explores the mechanisms of social action buoyed by the conviction that ordinary people require both habits of seeing *and* of speaking to effect change in the world.

Throughout this book, I addressed directly and explicitly the centrality of visuality, rhetoric, and place in social action. I spun out the consequences and ramifications of individuals transacting with a symbiotic knot, attending particularly to a symbiotic knot of silence, interweaving spectacle, rhetorical compliance, and monologic places; a knot of bodies, threading together animation, corporeal rhetoric, and lively places; and a knot of contradictions, featuring the intersections among antinomy, digressive rhetoric, and radical places. When individuals transact with the threads in each knot, coparticipating in the knot, particular forms of social action emerge: disengagement from a knot of silence, empathic social action from a knot of bodies, subversive social action from a knot of contradictions. Through the agencies afforded by each knot, ordinary people discover strategies that enable them to alter their realities directly, on a personal level; structurally, on an institutional level; or systemically, on a cultural level.

Two goals motivated *Vision, Rhetoric, and Social Action in the Composition Classroom.* As a scholar, I wanted to understand the nature of social action, particularly the interlacing of visual habit, rhetorical habit, and place as a source of social action. Then, as a teacher, I wanted to use that understanding to inform my teaching. If we teach, in James Berlin's words, a reality as well as a rhetoric, then the writing classroom constitutes a potential site for inviting compassionate modes of social action that serve compassionate ends. As bell hooks reminds us,

> teaching is a performative act. And it is that aspect of our work that offers space for change, invention, spontaneous shifts, that can serve as a catalyst drawing out the unique elements in each classroom. . . . Teachers are not performers in the traditional sense of the word in that our work is not

meant to be a spectacle. Yet it is meant to serve as a catalyst that calls everyone to become more and more engaged, to become active participants in learning. (*Teaching to Transgress* 11)

The *how* we teach and the *what* we teach implicate the kind of citizens our students may become. *How* we teach and *what* we teach also implicate the kind of vision we privilege and the kind of social action we sanction. As teachers, we can choose to grapple with the implications of symbiotic knots, offering opportunities that invite our students to be coparticipants in social action. As teachers, we can choose to be proactive, to shock ourselves into new ways of seeing and teaching, in the hope—the belief, despite uncertainty, in a good chance for a good outcome—that our students will take up our invitations to become citizens actively working toward a more equitable world. And so I have chosen the writing classroom as the locus of my symbiotic knots across *Vision, Rhetoric, and Social Action in the Composition Classroom*, connecting what I currently do in the classroom with the visually and rhetorically rich pedagogies developed by other compositionists.

In this final chapter, I consider where hope might next take us. Martin Luther King Jr. reminds us that hope drives life; its vitality keeps us going so that we can continue to dream. Because of hope in the face of setbacks, he continued to dream of racial equality achieved through peaceful means. After an exploration of three different symbiotic knots, of three different modes of social actions within which particular visual and rhetorical habits interface, I take King's faith in hope as both a call and a challenge. I use this last chapter to describe what we still might dream. First, I take the work of the current volume and extend it into my own classroom by considering how a symbiotic knot can transform my teaching. Inspired by a symbiotic knot of contradictions, I share key elements of a course I will soon be teaching, one that combines the intimacy of memoir writing with the public face of subversive social action. Second, I take the work of this book and extend its research agenda by suggesting two directions of exploration that will invigorate the discipline. Because much of the work in composition studies focuses on helping students know what to say or helping students, in Welch's words, "to be heard," we need to pay more attention to helping students know how they see (or are seen) and how those visual habits affect what they say (or cannot say). Filling this gap requires building a more in-depth understanding of visual epistemologies, a theory of vision as a way of knowing. It requires as well further exploration of specific visual habits. The greater our repertoire of visual habits, the more vigorous will be our composition teaching. For rhetoric and for composition to remain central to our students' and our communal well-being, teacher-scholars need to grapple with the challenges posed by visuality and by the interweaving of visuality with language in particular places.

Teaching with Hope

Throughout these chapters, I have described visual habits, analyzed their interactions with language, and traced the complex network of visual habit, rhetorical habit, and place in a symbiotic knot. Focusing specifically on one location—the composition classroom, both within academic settings and within a community-outreach program—I have sought to provide insight into pedagogical activities that encourage or discourage the evolution of a symbiotic knot. As I researched, sifted, organized, reorganized, deleted, and revised, a key question remained paramount for me: how might I more effectively and directly tie the rhetorical-visual focus in my current writing classrooms to social action on micro to macro levels? In this section, I outline a creative nonfiction course that I have revised according to a symbiotic knot of contradictions (antinomy, digressive rhetoric, and radical places). I choose to focus on this class, first, because the combination of subject matter and students make it one of my favorite classes and, second, because the subject matter initially appears to discourage a social-action component. So I seek to show the ways in which a symbiotic knot of contradictions can support the pedagogical goals of the course by integrating explicit attention to social action. Thus, my revised syllabus represents a generative negotiation between institutional course goals and my pedagogical commitment to activism arising from my work with this book. It invites students to write by facing two directions simultaneously: the private realm of personal writing and the public realm of social action.

ENC (English/Creative Writing) 4311: Advanced Article and Essay Workshop is an upper-division creative-writing class required of the eight hundred-plus undergraduate creative-writing majors at Florida State University. As the minimalist catalog description delineates, 4311 focuses on "a writer-editor relationship between student and instructor, designed specifically for writers who aspire toward publication." By tradition, the class aims to provide students with sophisticated workshop experiences and with training in creative nonfiction broadly construed to include anything from literary journalism to the personal essay. Prior to 4311, creative writing majors take a lower-division course focusing on article and essay techniques as a prerequisite to an upper-division course emphasizing application and extensive workshopping. In addition, to satisfy graduation requirements, creative-writing majors must complete two versions of 4311; thus, competition is fierce for a place in these courses. Everyone is admitted through an application process that requires individuals to submit work to an instructor who then gives permission for eighteen students (the course cap) to enroll. The students entering my class arrive with varied experiences in creative nonfiction and with well-defined expectations for my 4311.

I have in the past focused my syllabus on the memoir, a subset of the personal essay. In its previous incarnation, my class typically spent the first six weeks engaging in three activities: reading, responding to, and analyzing memoirs in weekly journals; creating snippets, which are short passages based on their own memories but using techniques they admired in the selections they read; and discussing in depth their reading and writing. The last eight weeks of the course consisted of a series of workshops in which four students per class period (seventy-five minutes) presented their evolving memoir projects in two stages: initial draft, followed by a recommended student-teacher conference and revision, followed by mandatory student-teacher conference. The course concluded with a mini-reading of portions of each student's final draft. In addition, I also required a pivotal visual assignment between the first draft and revision workshops. This image-based assignment has become the core for my new syllabus, a revision process informed by bricolage, paradox, and agenic invention, the perceptual practices central to a symbiotic knot of contradictions.

As I described in chapter 4, a symbiotic knot of contradictions, coevolving with our visually fragmented culture, interweaves antinomy, digressive rhetoric, and radical places through the shared practices of bricolage, paradox, and agenic invention. A knot of contradictions offers insight into the complexities of discursive and material transformation, moments when writers alter the patterns by which they think, compose meaning, and orient themselves in the world. By coparticipating in a knot of contradictions, community members on both micro and macro levels can begin to alter injurious situations by imagining different subjectivities and realities. A knot of contradictions provides an opportunity to destabilize the status quo by bringing individuals to a visual crisis, which they might potentially resolve by choosing radical change. Then, through digressive rhetoric, a means of persuasion that works via indirection, coparticipants in a symbiotic knot engage in subversive social action, altering the world around them on local and communal levels.

I chose a symbiotic knot of contradictions as the backbone of my revised course for a variety of reasons.[1] First, I retained my focus on memoir, and I believe that memoir aligns in intriguing ways with digressive rhetoric. As a form of rhetorical persuasion, memoir works on the slant, persuading indirectly through digression rather than direct attack. Thus, memoir writing offers interesting and unexplored options for subversive social action. In addition, as a memory stitched together in bits and pieces through the art of the imagination, memoir functions as a possible location of recovery where, by grappling with different interpretations of the past, authors have the chance to envision new futures and new identities. Memoir has the potential to bring the writer to an alchemical moment, opening up a good chance for a good outcome for writer and reader. By inviting students to teeter on the brink of transformative change in a writing moment, I hope to invite them to envision and possibly engage in activities that advocate for transformative change within a community beyond the classroom.

Second, a knot of contradictions provides a vehicle to destabilize students' preconceived notions of the memoir. While my students arrive in my class attuned to the private face of memoir, they frequently struggle with its public face, with what Phillip Lopate calls its "implicitly democratic bent" (xxiii). As a subset of the personal essay, the memoir concerns not only personal revelation, spotlighting the "writer's 'I' or idiosyncratic angle" (xxiv), but also communal revelation, spotlighting the idiosyncratic "I" as part of the larger "we." Memoir attends simultaneously to self and to self as a part of the human community; it uses the personal as an opportunity to articulate an insight important both to self and other. Memoir, then, is Janus-faced: looking toward the intimacy of self and toward the publicness of community. Vivid and evocative though their writing might be, many students entering my class have initial difficulty shuttling between the apparently paradoxical qualities of the personal and the communal in memoir. So a central goal of the revised course, one forwarded by a knot of contradictions, consists of helping my students write memoirs that, too, are Janus-faced: facing inward, toward the privacy of the writer's inner life, and outward, toward the publicness of active involvement in democratic life. Finally, as Lopate notes, conventions of the memoir coincide with a knot of contradictions, such as the techniques of digression (xl) and contrariety (xxx), as well as the importance of perception: "the practice of seeing" what others do not (xxxv). The overlap suggests that students as memoirists can benefit from a writing pedagogy structured according to the logic of a symbiotic knot of contradictions at the same time that this knot can issue invitations for engagement with subversive social action.

My forthcoming course focusing on memoir includes one key text—Dave Eggers's memoir, *A Heartbreaking Work of Staggering Genius*—and an array of short memoirs and critical essays selected for their inward-outward movement as well as their quality. Three central goals anchor my efforts to configure my creative writing classroom as a radical place. As I explain to students in my syllabus, I designed the course to help them

- develop a robust understanding of memoir as a genre and build a repertoire of writing techniques;
- connect the privacy of the memoir to the publicness of rhetoric;
- demonstrate expertise with memoir writing as a Janus-faced genre facing in and out by drafting, revising, and completing a fifteen-to-twenty-page memoir project throughout the semester.

Let me elaborate on each one of these course goals, describing the ways in which a symbiotic knot of contradictions guides goals and activities.

Goal 1: Develop a robust understanding of memoir as a genre and build a repertoire of writing techniques.

The first goal and the activities supporting that goal owe much to antinomy, or visual atom cracking. As I explain in chapter 4, through bricolage, paradox, and agenic invention, antinomy juggles the ongoing tensions between contradictory images and words in our visually fragmented culture; it juxtaposes those fragments to move the perceiver to a visual crisis, inviting the creation of new order. Antinomy helps individuals cut "across the bias" to develop a "new angle of vision" (Burke, *Permanence and Change* 154n1). Although students might be predisposed to develop antinomy outside of the classroom where they are bombarded by a continual barrage of fragmented images, they are less inclined to deploy that mode of seeing so tightly tied with popular literacy in the classroom where institutional literacy—discovering and supplying the right answer—gains them prestige and rewards. The textual orientation of an English classroom, with the accompanying emphasis on stable, agreed-upon textual meaning, reinforces their disinclination to rely on antinomy in that space. To encourage them to engage with texts guided by the destabilization of antinomy, I ask students to respond to assigned memoirs through a scrap-box journal, which involves approaching readings on the slant, indirectly rather than directly.

The tool for recording their thoughts, reactions, analyses, and conclusions related to their required reading, a scrap-box journal consists of pages stored in loose-leaf folder or cardboard container. For the first six weeks, students create and turn in weekly a set of responses that are put together as a bricolage: bits and pieces of drawings, snippets of handwritten and decorated texts, remixed texts, photographs, pictures, fabrics, strings, ribbons, small objects, dried flowers, remixed texts, and any other materials that express responses to and observations of their own reading. As I explain in my assignment prompt:

> To hone our understanding of and appreciation for the art of the memoir, we will be reading, analyzing, and discussing various examples of memoir, from Dave Eggers's *A Heartbreaking Work of Staggering Genius* to Adrienne Rich's "Split at the Root." But, rather than responding exclusively through words, you will be creating visual artifacts that evoke your reactions to significant ideas or powerful textual passages. Instead of the conventional reading journal, you will create what I call a scrap-box journal. For this, you'll need paper, idiosyncratic materials, and a lot of creativity because you will be creating "journal quilts" or "scrap

books" of your response. For instance, Mary Clearman Blew in "The Art of Memoir" uses the metaphor of quilt making to describe the process of writing a memoir. You have to be a "saver of fabric" to craft a successful memoir, she says. Therefore, we will begin that process of becoming a "saver of fabric" with our journals.

As you read the assigned material, you will be expected to contribute to your scrap-box journal in a variety of ways: analytical and/or responsive writing arranged in nonlinear patterns on your paper, experimental writing, in which we take an admired technique and make it our own, and quilting responses, in which we create predominantly nonverbal responses to or comments on the essay through bits and pieces of diverse materials: fabrics, small objects, segments of decorated, closely examined—even decorated—texts, photographs, pictures, or drawings pasted in deliberate patterns on the page.

I will be collecting your scrap-box journals either at the beginning or the end of every week, so make sure you have an appropriate container for your work. Please bring pages with you to class, also, because these will serve to initiate class discussion. Don't create anything that you would prefer not to share with the entire class.

Finally, keep an informal record of what you like and dislike about the scrap-box journal because the activity culminates at the end of the first six weeks with a short reflective essay on this mode of response, particularly in terms of what you were able to see and not see in the assigned reading with knowledge of this mode of response lurking in the background.

The connections to antinomy, especially bricolage, are obvious: the scrap-box journal emerges from the act of bricolage. It relies on cutting up the specious stability of the assigned memoirs into fragments and then reordering those fragments into new patterns. In addition, the journal's attention to both verbal and nonverbal responses draws on paradox, particularly the potential tension between words and images, images and images. As students respond with the assigned readings, they are invited to offer reactions that are visual as well as verbal, juxtaposing image and word in potentially generative ways.

To prime the pump, I offer my students an example from my own visual journal for the first week's reading, which consists of Phillip Lopate's introduction from *The Art of the Personal Essay* along with Annie Dillard's "To Fashion a Text" and Patricia Hampl's "Memory and Imagination." On a sheet of computer paper, I positioned a Xeroxed page of Egger's *HWSG* torn into pieces and partially glued to the page so that the Eggers's text resembles a semi-constructed puzzle. From the fragments tenuously connected to the board, strings extend to overlapping, chaotic images of intimacy, humor, idleness, and other elements that Lopate identifies as characteristic of the personal essay. The tension on the strings tugs the memoir—the fragmented page—into numerous different directions so that the memoir teeters on the edge of disintegration. This visual response is designed to jump-start discussion of the essays and provide an illustration of one incarnation of a scrap-box-journal response. Following my lead, students share on subsequent days their scrap-box journals, using these visuals to initiate discussion of the assigned material.

My hopes for the scrap-box journal are myriad. First, I seek to invite a different mode of close reading, one that does not focus on a surface summary of the assigned reading. Already adroit with language, my students have little difficulty in replicating the superficial meaning of a memoir or critical essay. But their written journals do not always show active minds seeking to peek beneath the outside shell of the page. Dislocating students from language, the scrap-box journal encourages them to engage with texts differently, reading from the perspective of both image and word, abstract ideas and material artifacts. Second, by shifting students between texts and physical materials of construction, the scrap-box journal encourages new modes of in-class discussion. My belief is that a more intense engagement with the assigned readings will enable students to participate more fully in the material implications of a text for action in the world.

Goal 2: Recognize the public face in the intimacy of the memoir and publicness of rhetoric.

The second goal draws explicitly on digressive rhetoric, or persuasion on the sly. Digressive rhetoric employs the technique of interrupting the logical progression of an argument with what seem to be non sequiturs, thus a rhetoric of fragmentation that persuades through misdirection. To paraphrase Emily Dickinson, digressive rhetoric tells the all truth but tells it slant. Two activities designed to poise students between intimacy and publicness draw on bricolage, paradox, and agenic invention in digressive rhetoric.

The first step in creating this tension involves helping students recognize the double nature of memoir; that recognition begins with the materials I have collected for them to read in association with Eggers's memoir. To help them see memoir as a door that opens on one side to the privacy of their own lives and on the other side to work in the world, I have juxtaposed with Eggers's memoir a set of readings—newspaper articles, Web sites, videos, and interviews—concerning Eggers's work with community literacy. As cofounder of 826 National, a nonprofit foundation that supports community-literacy programs in six cities throughout the country, Eggers works actively to advocate a creative, imaginative approach to literacy ("About 826"). I have scheduled the materials so that students read about Eggers's activism at the same time they read his intensely personal memoir. To further underscore the inward-outward dynamic, *HWSG* itself faces two directions simultaneously. It looks to the intimacy of traumatic family loss, which includes the death of Eggers's father from a fast-moving cancer followed within months by the death of his mother also from cancer; it focuses on the privacy of Eggers's hilarious, poignant efforts to raise his younger brother, Toph, while struggling with grief for his family's loss. *HWSG* also faces outward as Eggers in the second half of his memoir writes vividly of his start-up work with *Might* magazine and McSweeney's, a publication company that includes the magazine *McSweeney's* as well as other ventures. Thus, Eggers's memoir in conjunction with the texts reporting on his literacy outreach provides a starting point for examining the intimacy of Eggers's revelations within the context of his literacy activism, especially his emphasis on the importance of art, humor, and whimsy in the 826 National outreach programs.

Discussions of Eggers's materials revolve around the following questions, phrased to highlight the paradoxical tension in memoir writing: what intimate look into the memoirist's life are we provided, and how does that intimacy also possess a public face? I ask them to respond to this question through an entry in their scrap-box journal, an opportunity for agenic invention:

> Given what you learn about Dave Eggers in *HWSG*, create a set of materials that you might want to use as a volunteer at 826 Valencia in San Francisco where Eggers volunteers. What elements in the memoir—from Eggers's representation of himself as a guardian for Toph to his representation of himself as a writer for *Might*—help you envision yourself as a literacy advocate and community activist? Don't hesitate to substitute for literacy a different social problem or institution that might concern you. Include these materials in your scrap-box journal and be ready to share with the class your take on Eggers's private and public faces.

While I cannot demand that students engage in direct social action, a requirement beyond the bounds of and contrary to the focus of the course, I can request that they recognize the possibilities of social action implicit within each memoir they read. By helping them envision memoirists as agents of change, I also implicitly encourage them to act as agents of change. In addition, I reinforce their agency by asking them to grapple with the potential of their own writing to serve as subversive social action in the public sphere.

The first step in addressing my second goal—oscillating between the private and public faces of memoir via paradox—consists of recognition: providing opportunities for students to discover that oscillation in published memoirs. The second step—incorporation—builds on the first by initiating the same oscillation between private and public in their own evolving memoir projects. As students begin to shape their proposals for their memoir project, a process that starts in the fourth week of class, I ask them to commence work simultaneously on a parallel project: research on an issue related to some aspect of their memoir that serves as a site of collective action. Before engaging in social action, people need to know the range of available options for social action: what might they do, with whom, where, and how? To help students explore these questions in connection with their memoir project, I request that they conduct highly focused research and create a visual and written report that humanizes the results of that research.[2] A key question from the assignment prompt begins their project:

> What opportunities for advocacy, what commitment to acting in the world, always circulates under the surface of the memoir, the most intimate writing of all? To answer this question, identify an issue in your memoir and research local, national, or international social protest movements or advocacy organizations that work in the world to effect change relating to your issue. For instance, in previous semesters, a student has written about a relationship with a lesbian parent. A possible advocacy and support group connecting to that memoir is PFLAG: Parents, Family, and Friends of Lesbians and Gays. Another student, focusing on a destructive dynamic in her romantic relationship, discovers that a pattern of verbal abuse stems from her childhood experiences with an alcoholic parent. A possible advocacy group interfacing with that memoir includes Al-Anon or Alateen. The options are as plentiful as your imagination is limitless.

The culmination of incorporation consists of a visual project growing out of a close examination of the tools of protest used by the particular protest movement they study. Via any medium of their choice, students are asked to put a human face to collective action and the desired outcomes of that action. The aim of the visual project is twofold. First, it invites students to grapple with the material actions of their target organization. Second, it encourages students to evoke through images a key insight they develop about the human outcomes of the movement. Such an assignment does not require my students to join a particular protest movement. Rather the assignment asks them to become aware of the existence of these movements, study the various techniques employed by one specific group, and find linkages between techniques and goals. Finally, in a two-page reflection, students report on the results of their research and comment on the implications of their visual choices: what responsibility must they take for the images they select for their visual project? What are the implications of these representations of people, places, issues, and actions? These questions feed directly into their memoir project because memoir, too, is all about representation.

Students share the results of their research and the visual evocation of the protest movement on the same day they workshop the first draft of their memoir. My hope is that the combination of bricolage and paradox will open up gaps for agenic invention, leading to significant peer discussion about the student's work with the memoir and about connections between memoir and work in the world. My hope is that the tensions between intimacy and publicness will prove generative to them as writers and as actors in the world as they work through the implications of representation for their memoirs.

Goal 3: Demonstrate expertise with memoir writing as a Janus-faced genre facing in and out by drafting, revising, and completing a fifteen-to-twenty-page memoir project throughout the semester.

The third goal constitutes the culmination of their participation with bricolage, paradox, and agenic invention. In prior versions of my 4311, I have included an alternative-media project (AMP), a key element of their drafting/revising process. The AMP consists of a remixing of their nascent memoirs through a nonlinguistic medium. The prompt for the AMP consists of a brief explanation of the assignment as well as a brief rationale for the project. In short, they are asked to express what they believe constitutes the heart of their memoir, using any means of communication other than alphabetic language. Inviting them to communicate through an alternative medium provides an opportunity to generate new insights into that memoir. The prompt includes details concerning the contents of their reflective essays that will serve as the basis for their in-class workshop. Although students tend to be initially reluctant, the AMP has become one of the most powerful teaching tools I have discovered for eliciting substantive revision and for providing a focal point for peer responses. In their end of the semester evaluations, students have consistently mentioned the AMP as one of their most valuable writing activities from the semester, citing the unexpected discoveries they made through its production and through the class discussion the AMP evoked. Shared before they begin their first round of substantive revisions, the AMP helps them hone their sense of the center of their memoirs by destabilizing their in-progress narratives.

In the wake of *Vision, Rhetoric, and Social Action in the Composition Classroom*, I have revised my AMP to integrate more explicit attention to social action through agenic invention. I have retained the prompt I have always used with one significant change: students are required to integrate into their workshop (but not necessarily into the AMP) the visual project on activism they created and shared earlier in the semester. So they construct their AMP based on what they see as the "heart" of their memoir, but they re-present as well their work with social action in the world related to events or experiences in their memoir. At this moment in their work, they are juxtaposing two different visual projects and their textual memoir, creating a pool of potentially contradictory words, images, and stories. I hope for two outcomes from this welter of artifacts: to reinforce the connections between memoir and social action and open up more opportunities for students' agenic invention as writers and respondents. An experience that illuminates the limits of my traditional AMP and the hopes for my revised AMP comes from a recent article-and-essay workshop.

While the AMP brings students to the edge of difficult transformations, it sometimes falls short of helping them over the edge. The interaction between my students and one writer during my spring 2008 4311 highlights the weakness of my traditional AMP. Stephen came to my class near the end of his undergraduate career with a 4.00 GPA, well-established work habits, and dreams of graduate work in film. A talented writer older than the traditional undergraduate students, Stephen was also an Air Force veteran who had survived two tours of duty as a gunnery airman in Afghanistan. His memoir progressed from a long, vividly detailed, slightly rambling draft on brotherhood in the ranks to a poignant account of the loneliness of deployment for a short-term airman among a cadre of lifers. Contributing to his marginalization during his first tour was his status as a "virgin": he had yet to man the controls of an active bombing mission. After working steadfastly throughout the semester on three major revisions, Stephen concluded his outstanding memoir with a story of a nighttime mission: his crew had determined he would finally cross the line between novice and expert by targeting and releasing his first load of ordnance. The memoir, "Failure to Fire," ends in the dark, cold plane just after take off with Stephen checking the cords and hoses attached to his body "like hospital IV lines and chest tubes," only to realize that he and his crewmates all share the same breath, the same voices and words, the same danger, the same safety. The memoir's final image is of the "engines dron[ing] on as the plane drives halo-shaped holes into the sky," leaving uncertain the culmination of the night's mission.

Central to the memoir but also something never explicitly raised during the three full-class workshop discussions of Stephen's draft concerned the author's confrontation with his purpose in Afghanistan: to take out assigned enemy targets, including vehicles and people, by becoming the man dropping the bombs efficiently and accurately. While he and I discussed this in conferences, piecing together his loneliness, the Afghanistan landscape, and his reason for being there, the issue never arose in class. Both early drafts and his AMP allude to this purpose. Prior to the second of three revisions, Stephen presented his AMP, which consisted of a highly polished three-minute video artfully combining scenes from his tours in Afghanistan. Enriched by a haunting musical accompaniment, the film culminated in a final shot taken through the lens of a targeting mechanism. In real time, the viewer, in the position of the gunner on a live bombing run, lines up, releases, and verifies successful deployment of the load. The closing scenes of the AMP presents bombs silently exploding on unidentified subjects far below the airman's plane. However, the ambiguity of the memoir's end, contrasting with the stark clarity of the AMP's end, never initiated conversation in the full-group workshop. The crew's definition of a rite of passage, as blooding the novice, never became a tool for revision. The brooding sense of death lurked below the surface, but no one found (or took) an opportunity to highlight the contribution of that element to the loneliness at the heart of the memoir. During class workshopping, Stephen's classmates, perhaps intimidated by both his experience and his poise, danced around the question. Stephen also deflected the question. After his video, just before the class began discussing his AMP within the context of his memoir, Stephen passed around samples of MRE (meals ready to eat) pound cake, a military "treat" that he featured in his memoir. Students munched on bits of the cake as they discussed his memoir, but no one broached uncomfortable areas. An opportunity to bring a lurking tension to the fore, an opportunity to turn crisis into creative new order both in memoir and in the world passed us by.

My revision of the AMP potentially opens up moments of crisis, inviting agenic invention both in the memoir and in the larger community. By including with the student's work an explicit element of social action relating to the memoir, the revised AMP extends the memoir, if only intellectually, from the inside of class to the outside of class. For example, a potential activist project for Stephen might involve anything from antiwar protests to programs designed to support 9/11 survivors to calls for improving the care—medical, psychological, and financial—of returning vets. Any one of these connections holds the hope of moving discussions of Stephen's memoir into new territory, into public territory, where the intimacy of loneliness and the costs, individually and collectively, of war inform each other. The tensions between work in the world and work in the memoir can potentially lead to hard questions that effect a creative crisis and open up the possibility of subverting previously accepted realities, both real and textual.

In her article calling for increased attention to the visual as epistemic, art historian Johanna Drucker asks what academics might do to ensure that the visual gains a foothold in the academy. She answers: "by example, demonstration, the production of intelligently made projects that give proof of the intellectual value of this unique approach to knowledge" (5). ENC 4311 constitutes a deliberately designed effort to invite from my students thoughtful projects that give proof of the intellectual and emotional value of the visual. The course revision itself constitutes my own visual project, one informed by a symbiotic knot of contradictions. I look with hope to my forthcoming opportunity to teach 4311, believing, despite uncertainty (and some anxiety), that a good chance for a good outcome exists for my revised syllabus. By changing my way of seeing my classroom, by engaging with the options provided by a symbiotic knot of contradictions, I offer invitations to my students to be coparticipants in the knot as well. To draw them into social action indirectly, through memoir as persuasion on the slant, I seek to create a radical space out of my classrooms with activities and relationships that nurture subversive social action. I eagerly anticipate the many and varied ways that my students will respond as they determine how (and whether) to take up my invitation.

Researching with Hope

For me, my revision of 4311, inspired by a knot of contradictions, constitutes an act of hope. Hope is not just an intellectual stance; it is an emotion that impels people to action, even in the face of overwhelming odds. It drives women to dress in black and stand silently on street corners, quiescent in the face of heckling, steadfast in their commitment to peace. Hope pushes a divorcée with children to return to school and struggle with her panic in the writing classroom. It inspires a tweenager to create an alternative world where victim and villain rescue each other. Hope and change are inextricably tied up with the visual habits nested within a web of rhetorical habits and places. Changing the world on micro and macro levels involves changing the ways in which we see the world and speak the world, an agenda that brings me to necessary directions for future research.

To continue as a viable and vigorous discipline, composition studies and rhetoric need to address systematically the ways in which visuality and persuasion intersect in and out of the classroom. Much of the work we do as compositionists helps people know what to say, but our work is less successful at helping people understand the ways in which what they say intersects with how they see. As a result, people use language to change the world without realizing that they must use ways of seeing as well. Without research into the interface of visuality and rhetoric in social action, our choices as activists decline, and we reduce our chances of achieving a more equitable, just world. Likewise, without research into the interface of visuality and persuasion, we impoverish our choices as teachers, diminishing the possibility of crafting a pedagogy that invites multiple forms of agency in and out of the classroom. Uncertainty increases, and belief in a good chance of a good outcome decreases. I urge that we take up the challenge to theorize more fully the nature of the interface between ways of seeing and ways of speaking, extending the work started in *Vision, Rhetoric, and Social Action in the Composition Classroom*.

Perhaps the most urgent direction for scholarship growing out of this volume involves visuality as a way of knowing, as epistemic. "Perception (aesthesis) is a significant form of knowledge (episteme)," Barbara Maria Stafford argues, "perhaps even the constitutive form" (*Good Looking* 39), which means that perception itself is a knowledge-making enterprise. Thus, a crucial question to ask about imagery and social action includes the following: how is the viewer thinking through the image? Drucker echoes this sentiment, claiming that a theory of visuality as an epistemology needs to be our current "grail" quest (5):

> Visuality is a primary mode of understanding, but also of our produc-
> tion as social and cultural beings. Identity and authority are constituted
> through the systems of knowledge production embodied in visual forms.
> We know this. But how seriously does this centrality of vision translate
> into a theory of visuality? Not just the "reading" of visual representations,
> but an understanding of the cultural-cognitive foundation of visuality as
> a way of knowing? A challenge indeed. (4)

As teachers concerned with social action, we, too, need to be concerned with visuality as a mode of thinking, because a visual episteme constitutes a formidable tool for and constraint on social action.

Consider the reciprocal influence of visual epistemology and racism. As Linda Martín Alcoff points out, because racism occurs at the level of perception, it falls within the domain of visibility. Thus, to address racism through collective action, we have to identify and dismantle the "practices of visibility" that support racism (281). Such work requires attention to the visual not only as an array of images but also as a mode of racist thinking. Sue Hum takes up just such a challenge in her theory of the racialized gaze. Using the Disney film *Mulan* as her starting point, Hum describes practices of visibility that reinscribe and appropriate race and ethnicity in hegemonic White America. She identifies two key perceptual processes characterizing the racialized gaze. First, the racialized gaze reduces differences to a compendium of aesthetic and surface markers, such as iconography. This perceptual activity erodes awareness of the deep differences that result from historical oppressions and their material consequences. Second, the racialized gaze subsequently erases even those superficial markers by superimposing the assumption of universality, where all human beings are essentially the same in needs, desires, and aspirations. Appropriated and appropriating, the racialized gaze inculcates within cultural members a way of seeing that (re)confirms a racist order. Redressing the inequities of that racist order requires wrestling with the realities of the racialized gaze and the image artifacts that coevolve with it. For change to occur, we have to change vision and by so doing create the ability to produce new kinds of vision. Researching with hope, therefore, needs to include a robust theory of visual epistemology so that we better understand where to begin dismantling ways of seeing that support inequitable systems such as racism and sexism.

Another value of research on the visual as epistemic concerns the hope for multiple forms of agency. Without agency, social action is impoverished. As I highlight in chapter 1, Karlyn Kohrs Campbell argues persuasively that agency, among other qualities, is "'invented' by authors who are points of articulation," so it is a phenomenon of language. Campbell also points out that agency, in addition to being communal and participatory, is also materiality constrained, artistic, and protean (3). Implicit within Campbell's definition is the argument that I make explicit throughout *Vision, Rhetoric, and Social Action in the Composition Classroom*: agency is invented by authors who are also points of visualization. Agency is as much about imagery and ways of seeing as it is about language and ways of speaking. Thus, I have identified three different kinds of agency linked to visual habits: simulated agency (spectacle), embodied agency (animation), and antinomian agency (antinomy). Exploring systematically the epistemic nature of the visual offers hope of identifying and encouraging multiple ways to imagine, configure, and enact agency.

The current critical turn in rhetoric and composition studies underscores the role of the visual, especially the image artifact, in agency. For instance, in *Just Advocacy?* a collection of essays focusing on the representation of women and children in international advocacy efforts, coeditors Wendy S. Hesford and Wendy Kozol open their introduction with a critical analysis of a documentary based on a picture: the photograph of an unknown Afghan girl taken by Steve McCurry and gracing the cover of *National Geographic* in 1985. Through an examination of the ideology of the photo's appeal as well as the "politics of pity" circulating through the documentary, Hesford and Kozol emphasize the power of individual images to shape perceptions, beliefs, actions, and agency. Important to advocacy, to humanitarian efforts to ensure human rights around the globe for women and children, is control of representation: who does it, how it is done, and through what medium. A visual irony highlights the importance of agency in Hesford and Kozol's introduction. A second photograph of the Afghan girl, Shabat Gula, taken seventeen years after the first shows a figure wrapped in full burqa, any trace of specific identity consumed within the all-encompassing folds of the garment. The sole evidence of who might be within the burqa consists of a copy of Shabat Gula's 1985 *National Geographic* cover photo clutched in a hand hidden beneath the Afghan *chadri*. As Hesford and Kozol emphasize, what is visible, what is not, what is revealed, what is not, and who controls those revelations are conditions essential to understanding the persuasive power and the agency intertwined with individual images.

Although this laudable critical work focusing on imagery contributes essential insights into the mechanisms of agency in social action, it constitutes only a first step. Research in visual epistemology needs to go beyond critical analysis of images. It needs to wrestle with the question of visual habits: the means by which people think through imagery, endowing individual images with meaning, significance, and power. Visual habits already implicitly circulate through Hesford and Kozol's chapter. For instance, the impact of the picture of Shabat

Gula, both in 1985 and seventeen years later, depends on the mode of perception brought to bear on that image, but the mode of perception relates in part to the image deployed. Thus, as we analyze individual images and their persuasive appeal, we need to explore the range of specific visual habits—the different ways of thinking through images—that organize a culture at any particular historical moment in any one place. Both image and habits intersect with rhetoric and social action, as chapter 1 explains; therefore, to understand the persuasive impact of images, we need to understand the visual habits whereby we perceive those images and assign them value. I identified three in this book—spectacle, animation, and antinomy—tying each to literacy, rhetoric, social action, and the classroom, but that trio does not exhaust the important visual habits that unite with rhetoric and flow throughout the world. Let me offer two more tentative habits for consideration, both of which have implications for agency and social action: mirroring and the oppositional gaze (hooks).

Eileen, a former student, provides an initial preview of the visual habit of mirroring and a social action based on revamping the status quo. A few months after her graduation and three years after she was a member of my first-semester, required composition class, Eileen e-mailed me. "Dr. Fleckenstein," she wrote, "I just wanted to let you know that I am currently a 6th grade teacher! I am teaching in East Chicago, IN at Washington Elementary." As a poised eighteen-year-old, Eileen had entered the university committed to a career in elementary education; specifically, she wanted to teach underprivileged children in underfunded schools. She obtained her goal to teach in a disadvantaged area following her graduation. She chose a Title I school where 83 percent of students were receiving free lunches and where recruitment into local gangs flourished. Here, in her first teaching situation, she struggled to "establish a peaceful atmosphere for learning" in a classroom with more students than desks, more desks than room, and in a building "surrounded by railroad tracks and industrial companies spewing pollution." Through this struggle, Eileen hoped in some small way to rectify what she saw as a tragic social inequity.

Born in a family of strong social activists, Eileen configured herself, too, as an activist, and the arena of that activism lay with inner-city schools: "More than ever I realize that education cannot even begin to improve our society when support and funds are distributed so disproportionately," she wrote in her 2004 e-mail. Like her parents before her, she chose to focus her activist energies on changing inequities by working within the system. She deliberately decided to operate within the realm of institutional discourse, using language in and of the classroom to change the cultural context that creates inequitable education in the first place. The social action she enacts corresponds with her family's activist philosophies and their engagement with social movements supported by the Catholic Church.

As I sift through Eileen's course materials, her e-mails, and my memories of our long out-of-class conversations, I wonder if a culturally significant visual habit might exist that organizes realities by matching word and image in a harmonious alignment. Kenneth Burke suggests as much, claiming that much of what we do in life—our decisions (conscious and unconscious), our sense of aesthetic pleasure, ethics, subjectivities—derive from our effort to harmonize with images we encounter. Burke calls these images symbolic syntheses: "imaginative and conceptual imagery that 'locates' the various aspects of experience" (*Attitudes* 179). Coupled with the drive to imitate, symbolic syntheses serve to guide social purpose, providing cues as to what we should get, how we should try to get it, and how we should resign ourselves to renouncing things we cannot get.

By building on Burke and a detail-rich analysis of Eileen's choices of social action, we can begin to tease out the shape of mirroring. Through this visual habit, people evolve a vision of what can be, which includes a vision of their role in that change, and then they seek to match language and action to that vision. For example, the habit of mirroring leads Eileen to a protocol for rhetorical agency that reflects the one manifested by her parents' activism. Mirroring invites Eileen to match word and image, rhetorical habits and proactive behavior, in the belief that such performances will, in fact, have an analogous and equal impact on the world: saying effects changing. Mirroring implants the belief that a verbal act will evoke a parallel, visible change in a sphere of action. By extending our understanding of specific visual habits, we extend our understanding of rhetorical habits, agency, and potential modes of social action.

For now, mirroring merely constitutes a possibility, a tentative hypothesis that through research we can explore to determine its significance. We can track as well the limits of mirroring, for this visual habit might be localized to a specific segment of the population for whom image and word match consistently in their lives. Conversely, material existence for other members of a culture might undermine the evolution of mirroring at the same time that it fosters the evolution of different visual habits. One potential visual habit fostered by life experiences radically different from those of a White, upper-middle-class Midwestern Catholic girl consists of the oppositional gaze.

Drawing from raced and gendered positionality, hooks proposes that Black women develop the oppositional gaze as a means of survival in a racist and sexist culture. Hooks argues that racist Western culture punishes children and African Americans for staring, for employing "hard intense direct looks" ("Oppositional Gaze" 308). "There is power in looking," she says, and that power, like all power in a racist culture, is controlled by the dominant population (307). Robert Bernasconi concurs. He argues that Whites once saw African Americans without seeing, a phenomenon made possible by controlling the African

American gaze "so that Whites did not experience themselves as they were seen by Blacks" (287). By cultural dictates, African Americans could not look back; racist culture trained them to drop their eyes physically before making eye contact with Caucasians. These power politics played out in the perceptual system, hooks contends, resulting in the evolution of the oppositional gaze, an aggressive looking back: "Spaces for agency exist for Black people, wherein we can both interrogate the gaze of the other but also look back, and at one another, naming what we see" (308).

Although both Black men and women develop the oppositional gaze as a visual habit necessary for survival, hooks claims that it constitutes a particularly important way of looking for Black women because without it, Black women disappear. The mass media (particularly film and television) "constructs our [Black women's] presence as an absence, that denies the 'body' of the black female," hooks argues ("Oppositional Gaze" 310), echoing a concern discussed in chapter 3. Cinematic racism is especially virulent in its erasure of the Black female body, either by ensuring the total absence of the Black female body or by including it only in the guise of servant to the White female body (310). As a result of constant inroads on their identities, Black women, especially those most deeply resistant to practices of the dominant racist order, evolved the oppositional gaze (316).

Using broad strokes, hooks delineates the oppositional gaze according to its two different characteristics: critique and creation. Consisting predominantly of critique, the oppositional gaze includes contestation and confrontation, particularly in response to disempowering images circulated through television and film ("Oppositional Gaze" 308). However, the oppositional gaze does more than contest through critique. It also creates. As hooks describes, the oppositional gaze functions as social action: through its aegis, Black women "create alternative texts that are not solely reactions" (317). The creative element of the opposition gaze enables Black women to use history as a "counter-memory" to better understand the present and "to invent the future" (319).

While hooks provides insight into the oppositional gaze and into Black women as resistant spectators, she provides no close analysis of the contributing perceptual processes beyond resistance and invention. She explains that "as critical spectators, Black women participate in a broad range of looking relationship, contest, resist, revision, interrogate, and invent on multiple levels" (317), but the protocols by which that gaze operates remain a rich area for research, one that holds immense value for understanding agency and social action for marginalized members of a population.

As teachers and activists, we need to explore new ways of seeing so that our teaching and acting can be informed by that research. We can no more escape vision than we can escape language; blinding ourselves as Democritus supposedly did to gain greater intellectual insight does not prevent a way of seeing from becoming what Michel Foucault in *Birth of the Clinic* calls the pure gaze, the speaking eye (35). What we can do, however, is enlarge the scope of our vision, the quality of our vision, and bring both back to rhetoric in and out of the writing classroom. Marilyn Cooper in her editor's address to the December 2000 issue of *College Composition and Communication* defines the work of composition studies as a dialogic exploration of "ways of thinking, ways of being, ways with words" that we might find "so 'natural' that they are hard to explain" (185). I would add *ways of seeing* to this list of necessary work. By acknowledging the existence and the power of visual habits in a symbiotic knot, we can acknowledge and take responsibility for the visual field, social practices, and institutional spaces defined by that gaze. By exploring visual habits as they interweave with rhetorical habits in specific places, we have the possibility of hope for a social action of many forms and many agents who work toward a vision of the world as compassionate to and for all. We have a good chance of a good outcome.

NOTES
WORKS CITED
INDEX

Notes

Introduction: Vision and Rhetoric in Social Action

1. Cara A. Finnegan corroborates Alcoff's concern with the importance of the visual. Focusing on a nineteenth-century daguerreotype reproduction of Abraham Lincoln, Finnegan argues for the necessity of investigating the "social, cultural, and political work that visual communication is made to do" (33). She coins the term *image vernaculars* to highlight the way in which different periods develop different ways of seeing and talking about seeing. She then illustrates image vernaculars in action by analyzing letters published in *McClure's* magazine in 1895 and 1896 that responded to a newly discovered daguerreotype of Lincoln. Her careful analysis highlights the reciprocity between the visual and the rhetorical at a particular historical moment.

2. Although Stafford describes classical culture as oral-visual, Walter Ong categorizes it as oral-audio. The rise of print culture, he contends, occurred conterminously with the rise of visual culture.

3. Robert Hariman and John Louis Lucaites assert that particular photographs function as "iconic photographs." Pointing to the photograph of the flag raising on Mount Suribachi on Iwo Jima in World War II ("Performing") and the photograph of the young Vietnamese girl running from a napalm attack during the Vietnam war ("Public"), the authors argue that photographs can serve to shape national identity and community.

4. Nor are the partially sighted exempt from such visual dynamics. The more than 3.4 million Americans who are not fully sighted or who lack any sight are subject to the visual habits of the dominant culture as they adjust to and are expected, to a large extent, to function according to the ways of seeing that serve to organize the sighted population. Thus, visual regimes impinge on the lives of all individuals, sighted or not, dominant or marginalized, shaping what constitutes viable social action and what constitutes viable avenues to social action.

1. Stronger Hopes: Symbiotic Knots and Social Action

1. Burke is not alone in his concern with humanity's second naturing. Gregory Bateson refers to second naturing as the process of developing *habits*, a sinking of knowledge—"whether of action, perception, or thought"—to "deeper and deeper levels of mind," a phenomenon central to Zen (*Steps to an Ecology of the Mind* 134–35). Quoting Blaise Pascal, Bateson calls this complex layering of consciousness and unconsciousness "reasons of the heart" that are inaccessible to reason but make themselves at home in the discourse of the body. Both second naturing and habits also resonate to Pierre Bourdieu's definition of *habitus*. Derived from the Aristotelian notion of *hexis*, *habitus* offers Bourdieu a means of challenging structuralism and its representations of agents

as the bearers of cultural structure. In Bourdieu's hands, habitus becomes the point at which culture and body meld. Visual habits are one kind of second naturing, one kind of habitus.

2. Images, like any medium, possess what Gunther Kress calls *affordances*: characteristics that lend themselves to one kind of use, one kind of intellectual activity, over another (*Literacy in the New Media Age*). Anne Frances Wysocki, however, points out that humans tend to disregard an artifact's designed intent. So affordances, she claims, are not deterministic; rather, they are negotiated through the mediation of a human interpretant. See as well Johndan Johnson-Eilola.

3. Ann E. Berthoff argues that the looping of imagery and language generates all meaning making; thinking is intrinsically metaphoric. As she explains, we are constantly coping with two forms of abstraction: the first form is our image-making ability, an ability that enables us to stop the stream of life so that we can perceive it and reflect on it. The second form, discursive abstraction, occurs when we name our images by categorizing them and thus organizing our worlds. We interpret our interpretation; we generalize about our primary interpretations. However, no one-to-one correspondence exists between first-order and second-order interpretation. Because no perfect fit occurs, the movement between visual and discursive interpretations is always fresh, always generative, always reciprocal. This generativity serves as the foundation for Berthoff's transformative composition pedagogy.

4. Although I. A. Richards in *The Philosophy of Rhetoric* claims that images are not necessary for metaphors, his efforts to distance metaphors from imagery results in what I see as a misstep: he falls into proper-meaning superstition by erroneously assigning imagery a single, static meaning.

5. I am not the first to make this argument, nor am I the first to recognize the power of metaphor to effect (and to limit) social change, including change that is undesirable from the perspective of the status quo. For example, High Church prelates and politicos during the late seventeenth century sought to render the use of metaphors illegal in the sermons and speeches of radicals, including dissenting clergy. In 1660, Samuel Parker, an official licenser and later bishop of Oxford, argued, "Had we but an Act of Parliament to abridge Preachers the use of fulsome and luscious Metaphors, it might perhaps be an effectual Cure of all our present Distempers," for it is the "gawdy Metaphor" and "lascivious Allegories" that authorize the workings of private, and dissenting, conscience (qtd. in Cable, "Licensing Metaphor" 244). Seventeenth-century literary scholar Lana Cable argues that politicos feared figurative language, especially in the hands of resisters, believing that it would foment intellectual, political, and religious rebellion. Thus, to maintain the desired status quo, these politicos sought to deny the use of image-rich language to the elements of the population who most threatened that status quo. This effort to censor "gawdy Metaphor" highlights the deep-seated belief in the power of metaphor to effect change.

6. W. J. T. Mitchell suggests that the history of the Western world can be plotted according to image-word relationships, indicating, first, that these relationships exist and, second, that they shift historically. Jay David Bolter concurs; he argues that in this digital moment, "[w]ords no longer seem to carry conviction without the reappearance as pictures of imagery that was latent in the words" (260).

7. Sue Hum argues that approaches to difference emphasizing aesthetics habituates a visual habit she calls the "racialized gaze," a way of seeing that privileges superficial

dissimilarities and thus separates students of color so that they cannot and do not find a place for themselves in the dominant culture. (See, as well, the conclusion to the current volume.) Cosmetic multiculturalism, then, functions as eye candy that trivializes the material realities of students of color.

8. Although I list these levels of place separately, they all interact. For instance, possessing a particular kind of body can bar one from some public places and, thus, restrict that individual's right to speak in that place. As the rhetorical strategy from fifth-century B.C.E. Athens illustrates, dropping one's cloak in the agora or Assembly might have been a persuasive rhetorical habit for men, but it certainly excluded women from any public place of speaking because women's bodies did not carry the same persuasive weight. The configuration of one aspect of place implicates other aspects of place.

9. Perhaps this is why Fusco has chosen to protest these same issues via different modes, for instance, the 2002 protest march in Washington, D.C., organized in conjunction with the Women in Black International Art Project and Electronic Disturbance Theater (see chapter 3). The protest integrates a physical march, with a performance-art component, a virtual march through visual chat rooms, a virtual sit-in, and an online petition.

10. Michel Foucault's critique of Jeremy Bentham's Panopticon in *Discipline and Punish* spins out in more detail the intricate threads uniting design of place with the flourishing of a particular visual habit.

11. A similar dynamic by which place coevolves with visual and rhetorical habits occurs in the traditional classroom where desks align vertically and horizontally, occasionally bolted in rows to ensure that students face the teacher's desk, which may even be positioned on a raised dais. Students are caged, held immobile, in a small space; they can be comfortable only facing the front of the classroom. This design hones visual and rhetorical habits resistant to change. When teachers arrange students in a circle, they many times continue to function as if they were sitting in rows. Trained to inhabit a particular place and exercise a particular visual habit there, students act according to that habit when the environment is reordered. Thus, when in a circle, they direct their eyes to the teacher, incline their bodies toward the teacher, and speak to the teacher.

12. King's "Letter from the Birmingham Jail," another jeremiad, also presents an example of the crossover of place and rhetorical habit. Finally, the decision of Malcolm X to critique and reject the jeremiad, which is the focus of Miller's article, also highlights my point, for Malcolm X spoke in places where the audiences consisted exclusively of African Americans. He and King configured different public spheres and different responsive audiences, which affected the strategies they deployed.

13. Welch associates the shrinking public sphere with issues of class, a connection that Linda Brodkey also emphasizes in "Writing in Designated Areas," arguing that space organizes itself along the fault lines of class.

2. A Knot of Silence: Spectacle, Rhetorical Compliance, and the Struggle for Agency

1. The silence I explore here is what Krista Ratcliffe calls "dysfunctional silence," one that is imposed rather than voluntarily pursued. The generativity of silence as well as its rhetorical power I explore in chapter 3.

2. Even the growing phenomenon of interactive television programs, programs where viewers assess performances by calling in or text messaging, such as *American Idol* or *Dancing with the Stars*, or educational programming akin to *Sesame Street* and

Zoom, is subject to the same addictive dynamic as noninteractive programs. The formal features of all televised images solicit the attention without cuing critical perception.

3. The Situationist Internationale was established in the mid-1950s and disbanded in 1972. It consisted of critics of modern society who evolved new methods of social action, methods that contributed significantly to the 1968 May revolt in France. Guy Debord was a central figure in the movement, defining its precepts and offering strategies for enacting those precepts. His work had considerable influence on Jean Baudrillard and Jean-François Lyotard.

4. The first French edition of *Society* was published in 1967. It was not translated into English until 1992. *Comments on Society of the Spectacle*, published in 1988, extends Debord's agenda.

5. Kevin Michael DeLuca points out definitions for the term *image event* that differ significantly from Debord's, especially Debord's emphasis on the passivity fostered by image events. DeLuca, in fact, explores image events as powerful and effective rhetorical appeals. I address this aspect of image in chapter 3.

6. The impact of YouTube and similar Web sites on spectacle has yet to be assessed. At first glance, the egalitarian YouTube seems to challenge spectacle by distributing expertise and celebrating difference in a chaotic outpouring. In addition, the rise of guerrilla television in the mid-1960s defied the "conditioning" of spectacle by celebrating the creative contributions of ordinary people. As Deidre Boyle explains, guerrilla television, so named in a manifesto by Michael Shamberg, aimed to "decentralize" television by making available "narrowcast" videos created "by and for people" (xi–xii).

7. Following a widely televised meeting with the CHA director and a gymnasium full of community protestors, Sadie Evans withdrew from the community action, explaining to Obama that, after the television exposure, her husband felt she should focus her time and attention on their family.

8. Obama first hears the phrase "audacity of hope" in a sermon by Reverend Jeremiah Wright at Trinity United Church of Christ. This phrase becomes the title and the core to his 2004 Democratic Convention Keynote Address and *The Audacity of Hope: Thoughts on Reclaiming the American Dream*, in which he expands on the issues introduced in that speech.

9. See Kevin Maness, "Teaching Media-Savvy Students about Popular Media," for evidence of a similar assumption.

10. The three strategies creating a monologic classroom also resemble the classroom praxis associated with current-traditional rhetoric, a methodology that Sharon Crowley claims remained dominant in twentieth-century composition classrooms.

11. Kiefer is less sanguine, concluding her essay with a call to "ask ourselves, finally, whether we should continue to teach writing through an instructional mode that seems so much at odds with our full range of goals for writing instruction" (151).

12. For example, *Strategies for Teaching First-Year Composition* has an entire chapter devoted to various ways of shaping writing assignments. The fourth edition of *The Writing Teachers Sourcebook* similarly devotes a chapter on writing assignments, including four professional essays that while approaching the task from different angles jointly and individually highlight the value of the endeavor. Finally, Traci Gardner's *Designing Writing Assignments* explores in depth the importance of well-crafted writing prompts.

13. Kiefer also associates disengaged writing with students' market model of education. Because many perceive education as a commodity that they consume in "dispos-

able units of education (credits)," they bring to the classroom, particularly the online classroom, pragmatic goals that reduce writing assignments to get it, get it done, get it graded (147–48). Stroupe ("Making Distance Presence") connects disengaged writing with prompts that ineffectively layer print-based genres onto an online environment.

3. A Knot of Bodies: Visual Animation and Corporeal Rhetoric in Empathic Social Action

1. Artist activist Coco Fusco (see chapter 1) organized the march in conjunction with the Electronic Disturbance Theater (see chapter 4). Her play, *The Incredible Disappearing Woman*, was inspired by and dedicated to these lost and murdered women. For the march, Fusco sent out a call inviting other artist-activists to suggest alternative modes of social action, both real world and virtual world (Jenik, "Re: 2002 DC March"). An online petition and a virtual sit-in organized by the Electronic Disturbance Theater supported the street action with ten thousand virtual participants (*Electronic Civil Disobedience*).

2. This vulnerability functions in conjunction with two other qualities: an assessment of the nontrivial quality of another's dilemma and an assessment of the individual's or group's degree of responsibility for the dilemma.

3. See Fleckenstein, "Testifying" for an exploration of the interinanimation of visual habit, language, and image.

4. For instance, N. Katherine Hayles describes the changes in proprioception—our sense of our bodies in space and time—that occur when we work with computers on a daily basis. As Hayles describes, "an experienced computer user feels proprioceptive coherence with the keyboard, experiencing the screen surface as a space into which her subjectivity can flow" ("Condition of Virtuality" 88). Because of tactile and kinesthetic feedback loops, the computer user feels "physically attached" to the onscreen page, changing the patterns of body-text interactions. The act of coordinating the physical body with the virtual page instills new ways of perceiving—and being in—the world. Life on the screen permeates life in front of the screen, something that Sherry Turkle points out in her landmark study of identity and digital worlds. In the decade-plus since the publication of Turkle's *Life on the Screen* in 1995, numerous accounts and descriptions of the interface between screen life and real life have surfaced, from the replication of racist behavior in online chat rooms to the use of avatars to heal psychological and physiological wounds. Participation in screen life (or lives), characterized by highly interactive images and textual experiences that blur virtual life and real life, predisposes the user to develop the visual habit of animation. However, see Fusco for a divergent view (*Bodies*).

5. Experiences with interactive imagery are not limited to a small fraction of the population, to an isolated community of Internet geeks, hackers, and netheads. Rather, frequent and extended play with interactive imagery is becoming the norm, not the exception, in a variety of ways among many segments of the population, but especially among the three-to-seventeen-year-old age group, where Internet use has increased from 22 percent in 1997 to 42 percent in 2003 ("Home Computer Access"). Those interactive experiences run the gamut from online role-playing games where users create and control a graphic-user interface and navigate a reality while sitting in front of a computer in real time inhabiting a blood-and-bone body to social-networking sites such as MySpace and Facebook where users both create their own interactive sites and

browse those created by others. According to a Pew Internet report, the popularity of such sites has exploded to the extent that tens of millions of online users, including a whopping 55 percent of all online teens between twelve to seventeen, engage in online social networking ("Social").

6. See Desktop Theater's Web site, http://www.desktoptheater.org, for images, scripts, and videos of performances.

7. While Fishman and Lunsford connect performing literacies with new media, they theorize their approach to performance with work in performance studies, which, they explain, emerged as a formal discipline in the 1950s ("Performing Writing" 227) and predates the evolution of digital interactivity. Performance studies "has much to contribute to composition studies," they argue, including insights into such shared concerns as the "relationships between language and the body, individuals and communities, and social norms and forms of resistance" (227). I would argue that the groundswell from which new media emerged involves not only the rise of performance studies but also the rise of cybernetics and interactivity. See N. Katherine Hayles, *How We Became Posthuman: Virtual Bodies in Cybernetics, Literature, and Informatics.*

8. Fishman and Lunsford introduced their concept of performing literacy at the 2005 Conference on College Composition and Communication through a panel presentation during which two Stanford undergraduates, Mark Otuteye and Beth McGregor, offered vivid examples. The panel participants later transformed their papers into an article, published in *College Composition and Communication*, which was accompanied by a video of the students' performances through "*CCC* Online Archive," http://inventio.us/ ccc/2005/12/index.html. Thus, in person, in print, and in pictures, Otuteye and McGregor exemplify the interface between visual animation and literacy.

9. See Nussbaum as well for the differences between definitions of empathy and compassion and for her rationale for choosing compassion. See Fleckenstein, "Once More with Feeling," for a rationale for choosing empathy.

10. Hoffman's concepts of self and other focus are heavily visual and kinesthetic; these qualities manifest depending on our ability to visualize another's situation and place ourselves imaginatively within that situation. Others working with empathy, however, have emphasized the importance of listening. For instance, Susan McLeod's account of empathy in the classroom, which draws on the work of Carl Rogers, highlights the value of teachers' careful listening. Kia Richmond similarly underscores the need for careful listening, outlining an ethical framework for such empathic listening. Dale Jacobs, concerned with establishing affective ties in the classroom advocates "deep listening," which he relates to Krista Ratcliffe's rhetorical listening.

11. I am not the first to posit a connection between the writing classroom and peaceful persuasion. Mary Rose O'Reilley in *The Peaceable Classroom* highlights a similar connection, although her starting point is the linkage between pedagogy and violence. Inspired by Ihab Hassan's question, "Is it possible to teach English so that people stop killing one another?" O'Reilley contends that the pedagogy we enact within classrooms can nurture peaceful means of living in the world and peaceful means of acting for a change. I similarly believe that our literacy pedagogy, especially one organized by visual animation and corporeal rhetoric, has the potential to foster peaceful living and peaceful changing.

12. The cutoff age for participants was twenty (18).

13. Imaginal interactions have an important mental element, Worthman contends,

resonating to Beth McGregor's inner drama in her writing process. Drawing on Susan Aylwin's work in *Structures in Thought and Feeling,* Worthman explains that imaginal interactions are enacted in both exterior and interior worlds. Such performances, I would argue, habituate a predisposition for visual animation and corporeal rhetoric.

14. Such an agenda resonates with a similar one Fishman and Lunsford articulate. In asking how teachers might "incorporate performance into our classrooms and our pedagogies," they, like Shipka, urge greater attention to delivery. "It is as though, if we picture the rhetorical triangle among sender, receiver, and message, our eyes should no longer rest on any one role, but should instead focus on the lines that connect them, lines that seem to shimmer and hum with the dynamism of those interrelationships" (247).

15. Noting Mulvey's reliance on the male/female binary in "Visual Pleasure and Narrative Cinema," Jane Gaines argues for a more nuanced sense of spectatorship, pointing out that "Male/female is a powerful, but sometimes blinding construct" (294). Unassimilated into the binary are differences arising out of sexual orientation and race, a point bell hooks makes concerning women of color. I address this more fully in my conclusion.

16. Through objectification, women's bodies become not just a consumable resource but also what Janie Leatherman calls a "loot-able resource" (55). She emphasizes the importance of patriarchal ideologies and perception in wartime violence aimed at women: "At the crux of the problem are patriarchal systems of privilege that construct violence against women as permissible, along with other forms of violence" (57). She suggests that sexual violence against women emerges from a belief system "where the female body is seen as a 'territory' to be owned and controlled by the male" (Manuela Colombini qtd. in Leatherman 57). Thus, women's bodies become tools of war rather than signs of peace because they are perceived as objects without feelings, identities, or intrinsic worth.

17. An additional layer of invisibility occurs when sexism and racism interweave. Repeatedly, hooks has argued in a range of venues that "racism and sexism are interlocking systems of domination which uphold and sustain one another" (*Yearning* 59). Infused with sexist ideologies, scopophilia intertwines with racial invisibility to render women of color doubly invisible, first through racism and then through sexism. Subject to the Black male gaze "that had a different scope from that of the black female," the bodies of women of color become objects to dominate and use, not bodies to respond to responsibly and empathically ("Oppositional Gaze" 310). Thus, women of color disappear as bodies and as bodies warranting answerability.

4. A Knot of Contradictions: Antinomy and Digressive Rhetoric in Subversive Social Action

1. Composition scholars are just beginning to explore audio imagery and its contribution to meaning, both alone and in conjunction with images. See, especially, Heidi McKee, who, through an analysis of Flash poetry, begins the process of creating a taxonomy for sound. See also Fleckenstein, "Words Made Flesh," which makes the argument that visual imagery is multisensual, yielding a polymorphic rather than merely a visual literacy.

2. See, also, Ann E. Berthoff, *Sense of Learning,* on seeing and composing.

3. She notes as well the magic of visual art where in high school she would escape to art class. In that world, hooks remembers, she and her fellow escapees could, momentarily, be "whatever we wanted to be" (*Art on My Mind* 1).

4. In chapter 3 of *Pedagogy of the Oppressed*, Paulo Freire describes the process of conscientization in which a team enters a village, conducts field work on the life of the village by interacting with community members, and then returns with an array of artifacts—usually photos and sketches—that serve as the subject of decoding: discussions in which the villagers experience the paradox—the contradiction between—their beliefs about reality and their experiences of reality. I would argue that this is an unknowing effort to develop among the villagers the habit of antinomy.

5. Scholars situate themselves variously to the reciprocity of imagery and narrative. For instance, on the one hand, Fleckenstein argues that image and narrative are mutually dependent ("Image, Word, and Narrative Epistemology"). On the other hand, Gunther Kress argues that imagery disrupts narrative.

6. The differences between imagery and word as well as their inextricability from each other are explored in and central to Fleckenstein's *Embodied Literacies* and "Body-signs."

7. Craig Stroupe argues that this visual-verbal contradiction within digital communication results in image illuminating rather than illustrating language. Images and words are and are not the same; images and words cannot exist without being both complementary and contradictory simultaneously ("Visualizing English").

8. While Cotterill alludes to seventeenth-century visual culture, she does not systematically relate the evolution and use of *digressio* in the seventeenth century to dominant visual habits.

9. Cyberactivism involves the use of digital technologies to support political action in the real world (RW) and hacktivism involves the use of digital technologies to support political action in the virtual world. Cyberactivism is best exemplified by the 1994 Zapatista insurrection in southern Mexico, which, to add to the confusion of terminology, Lester Faigley labels hacktivism, but which is, in fact, an early form of transgressive cyberactivism. The *Ejercito Zapatista de la Liberacion Nacional* (EZLN)—the Zapatistas—rebelled against an unresponsive Mexican government by occupying seven towns in Chiapas, a southern poverty-stricken Mexican province with a large population of indigenous Mayans. Particularly noteworthy about this military action was the Zapatistas' adroit use of the Internet and other modern media to publicize their military action. Coterminous with the armed rebellion, the Zapatistas flooded the media with manifestos, reports, and other communiqués concerning the rebellion. They used fax machines to contact major news outlets and consulates, garnering and directing the spin of international news coverage. The initial armed forays in the state of Chiapas, as well as the media blitz via electronic technologies, were systematically followed up with canny use of online technologies, from Web sites with timely postings to bulletin boards to email listservs (Swindle).

In short, cyberactivism uses the Internet as a tool for disseminating information to a wide audience through different kinds of discourse. Without a doubt, the Zapatista-led cyber rebellion constitutes what Stephen Wray calls a transgression or paradigmatic shift in online activism. Prior to the Zapatista media action, the Internet was perceived (and used) as a medium of communication, a way to connect politically attuned individuals via such listservs as PeaceNet. However, with the Zapatista media action, the Internet infrastructure became both a medium for communication and a site for action. Barack Obama's highly effective use of the Internet during his 2008 presidential campaign reflects the growing importance of cyberactivism in politics. As Sarah Lai Stirland points out, Obama's canny use of Web-based technologies, from Web site to social networking, "proved key to his winning the presidency." Beyond organizing phone-banking events and generating community activities, the Obama campaign shattered fund-raising records through its "Web savviness," receiving a "seemingly inexhaustible" influx of cash through small donations contributed over the Internet. Internet Fund-raising. As Micah Sifry, cofounder of *TechPresident.com*, noted, Obama used the affordances of the Internet almost to perfection, setting new benchmarks for both the Democratic and Republican parties.

10. Samuel carefully distinguishes hacktivism from cracktivism, a distinction important to my argument concerning the ends-means reciprocity necessary in compassionate social action. Unlike hacktivism, cracktivism achieves its political goals without consideration of the impact of its tools. In a carefully nuanced argument, Samuel claims that hacktivism derives from two political cultures: the cracktivist culture and the postmodern left. She then subdivides these two cultures into outlaw and transgressive orientations. Outlaw cracktivism gives rise to the work of political crackers who possess an essentially outlaw attitude, which leads them to act individually, anonymously, and with reduced accountability. While transgressive cracking leads to political cracking, which includes the creation and distribution of political coding designed to disrupt firewalls in countries such as China where access to the Internet is carefully controlled, it slips easily from social action to vandalism, Samuel argues (36).

Hacktivism also falls into outlaw and transgressive categories. Guertin associates outlaw hacktivism with cyberterrorism: the deliberate destruction of online venues or the theft and distribution of highly sensitive information throughout the real world. The aim of cyberterrorism is harm, both in the virtual world and the real world. Guertin notes that hacktivism "should not be confused with its adolescent and illegal cousins, cracktivism—code cracking, vandalism, data blockades (DDOs) and the loss of digital data—or cyberterrorism—acts and agents of wanton destruction including worms and viruses." However, pomo-left hacktivism consists of transgressive hacktivists whose aims and strategies are deliberately and consciously nonviolent, constituting a sharp contrast to the work of cracktivism. See Dorothy Denning for an alternative view, for she categorizes all hacktivism, regardless of style, as a form of cyberterrorism.

11. The limited work on hacktivism has focused on the politically liberal postmodern left. But the playbook, which is Samuel's term for hacktivists' strategies, is a means of social action that is available to any group seeking to fragment a coherent reality. Thus, Holocaust deniers have hacked into the Holocaust Web sites. Pro-Israeli hackers have defaced pro-Palestinian Web sites, while pro-Palestinian hackers have responded in kind. While this mode of social action is available to any group, the most organized practitioners of hacktivism, such as EDT and Electronic Civil Disobedience, tend to support liberal causes.

12. Suck sites are less subtle in their contradictions. Suck sites operate on the same logic but contain in their URL the domain name attached to "sucks" so that anyone typing in the domain name into a search engine will access both the original site and the suck site.

13. See Fleckenstein, "Whose Writing?" for an analysis of the participatory/interactive quality of Abrahams's work.

14. The nature of the course invited such personal writing. Writing-program policy mandated that the first-semester composition course focus on writing that drew on students' personal experiences in the world.

15. I explore more fully in my conclusion specific classroom practices that can encourage transformation through bricolage, paradox, and agenic invention.

Conclusion: The Possibility of Hope

1. I have revised a second course, an upper-division undergraduate elective in composition theory, in accordance with a knot of bodies. Called "*Placida Persuasio*," the class examines options for nonviolent rhetoric using the interface of animation, corporeal rhetoric, and lively places as a lens. The course currently consists of three main components: case studies in historical and present-day examples of peaceful persuasion; experimentation with secular contemplative practices designed to nurture a "peaceful mind" (walking meditation, silence, *Metta bhavana*, deep listening, and *lectio divina*); and student-developed public forums on campus or within the local community aimed to foster nonadversarial deliberative dialogue on an advocacy issue of their choice (see William N. Isaacs, *Dialogue and the Art of Thinking Together*).

2. To help them get started, I provide information about university and community organizations. Then, we spend time in class generating a list by searching the Internet, including MySpace, using the string "social action," subsequently narrowing down "social action" to specific issues, methods, and venues; that is, social action, social action protesting violence against women, nonviolent social action protesting violence against women, and nonviolent social action protesting violence against women in Tallahassee, Florida.

Works Cited

"About 826." *826 National*. 30 Apr. 2008 <http://www.826valencia.org/about/>.

"About WIB." *Women in Black: For Justice. Against War*. 9 Sept. 2006 <http://www.womeninblack.org/about.html>.

Abrahams, Annie. "karaoke." *being alive*. 6 March 2007 <http://www.bram.org/karaoke/karaoke.htm>.

"Action August 14, 2002 on Women Murdered in Ciudad Juarez: On the Streets and On-line." *Electronic Civil Disobedience*. 23 Feb. 2007 <http://www.thing.net/~rdom/ecd/JuarezCall.html>.

Adorno, Theodor W. *The Culture Industry: Selected Essays on Mass Culture*. Ed. J. M. Bernstein. New York: Routledge, 2001.

Alcoff, Linda Martín. "Toward a Phenomenology of Racial Embodiment." *Race*. Ed. Robert Bernasconi. Malden, MA: Blackwell, 2001. 267–83.

"Animation." Def. *Oxford English Dictionary*. Online. 6 May 2007.

"Antimony." Def. *Oxford English Dictionary*. Online. 12 Feb. 2007.

Anzaldúa, Gloria. *Borderlands/LaFrontera: The New Mestiza*. San Francisco: Aunt Lute, 1987.

———. "Speaking in Tongues: A Letter to Third World Women Writers." *This Bridge Called My Back: Writings by Radical Women of Color*. Ed. Cherrie Moraga and Gloria Anzaldúa. New York: Kitchen Table, 1981. 165–74.

Atwood, Margaret. "Spelling." *True Stories*. Toronto: Oxford UP, 1981. 13. *The Norton Anthology of Literature by Women: The Tradition in English*. Ed. Sandra M. Gilbert and Susan Gubar. New York: Norton, 1985. 1298–99.

Aylwin, Susan. *Structure in Thought and Feeling*. London: Methuen, 1985.

Barthes, Roland. *Mythologies*. Trans. Annette Lavers. New York: Hill, 1972.

Bateson, Gregory. *Mind and Nature: A Necessary Unity*. Cresskill, NJ: Hampton, 2002.

———. *Steps to an Ecology of the Mind. Collected Essays in Anthropology, Psychiatry, Evolution, and Epistemology*. 1972. Northvale, NJ: Aronson, 1987.

Bawarshi, Anis. *Genre and the Invention of the Writer: Reconsidering the Place of Invention in Composition*. Logan: Utah State UP, 2003.

Berger, John. *Ways of Seeing*. London: BBC, 1972.

Berlin, James. *Rhetoric and Reality: Writing Instruction in American Colleges, 1900–1985*. Carbondale: Southern Illinois UP, 1987.

Berman, Morris. *Coming to Our Senses: Body and Spirit in the Hidden History of the West*. New York: Simon, 1989.

Bernasconi, Robert. "The Invisibility of Racial Minorities." *Race*. Ed. Bernasconi. Malden, MA: Blackwell, 2001. 284–99.

Berthoff, Ann E. *Sense of Learning*. Portsmouth, NH: Heinemann, 1990.

Bitzer, Lloyd. "The Rhetorical Situation." *Philosophy and Rhetoric* 1 (1968): 1–14.

Blade Runner. Dir. Ridley Scott. Warner Brothers Studio, 1982.

Blitefield, Jerry. "Kairos and the Rhetorical Place." *Professing Rhetoric: Selected Papers from the 2000 Rhetoric Society of America Conference*. Ed. Frederick J. Antczak, Cinda Coggins, and Geoffrey D. Klinger. Mahwah, NJ: Erlbaum, 2002. 69–76.

Bolles, Edmund Blair. *A Second Way of Knowing: The Riddle of Human Perception*. New York: Prentice, 1991.

Bolter, Jay David. "Ekphrasis, Virtual Reality, and the Future of Writing." *The Future of the Book*. Ed. Geoffrey Nunberg. Berkeley: U of California P, 1996. 253–72.

Bourdieu, Pierre. *Outline of a Theory of Practice*. Trans. Richard Nice. Cambridge: Cambridge UP, 1977.

Boyle, Deirdre. *Subject to Change: Guerrilla Television Revisited*. New York: Oxford UP, 1996.

Britton, James. "Spectator Role and the Beginning of Writing." *Prospect and Retrospect: Selected Essays of James Britton*. Ed. Gordon M. Pradl. Montclair, NJ: Boynton-Cook, 1982. 46–67.

Brodkey, Linda. "Writing Permitted in Designated Areas Only." *Writing Permitted in Designated Areas Only*. Minneapolis: U of Minnesota P, 1996. 130–49.

Brummett, Barry S. *Rhetorical Dimensions of Popular Culture*. Tuscaloosa: U of Alabama P, 1991.

Burke, Kenneth. *Attitudes toward History*. Boston: Beacon, 1937.

———. *A Grammar of Motives*. Berkeley: U of California P, 1945.

———. *Language as Symbolic Action: Essays on Life, Literature, and Method*. Berkeley: U of California P, 1966.

———. *Permanence and Change: An Anatomy of Purpose*. Indianapolis, IN: Bobbs-Merrill, 1965.

———. *A Rhetoric of Motives*. Berkeley: U of California P, 1969.

Cable, Lana. "Licensing Metaphor: Parker, Marvell, and the Debate over Conscience." *Books and Readers in Early Modern England*. Ed. Jennifer Andersen and Elizabeth Sauer. Philadelphia: U of Pennsylvania P, 2002. 243–60.

Campbell, Karlyn Kohrs. "Agency: Promiscuous and Protean." *Alliance of Rhetoric Societies Conference*. May 2003. Evanston, IL. 14 December 2004. <http://www.rhetoricalliance.org/>.

Canter, H. V. "Digressions in the Orations of Cicero." *American Journal of Philology* 52 (1931): 351–61.

Certeau, Michel de. *The Practice of Everyday Life*. Trans. Steven Rendall. Berkeley: U of California P, 1984.

Cicero. "*Pro Archia*" [In Defense of Archia]." *Selected Works of Cicero*. Roslyn, NY: Black, 1948. 142–56.

Class Dismissed: How TV Frames the Working Class. Dir. Loretta Alper. Written and coproduced by Alper and Pepi Leistyna. Media Education Foundation, 2007.

Cockburn, Cynthia. "Women in Black, Gulf Coast, Florida: Letting Silence Speak." File: PROFILEGulfCoast211204.doc, Research profile 5, Florida: WiB—Letting Silence Speak. *notowar: Cynthia Cockburn's Weblog*. 19 Sept. 2005 <http://www.cynthiacockburn.org/Floridablog.pdf>.

———. "Why Feminist Anti-Militarism?" 1 Mar. 2003. *Women in Black UK*. 19 Sept. 2005 <http://www.womeninblack.org.uk/Feminist%20Antimilitarism.htm>.

Cooper, Marilyn. From the Editor. *College Composition and Communication* 52 (2000): 185–87.

Cooper, Marilyn M., and Michael Holzman. *Writing as Social Action*. Portsmouth, NH: Boynton/Cook, 1989.

Corder, Jim. "Argument as Emergence, Rhetoric as Love." *Rhetoric Review* 4 (1985): 16–32.

Cotterill, Anne. *Digressive Voices in Early Modern Literature*. Oxford: Oxford UP, 2004.

Crowley, Sharon. *The Methodical Memory: Invention in Current-Traditional Rhetoric*. Carbondale: Southern Illinois UP, 1990.

Crusius, Timothy W. *Kenneth Burke and the Conversation after Philosophy*. Carbondale: Southern Illinois UP, 1999.

Cushman, Ellen. "The Public Intellectual, Service Learning, and Activist Research." *College English* 61 (1999): 328–36.

Dalton, Jennifer. "Look at Me: Self-Portrait Photography after Cindy Sherman." *PAJ: A Journal of Performance and Art* 22.3 (2000): 47–56.

Davidson, James N. *Courtesans and Fishcakes: The Consuming Passions of Classical Athens*. New York: Harper, 1999.

Debord, Guy. *Comments on the Society of the Spectacle*. 1988. Trans. Malcolm Imrie. London: Verso, 1998.

———. "Report on the Construction of Situations and on the International Situationist Tendency's Conditions of Organization and Action." *Situationist International Anthology*. Ed. and trans. Ken Knabb. Berkeley, CA: Bureau of Public Secrets, 1996.

———. *The Society of the Spectacle*. 1967. Trans. Donald Nicholson-Smith. New York: Zone, 1995.

Deemer, Charles. "English Composition as a Happening." *College English* 29 (1967): 121–26.

DeLuca, Kevin Michael. *Image Politics: The New Rhetoric of Environmental Activism*. New York: Guilford, 1999.

Denning, Dorothy E. "Activism, Hacktivism, and Cyberterrorism: The Internet as a Tool for Influencing Foreign Policy." Arquilla and Ronfeldt 239–88.

DeStigter, Todd. "Public Displays of Affection: Political Community through Critical Empathy." *Research in the Teaching of English* 33 (1999): 235–44.

———. *Reflections of a Citizen-Teacher: Literacy, Democracy, and the Forgotten Students of Addison High*. Urbana, IL: NCTE, 2001.

———. "The *Tesoros* Literacy Project: An Experiment in Democratic Communities." *Research in the Teaching of English* 32 (1998): 10–42.

Dick, Philip K. *Do Androids Dream of Electric Sheep?* New York: Ballantine, 1968.

Drucker, Johanna. "Who's Afraid of Visual Culture?" *Art Journal* 58.4 (1999): 37–47.

Dyson, Anne Haas. "Coach Bombay's Kids Learn to Write: Children's Appropriation of Media Material for School Literacy." *Research in the Teaching of English* 33 (1999): 367–402.

Ebert, Teresa. *Ludic Feminism and After: Postmodernism, Desire, and Labor in Late Capitalism*. Ann Arbor: U of Michigan P, 1996.

Eggers, Dave. *A Heartbreaking Work of Staggering Genius*. New York: Simon, 2000.

Electronic Civil Disobedience. 23 Feb. 2007 <http://www.thing.net/~rdom/ecd/ecd. html>.

Erhlich, Paul R. "CoEvolution and the Biology of Communities." *Ten Years of* CoEvolution Quarterly: *News That Stayed News 1974-1984.* Ed. Art Kleiner and Stewart Brand. San Francisco: North Point, 1986. 3-9.

Estren, Mark James. *A History of Underground Comics.* San Francisco: Straight Arrow, 1974.

Evans, Jessica. Introduction to part 1. *Visual Culture: The Reader.* Ed. Evans and Stuart Hall. London: Sage, 1999. 11-20.

Ewen, Stuart. *All Consuming Images: The Politics of Style in Contemporary Culture.* San Francisco: Harper, 1990.

Faigley, Lester. "Understanding Popular Digital Literacies: Metaphors for the Internet." *Popular Literacy: Studies in Cultural Practices and Poetics.* Ed. John Trimbur. Pittsburgh, PA: U of Pittsburgh P, 2001. 248-63.

Finnegan, C. A. "Recognizing Lincoln: Image Vernaculars in Nineteenth-Century Visual Culture." *Rhetoric & Public Affairs* 8 (2005): 31-58.

Fishman, Jenn, Andrea Lunsford, Beth McGregor, and Mark Otuteye. "Performing Writing, Performing Literacy." *College Composition and Communication* 57.2 (2005): 224-52. <http://inventio.us/ccc/2005/12/index.html>.

Fleckenstein, Kristie S. "Bodysigns: A Biorhetoric for Changes." *JAC* 21 (2002): 761-90.

———. *Embodied Literacies: Imageword and a Poetics of Teaching.* Carbondale: Southern Illinois UP, 2003.

———. "Image, Word, and Narrative Epistemology." *College English* 58 (1996): 914-33.

———. "Once More with Feeling: Empathy in Deliberative Discourse." *JAC* 27 (2007): 701-16.

———. "Testifying: Seeing and Saying in World Making." Fleckenstein, Hum, and Calendrillo 3-30.

———. "Who's Writing? Aristotelian *Ethos* and the Author Position in Digital Poetics." *Kairos: Rhetoric, Technology, Pedagogy* 11.3 (May 2007). 8 Apr. 2008 <http://kairos. technorhetoric.net/11.3/topoi/fleckenstein/index.html>.

———. "Words Made Flesh: Fusing Image and Language in a Polymorphic Literacy." *College English* 66 (2004): 612-31.

———. "Writing Bodies: Somatic Mind in Composition Studies." *College English* 61 (1999): 281-306.

Fleckenstein, Kristie S., Sue Hum, and Linda Calendrillo, eds. *Ways of Seeing, Ways of Speaking: The Integration of Rhetoric and Vision in Constructing the Real.* West Lafayette, IN: Parlor, 2007.

Foucault, Michel. *The Birth of the Clinic: An Archaeology of Medical Perception.* Trans. A. M. Sheridan Smith. New York: Vintage, 1994.

———. *Discipline and Punish: The Birth of the Prison.* Trans. Alan Sheridan. New York: Vintage, 1979.

Fox, Roy F. *MediaSpeak: Three American Voices.* Westport, CT: Praeger, 2001.

Freedberg, David. *The Power of Images: Studies in the History and Theory of Response.* Chicago: U of Chicago P, 2001.

Freedman, Sarah Warshauer, and Arnetha F. Ball. "Ideological Becoming: Bakhtinian Concepts to Guide the Study of Language, Literacy, and Learning." *Bakhtinian Perspectives on Language, Literacy, and Learning.* Cambridge: Cambridge UP, 2004. 3-33.

Freire, Paulo. *Pedagogy of the Oppressed*. Trans. Myra Bergman Ramos. New York: Continuum, 1985.

Fulkerson, Richard. "Four Philosophies of Composition." *College Composition and Communication* 30 (1979): 343–48.

Fusco, Coco. *The Bodies That Were Not Ours*. London: Routledge, 2001.

———. "In Conversation: Coco Fusco and John Akomfrah." *Iniva: Institute of International Visual Arts*. 21 July 2007 <http://www.iniva.org/library/archive/people/f/fusco_coco/gallery/coco_fusco_in_discussion_with_john_akomfrah>.

———. "The Incredible Disappearing Woman." Forums. *Hemispheric Institute of Performance and Politics*. 17 July 2007 <http://hemi.nyu.edu/eng/newsletter/issue6/pages/idw.shtml>.

———. "The Incredible Disappearing Woman." Unpublished ms. 2003.

Gaines, Jane. "White Privilege and Looking Relations: Race and Gender in Feminist Film Theory." *Feminist Film Theory: A Reader*. Ed. Sue Thornham. Edinburgh, UK: Edinburgh UP, 1999. 293–306.

Galtung, Johan. "Cultural Violence." *Journal of Peace Research* 27 (1990): 291–305.

Gandhi, Mahatma. *All Men Are Brothers: Life and Thoughts of Mahatma Gandhi as Told in His Own Words*. New York: Columbia UP, 1958.

Gardner, Andrew. "Introduction: Social Agency, Power, and Being Human." *Agency Uncovered: Archaeological Perspectives on Social Agency, Power, and Being Human*. Ed. Andrew Gardner. London: U College London P, 2004. 1–15.

Gardner, Traci. *Designing Writing Assignments*. Urbana, IL: NCTE, 2008.

Garoian, Charles R. *Performing Pedagogy: Towards an Art of Politics*. Albany: State U of New York P, 1999.

Geisler, Cheryl. "How Ought We to Understand the Concept of Rhetorical Agency? Report from the ARS." *Rhetoric Society Quarterly* 34 (2004): 9–17.

George, Diana. "Changing the Face of Poverty: Nonprofits and the Problem of Representation." *Popular Literacy: Studies in Cultural Practices and Poetics*. Ed. John Trimbur. Pittsburgh, PA: U of Pittsburgh P, 2001. 209–28.

———. "From Analysis to Design: Visual Communication in the Teaching of Writing." *College Composition and Communication* 54 (2002): 11–39.

Goldhill, Simon. "Refracting Classical Vision: Changing Cultures of Views." *Vision in Context: Historical and Contemporary Perspectives on Sight*. Ed. Teresa Brennan and Martin Jay. New York: Routledge, 1996. 17–28.

Gombrich, E. H. *Art and Illusion: A Study in the Psychology of Pictorial Representation*. Boston: Phaidon, 2004.

Gorsevski, Ellen. *Peaceful Persuasion*. Albany: State U of New York P, 2004.

Gramsci, Antonio. *Prison Notebooks*. New York: Columbia UP, 1992.

Guertin, Carolyn. "From Cyborgs to Hacktivists: Postfeminist Disobedience and Virtual Communities." 27 Jan. 2005. *Electronic Book Review*. 15 Dec. 2007 <http://www.electronicbookreview.com/thread/writingpostfeminism/concurrent>.

Haraway, Donna J. *How Like a Leaf: An Interview with Thyrza Nichols Goodeve*. New York: Routledge, 2000.

———. *Simians, Cyborgs, and Women: The Reinvention of Nature*. New York: Routledge, 1991.

Hariman, Robert, and John Louis Lucaites. "Performing Civic Identity: The Iconic Photograph of the Flag Raising on Iwo Jima." *Quarterly Journal of Speech* 88 (2002): 363–92.

———. "Public Identity and Collective Memory in U.S. Iconic Photography: The Image of 'Accidental Napalm.'" *Critical Studies in Media Communication* 20 (2003): 35–66.

Harvey, David. *Spaces of Hope*. Berkeley: U of California P, 2000.

Hastings, Tom H. Foreword. *Peaceful Persuasion*. By Ellen W. Gorsevski. Albany: State U of New York P, 2004. xvii–xxiv.

Hauser, Gerard A. *Introduction to Rhetorical Theory*. Long Grove, IL: Waveland, 1986.

Hayles, N. Katherine. "The Condition of Virtuality." *The Digital Dialectic: New Essays on New Media*. Ed. Peter Lunenfeld. Cambridge: MIT P, 2000. 68–95.

———. *How We Became Post-Human: Virtual Bodies in Cybernetics, Literature, and Informatics*. Chicago: U of Chicago P, 1999.

———. "The Materiality of Informatics." *Configurations* 1 (1992): 147–70.

Hebdige, Dick. *Subculture: The Meaning of Style*. New York: Routledge, 1981.

Herr, Norman. "Television & Health." Sourcebook. *Teaching Science*. 14 Mar. 2007 <http://www.csun.edu/science/health/docs/tv&health.html>.

Herrick, James A. *The History and Theory of Rhetoric: An Introduction*. 3rd ed. Boston: Pearson, 2005.

Hesford, Wendy S. "*Kairos* and the Geopolitical Rhetorics of Global Sex Work and Video Advocacy." Hesford and Kozol, *Just Advocacy?* 146–72.

Hesford, Wendy S., and Wendy Kozol. Introduction. Hesford and Kozol 1–29.

———, eds. *Just Advocacy? Women's Human Rights, Transnational Feminisms, and the Politics of Representation*. New Brunswick, NJ: Rutgers UP, 2005.

Hillocks, George. *Research on Written Composition*. Urbana, IL: NCTE, 1986.

Hocks, Mary E. "Understanding Visual Rhetoric in Digital Writing Environments." *College Composition and Communication* 54 (2003): 629–56.

Hoffman, Martin L. "Empathy and Prosocial Activism." *Social and Moral Values: Individual and Societal Perspectives*. Ed. Nancy Eisenberg, Janusz Reykowski, and Ervin Staub. Hillsdale, NJ: Erlbaum, 1989. 65–85.

———. "Interaction of Affect and Cognition in Empathy." *Emotions, Cognition, and Behavior*. Ed. Carroll E. Izard, Jerome Kagan, and Robert B. Zajonc. Cambridge: Cambridge UP, 1984. 103–31.

"Home Computer Access and Internet Use." *Child Trends Databank*. 6 Sept. 2006 <http://www.childtrendsdatabank.org/indicators/69HomeComputerUse.cfm>.

hooks, bell. *Art on My Mind: Visual Politics*. New York: New, 1995.

———. *Killing Rage: Ending Racism*. New York: Holt, 1995.

———. "The Oppositional Gaze: Black Female Spectators." *Feminist Film Theory: A Reader*. Ed. Sue Thornham. Edinburgh, UK: Edinburgh UP, 1999. 307–20.

———. *Outlaw Culture: Resisting Representations*. New York: Routledge, 1994.

———. *Teaching to Transgress: Education as the Practice of Freedom*. New York: Routledge, 1994.

———. *Yearning: Race, Gender, and Cultural Politics*. Boston: South End, 1990.

Hum, Sue. "The Racialized Gaze: Authenticity and Universality in Disney's *Mulan*." Fleckenstein, Hum, and Calendrillo 107–30.

"Internet Fund-Raising Comes of Age." *Time* 17 Nov. 2008: 53.

Isaacs, William N. *Dialogue and the Art of Thinking Together: A Pioneering Approach to Communicating in Business and in Life*. New York: Currency, 1999.

Jackson, Cindy. *Cindy Jackson*. 26 Feb. 2008 <http://www.cindyjackson.com/>.

Jacobs, Dale. "Being There: Revising the Discourse of Emotion and Teaching." *JAEPL: Journal of the Assembly for Expanded Perspectives on Learning* 7 (2001–2): 42–52.

Jay, Martin. *Downcast Eyes : The Denigration of Vision in Twentieth-Century French Thought*. Berkeley: U of California P, 1994.

———. "Scopic Regimes of Modernity." *Vision and Visuality*. Ed. Hal Foster. Seattle: Bay, 1988. 3–23.

Jenik, Adriene. "Desktop Theater: Keyboard Catharsis and the Masking of Roundheads." *TDR* 45 (2001): 95–112.

———. "Re: 2002 DC March with Women in Black Art Project." E-mail to author. 5 Mar. 2008.

Johnson, T. R. "School Sucks." *College Composition and Communication* 52 (2001): 620–50.

Johnson-Eilola, Johndan. *Datacloud: Toward a New Theory of Online Work*. Cresskill, NJ: Hampton, 2005.

Juzwik, Mary. "Towards an Ethics of Answerability: Reconsidering Dialogism in Sociocultural Literacy Research." *College Composition and Communication* 55 (2004): 536–67.

Keller, Evelyn Fox. *A Feeling for the Organism: The Life and Work of Barbara McClintock*. San Francisco: Freeman, 1983.

Kiefer, Kate. "Do Students Lose More Than They Gain in Online Writing Classes?" *Brave New Classrooms*. Ed. Joe Lockard and Mark Pegrum. New York: Lang, 2006. 141–51.

King, Martin Luther, Jr. *The Strength to Love*. New York: Harper, 1959.

———. *The Trumpet of Conscience*. New York: Harper, 1967.

Kirsch, Gesa. *Ethical Dilemmas in Feminist Research: The Politics of Location, Interpretation, and Publication*. Albany: State U of New York P, 1999.

Kosinski, Jerzy. *Being There*. 1971. New York: Grove, 1999.

Kreimer, Seth F. "Technologies of Protest: Insurgent Social Movements and the First Amendment in the Era of the Internet." *University of Pennsylvania Law Review* 150 (2001): 119–71.

Kress, Gunther. "'English' at the Crossroads: Rethinking the Curricula of Communication in the Context of the Turn to the Visual." *Passions, Pedagogies, and 21st Century Technologies*. Ed. Gail E. Hawisher and Cynthia Selfe. Logan: Utah State UP and NCTE, 1999. 66–88.

———. *Literacy in the New Media Age*. London: Routledge, 2003.

Kubey, Robert, and Mihály Csikszentmihályi. "Television Addiction Is No Mere Metaphor." *Scientific American* Feb. 2002: 74–80.

———. *Television and the Quality of Life: How Viewing Shapes Everyday Experience*. Hillsdale, NJ: Erlbaum, 1990.

Lanham, Richard A. *The Economics of {Attention}: Style and Substance in the Age of Information*. Chicago: U of Chicago P, 2006.

———. *The Electronic Word: Democracy, Technology, and the Arts*. Chicago: U of Chicago P, 1993.

———. *Style: An Anti-Textbook*. New Haven, CT: Yale UP, 1974.

Larson, Richard L. "Teaching Before We Judge: Planning Assignments in Composition." *English Leaflet* 66 (1967): 3–15.

Leatherman, Janie. "Sexual Violence and Armed Conflict: Complex Dynamics of Re-Victimization." *International Journal of Peace Studies* 12 (2007): 53–71.

Le Dœuff, Michèle. *The Philosophical Imaginary*. Trans. Colin Gordon. Stanford, CA: Stanford UP, 1989.

Lenhart, Amanda, and Mary Madden. "Social Networking Websites and Teens: Overview." 7 Jan. 2007. *Pew Internet*. 2 Mar. 2007 <http://www.pewinternet.org/PPF/r/198/report_display.asp>.

Lettvin, Jerome Y., Humberto R. Maturana, Warren S. McCulloch, and Walter H. Pitts. "What the Frog's Eye Tells the Frog's Brain." *Embodiments of the Mind*. By Warren S. McCulloch. Cambridge, MA: MIT P, 1989. 230–55.

Lévi-Strauss, Claude. *The Savage Mind*. Trans. John Weightman and Doreen Weightman. Chicago: U of Chicago P, 1966.

Lopate, Phillip. Introduction. *The Art of the Personal Essay: An Anthology from the Classical Era to the Present*. Ed. Phillip Lopate. New York: Anchor, 1995. xxiii–xlv.

Maness, Kevin. "Teaching Media-Savvy Students about Popular Media." *English Journal* 93 (2004). 46–51.

McKee, Heidi. "Sound Matters: Notes toward the Analysis and Design of Sound in Multimedia Webtexts." *Computers and Composition* 23 (2006): 335–54.

McLeod, Susan H. *Notes on the Heart: Affective Issues in the Writing Classroom*. Carbondale: Southern Illinois UP, 1997.

McLuhan, Marshall. *Understanding Media: The Extensions of Man*. Cambridge, MA: MIT P, 1994.

Meyers, Diana Tietjens. *Being Yourself: Essays on Identity, Action, and Social Life*. Lanham, MD: Rowman, 2004.

———. *Gender in the Mirror: Cultural Imagery and Women's Agency*. Oxford: Oxford UP, 2004.

Miller, Carolyn. "Genre as Social Action." *Quarterly Journal of Speech* 70 (1984): 151–67.

Miller, Keith D. "Plymouth Rock Landed on Us: Malcolm X's Whiteness Theory as a Basis for Alternative Literacy." *College Composition and Communication* 56 (2004): 199–223.

Mirzoeff, Nicholas. *An Introduction to Visual Culture*. London: Routledge, 1999.

Mitchell, W. J. T. *Iconology: Image, Text, Ideology*. Chicago: U of Chicago P, 1987.

Mulvey, Laura. "Visual Pleasure and Narrative Cinema." *Screen* 16 (1975): 6–18. 10 July 2002 <http://www.bbk.ac.uk/hafvm/staff_research/visua11.html>.

Myers, Nancy A. "Acting On or Acting With: Academe's Promotion of Exclusionary Participation in the Virtual Sphere." *Kairos Rhetoric, Technology, Pedagogy* 6.2 (2001). 8 Apr 2008 <http://english.ttu.edu/KAIROS/6.2/binder2.html?coverweb/ecac/myers/index.htm>.

"National Barbie-in-a-Blender Day." *Freeculture.org*. 27 Feb. 2008 <http://barbieinablender.org/>.

Nussbaum, Martha C. *Upheavals of Thought: The Intelligence of Emotions*. Cambridge: Cambridge UP, 2001.

Obama, Barack. *The Audacity of Hope: Thoughts on Reclaiming the American Dream*. New York: Crown, 2006.

———. *Dreams from My Father: A Story of Race and Inheritance*. New York: Three Rivers, 1995.

———. "2004 Democratic National Convention Keynote Address" [The Audacity of Hope]. 27 July 2004, Fleet Center, Boston. *American Rhetoric: Online Speech Bank*. 15 Feb. 2008 <http://www.americanrhetoric.com/speeches/convention2004/barackobama2004dnc.htm>.

Ong, Walter J. *Orality and Literacy: The Technologizing of the Word.* London: Routledge, 1982.

Orange, Carolyn M., and Amiso M. George. "Child Sacrifice: Black America's Price of Paying the Media Piper." *Journal of Black Studies* 30 (2000): 294–314.

O'Reilley, Mary Rose. *The Peaceable Classroom.* Portsmouth, NH: Boynton-Cook, 1993.

"Our Mission." *Women in Black.* 16 July 2005 <http://www.womeninblack.net/mission.html>.

Papert, Seymour. *Mindstorms: Children, Computers, and Powerful Ideas.* 2nd ed. New York: Basic, 1993.

Parekh, Bhikhu. *Gandhi.* New York: Oxford UP, 1997.

Perry, Alan E. "PowerPoint Presentations: A Creative Addition to the Research Process." *English Journal* 92 (2003): 64–69.

Postman, Neil. *Amusing Ourselves to Death: Public Discourse in the Age of Show Business.* 20th anniversary ed. New York: Penguin, 2006.

Poulakos, John. "A Sophistic Definition of Rhetoric." *Philosophy and Rhetoric* 16 (1982): 35–48. Rpt. in *Contemporary Rhetorical Theory: A Reader.* Ed. John Louis Lucaites, Celeste Michelle Condit, and Sally Caudill. New York: Guilford, 1999. 25–34.

Press, Andrea L. *Women Watching Television: Gender, Class, and Generation in the American Television Experiences.* Philadelphia: U of Pennsylvania P, 1991.

Putnam, Robert D. *Bowling Alone: The Collapse and Revival of American Community.* New York: Simon, 2000.

Rapping, Elayne. "You've Come Which Way, Baby? The Road That Leads from June Cleaver to Ally McBeal Looks a Lot like a U-Turn." *Women's Review of Books* 17.10–11 (2000): 20–22.

Ratcliffe, Krista. *Rhetorical Listening: Identification, Gender, Whiteness.* Carbondale: Southern Illinois UP, 2005.

Rice, Jeff. *The Rhetoric of Cool: Composition Studies and New Media.* Carbondale: Southern Illinois UP, 2007.

Rich, Adrienne. "Cartographies of Silence." *The Dream of a Common Language: Poems, 1974–77.* New York: Norton, 1993. 16–20.

Richards, I. A. *The Philosophy of Rhetoric.* London: Oxford UP, 1965.

Richmond, Kia Jane. "The Ethics of Empathy: Making Connections in the Writing Classroom." *JAEPL: Journal of the Assembly for Expanded Perspectives on Learning* 5 (1999–2000): 37–46.

Ronfeldt, David, and John Arquilla. "Emergence and Influence of the Zapatista Social Netwar." Ronfeldt and Arquilla 171–98.

———, eds. *Networks and Netwars: The Future of Terror, Crime, and Militancy.* Santa Monica, CA: Rand, 2001. 1 Dec. 2006 <http://www.rand.org/pubs/monograph_reports/MR1382/>.

Rorty, Richard. "The Contingency of Language." *Contingency, Irony, and Solidarity.* New York: Cambridge UP, 1989. 3–22.

Rosenblatt, Louise. "The Reading Transaction: What For?" *Developing Literacy.* Ed. Robert P. Parker and Frances A. Davis. Newark, DE: Intl. Reading Assn., 1983. 118–35.

Royster, Jacqueline Jones. "When the First Voice You Hear Is Not Your Own." *College Composition and Communication* 47 (1996): 29–40.

Sacks, Oliver. *An Anthropologist on Mars: Seven Paradoxical Tales.* New York: Knopf, 1995.

Samuel, Alexandra. *Hacktivism and the Future of Political Participation.* Diss. Harvard U, 2004. 4 Jan. 2007 <http://www.alexandrasamuel.com/dissertation>.

Schachtel, Ernest G. *Metamorphosis: On the Development of Affect, Perception, Attention, and Memory.* New York: Basic, 1959.

Schemann, Naomi. *Engenderings: Constructions of Knowledge, Authority, and Privilege.* New York: Routledge, 1993.

Sennett, Richard. *Flesh and Stone: The Body and the City in Western Civilization.* New York: Norton, 1996.

Seyhan, Azade. "Visual Citations: Walter Benjamin's Dialectic of Text and Image." *Languages of Visuality: Crossings between Science, Art, Politics, and Literature.* Ed. Beate Allert. Detroit, MI: Wayne State UP, 1996. 229–41.

Shipka, Jody "A Multimodal Task-based Framework for Composing." *College Composition and Communication* 57 (2005): 277–306.

Shohat, Ella. *Taboo Memories, Diasporic Voices.* Durham, NC: Duke UP, 2006.

Shrum, L. J., Robert S. Wyer Jr., and Thomas C. O'Guinn. "The Effects of Television Consumption on Social Perceptions: The Use of Priming Procedures to Investigate Psychological Processes." *Journal of Consumer Research* 24 (1998): 447–58.

Sifry, Micah. "What Happens to Obama's Online Community?" *Weekend Edition.* Host Scott Simon. *NPR.* WFSU, Tallahassee, FL. 8 Nov. 2008 <http://www.npr.org/templates/story/story.php?storyId=96778342>.

Sirc, Geoffrey. *English Composition as a Happening.* Logan: Utah State UP, 2002.

Sloane, Thomas O. *Encyclopedia of Rhetoric.* Oxford: Oxford UP, 2001.

Smith, Jeff. "Against 'Illegeracy': Toward a New Pedagogy of Civic Understanding." *College Composition and Communication* 45 (1994): 200–19.

Soja, Edward W. *Postmodern Geographies: The Reassertion of Space in Critical Social Theory.* London: Verso, 1989.

Sothern, Billy. "A Cruel and Unusual Punishment." *Nation.* 24 Apr. 2007. 18 Apr. 2008 <http://www.thenation.com/doc/20070507/sothern>.

Stafford, Barbara Maria. *Artful Science: Enlightenment Entertainment and the Eclipse of Visual Education.* Cambridge, MA: MIT P, 1996.

———. *Good Looking: Essays on the Virtue of Images.* Cambridge, MA: MIT P, 1998.

Stewart, Kathleen C. "An Occupied Place." *Senses of Place.* Ed. Steven Feld and Keith H. Basso. Santa Fe, NM: School of Amer. Research, 1996. 137–66.

Stirland, Sarah Lai. "Propelled by Internet, Barack Obama Wins Presidency." 4 Nov. 2008. *Wired.* 16 Nov. 2008 <http://www.wired.com/threatlevel/2008/11/propelled-by-in/>.

Strategies for Teaching First-Year Composition. Ed. Duane Roen, Veronica Pantoja, Lauren Yena, Susan K. Miller, and Eric Waggoner. Urbana, IL: NCTE, 2002.

Stroman, Carolyn A. "Television's Role in the Socialization of African American Children and Adolescents." *Journal of Negro Education* 60 (1991): 314–27.

Stroupe, Craig. "Making Distance Presence: The Composition Voice in Online Learning." *Computers and Composition* 20 (2003): 255–75.

———. "Visualizing English: Recognizing the Hybrid Literacy of Visual and Verbal Authorship on the Web." *College English* 62 (2000): 607–32.

Swindle, Mark. "The Changing Face of Online Environmental Activism: New Tools and Their Effect on Environmental Policy." 1 Dec. 2006 <www.shockandawe.us.globalization/Paper.doc>.

Tardy, Christine M. "Expressions of Disciplinarity and Individuality in a Multimodal Genre." *Computers and Composition* 22 (2005): 319–36.

Totenberg, Nina. "Justices Weigh Death Penalty for Child Rape." *NPR*. 16 Apr. 2008. 18 Apr. 2008 <http://www.npr.org/templates/story/story.php?storyId=89660806>.

Trimbur, John. "Popular Literacy: Caught between Art and Crime." *Popular Literacy: Studies in Cultural Practices and Poetics*. Ed. Trimbur. Pittsburgh, PA: U of Pittsburgh P, 2001. 1–16.

Turkle, Sherry. *Life on the Screen: Identity in the Age of the Internet*. New York: Simon, 1995.

Vision Problems in the U.S. 21 Mar. 2002. 25 July 2004 <http://www.preventblindness.org/vpus/vpus_page2.html>.

Walker, Alice. *In Search of Our Mother's Gardens: Womanist Prose*. San Diego, CA: Harcourt, 1983.

Walworth, Candace. "Engaged Buddhism and Women in Black: Our Grief Is Not a Cry for War." *JAEPL: Journal of the Assembly for Expanded Perspectives on Learning* 9 (2003–4): 20–31.

Webb, Ruth. "The Aesthetics of Sacred Space: Narrative, Metaphor, and Motion in Ekphraseis of Church Buildings." *Dumbarton Oaks Papers* 53 (1999): 59–74.

Weisman, Leslie Kanes. *Discrimination by Design: A Feminist Critique of the Man-Made Environment*. Urbana: U of Illinois P, 1992.

Welch, Nancy. "Living Room: Teaching Public Writing in a Post-Publicity Era." *College Composition and Communication* 56 (2005): 470–92.

———. *Living Room: Teaching Public Writing in a Privatized World*. Portsmouth, NH: Boynton, 2008.

———. "Who's Afraid of Politics? The Feminist Body in the New World Order." Interchange on Rhetoric and War. *College Composition and Communication* 55 (2003): 348–51.

Wells, Susan. "Rogue Cops and Health Care: What Do We Want from Public Writing?" *College Composition and Communication* 47 (1996): 325–41.

Williams, Bronwyn T. *Tuned In: Television and the Teaching of Writing*. Portsmouth, NH: Boynton, 2002.

"Women in Black Art Project." *ArtWomen.Org*. 2002. 23 Feb. 2007 <http://www.artwomen.org/wib/index.htm>.

Worthman, Christopher. *"Just Playing the Part": Engaging Adolescents in Drama and Literacy*. New York: Teachers College P, 2002.

Wray, Stefan. "On Electronic Civil Disobedience." *Defining Lines: <Breaking Down Borders>*. Socialist Scholars Conference. Mar. 1998. New York, NY. 15 Dec. 2007 <http://cristine.org/borders/Wray_Essay.html>.

Writing Teacher's Sourcebook, The. Ed. Edward P. J. Corbett, Nancy Myers, and Gary Tate. 4th ed. New York: Oxford UP, 2000.

Wysocki, Anne Frances. "awaywithwords: On the Possibilities in Unavailable Designs." *Computers and Composition* 22 (2005): 55–62.

Yates, Frances A. *The Art of Memory*. Chicago: U of Chicago P, 1966.

Zaeske, Susan. "Susan Zaeske's Position Paper on Agency." Alliance of Rhetoric Societies Conference. May 2003. Evanston, IL. 12 Dec. 2004. <http://www.comm.umn.edu/ARS/Zaeske%20agency.htm>. (Site now discontinued)

Index

Page numbers in italics indicate figures.

Kristie S. Fleckenstein is an associate professor of English at Florida State University, where she teaches rhetoric and composition classes in the undergraduate and graduate programs. She is the author of *Embodied Literacies* (2003), recipient of the 2005 Conference on College Composition and Communication Outstanding Book of the Year Award, and the coeditor of two collections on imagery, rhetoric, and teaching. Her work has appeared in *College English, College Composition and Communication, JAC, Rhetoric Review, Computers and Composition,* and other journals.